Praise for Retired Racing Greyhounds For Dummies:

"*Retired Racing Greyhounds For Dummies* is one of the best dog books ever written and one of the best-written dog books."

— Ian Dunbar, Ph.D., author of *How to Teach an Old Dog New Tricks*

"This is an absolutely wonderful book written by an expert on the subject. The book is full of important and practical information that will be useful to anyone contemplating adopting a retired racer. And it's a delight to read, filled with humor, anecdotes, and illuminating examples. I smiled my whole way through the book!"

— Dani Weinberg, Dogs & Their People, Albuquerque, NM

"What an insightful and delightful book. I would recommend this book to anyone contemplating adopting a retired racing Greyhound, and I would encourage all adoption/placement groups to make reading of this book part of the applicant's prerequisite."

— Linda Reiha, Retired President, Michigan Greyhound Connection

"*Retired Racing Greyhounds For Dummies* should be required reading for anyone adopting a sighthound. It is an excellent reference for both novice and experienced dog owners. In addition to information on the unique aspects of owning a Greyhound, it is full of sensible tips that will benefit owners of any breed. The training sections present humane, practical tips that are effective and designed to be fun for owner and dog alike. This book certainly will be included on my clients' suggested reading list."

— Lore I. Haug, DVM, Resident, Companion Animal Behavior, Texas A&M University Veterinary Teaching Hospital

"This is not just a book for Greyhound admirers and owners. It's for every pet owner of every breed and mix. This is a delightful, easy journey toward gentle, humane communication with the dogs who share our lives."

— Debi Davis, Service Dog User/Trainer and National Service Dog of the Year Award Winner

"I wish that this book had existed when I adopted my first Greyhound many years ago. It provides so much excellent information on all aspects of Greyhound ownership, from introduction to your family to possible medical problems. I have obedience-trained Greyhounds since the 1960s, and I still found some new and useful ideas here. This is a book I would heartily recommend to anyone getting a Greyhound, whether it's an adoption dog or an AKC champion."

> — Laurel Drew, A Place For Us Greyhound Adoption and
> El-Aur Greyhounds

"Lee Livingood does it again! With a combination of humor and straight talk, her latest creation provides a no-nonsense guide to the joys and pit-falls of adopting the retired racing Greyhound. Not only useful to the prospective adopter, current owners will find the book rife with tips and tricks, both new and long forgotten. A must read! Considering adoption? Already taken the leap? Don't miss this one!"

> — Bruce Skinner, Editor in Chief, *A Breed Apart*

"Lee Livingood's book, *Retired Racing Greyhounds For Dummies,* is a non-judgmental, no-nonsense guide to living with one of the more extraordinary members of the canine kingdom. Starting with the most important practical consideration — is a Greyhound the right dog for you — she covers all of the nitty-gritty questions that a first-time Greyhound owner inevitably has. Her extensive discussion of dog behavior and how to manage your Greyhound to become the best companion ever to walk on four feet addresses all of the problems dog owners have wrestled with since the first dog sneaked into the tent 60,000 years ago. *Retired Racing Greyhounds For Dummies* is the next best thing to having an experienced Greyhound owner living with you."

> — Joan Belle Isle, President, Greyhound Project

 ™

References for the Rest of Us!®

BESTSELLING BOOK SERIES

Do you find that traditional reference books are overloaded with technical details and advice you'll never use? Do you postpone important life decisions because you just don't want to deal with them? Then our *For Dummies®* business and general reference book series is for you.

For Dummies business and general reference books are written for those frustrated and hard-working souls who know they aren't dumb, but find that the myriad of personal and business issues and the accompanying horror stories make them feel helpless. For Dummies books use a lighthearted approach, a down-to-earth style, and even cartoons and humorous icons to dispel fears and build confidence. Lighthearted but not lightweight, these books are perfect survival guides to solve your everyday personal and business problems.

> *"...Dummies books consistently live up to their brand-name promise to transform 'can't into can.' "*
> — Ottawa Citizen

> *"...clear, straightforward information laced with a touch of humour."*
> — The Toronto Star

> *"...set up in bits and bites that are easy to digest, full of no-nonsense advice."*
> — The Calgary Herald

Already, millions of satisfied readers agree. They have made For Dummies the #1 introductory level computer book series and a best-selling business book series. They have written asking for more. So, if you're looking for the best and easiest way to learn about business and other general reference topics, look to For Dummies to give you a helping hand.

Wiley Publishing, Inc.

Retired Racing Greyhounds FOR DUMMIES®

by Lee Livingood

John Wiley & Sons, Inc.

Retired Racing Greyhounds For Dummies®

Published by
John Wiley & Sons, Inc.
111 River Street
Hoboken, NJ 07030
www.wiley.com

Copyright © 2002 by John Wiley & Sons, Inc., Hoboken, New Jersey

Published by John Wiley & Sons, Inc., Hoboken, New Jersey

Published simultaneously in Canada

Library of Congress Cataloging-in-Publication Data:

Library of Congress Control Number: 00-104217

ISBN: 978-0-7645-5276-2 (pbk); ISBN 978-1-118-05365-2 (ebk); ISBN 978-1-118-05604-2 (ebk)

Manufactured in the United States of America

20 19

WILEY

About the Author

Like most dog lovers, **Lee Livingood** has been owned by a dog since the day she was born. Lee has been training dogs since she borrowed a book on dog training from the library more than forty years ago. Rescuing and training adult companion dogs became a hobby and a passion for her.

A number of years ago, Lee and her husband met their first retired racer, and it was love at first sight. She was immediately taken with the Greyhound's quiet elegance and gentle disposition. A new passion was born.

Several years ago, Lee was able to combine her commitment to rescue dogs and her childhood dreams of being a writer and working with animals into a successful second career. In addition to running a companion animal training and behavioral modification business, Lee writes on dog and cat behavior and training for a variety of publications. Her work has appeared nationally in Celebrating Greyhounds; in Forward, the publication of the National Association of Dog Obedience Instructors; and online at *A Breed Apart* (a Greyhound magazine) and Bengaland (a Web site devoted to Bengal cats). She is a professional member of the Association of Pet Dog Trainers. She has a B.A. from Franklin and Marshall College.

Lee and her husband volunteer with a local Greyhound adoption group and were named volunteers of the year by Personalized Greyhounds, Inc. She also donates her time and behavioral expertise to local rescue and shelter groups. Her Web page, www.retiredracinggreyhounds.com is devoted to issues and resources related to training and living with retired racers.

Retired Racing Greyhounds For Dummies is Lee's third book and her second book on retired racing Greyhounds. Her first Greyhound book, *Running with the Big Dogs,* was self-published and is acclaimed by adoption groups in the U.S. and Canada. She has donated a significant portion of her profits to further the cause of Greyhound adoption. Lee is currently writing a guide to training and retraining adult dogs, *Lassie Doesn't Live Here Anymore.*

She shares her home with her very tolerant husband, Ben. Their family consists of two retired racers, Chaco and Cheyenne; a beagle/sheltie mix, Clancy; and a Bengal kitten, Kokopelli.

About Howell Book House
Committed to the Human/Companion Animal Bond

Thank you for choosing a book brought to you by the pet experts at Howell Book House, a division of Wiley Publishing, Inc. And welcome to the family of pet owners who've put their trust in Howell books for nearly 40 years!

Pet ownership is about relationships — the bonds people form with their dogs, cats, horses, birds, fish, small mammals, reptiles, and other animals. Howell Book House/Wiley understands that these are some of the most important relationships in life, and that it's vital to nurture them through enjoyment and education. The happiest pet owners are those who know they're taking the best care of their pets — and with Howell books owners have this satisfaction. They're happy, educated owners, and as a result, they have happy pets, and that enriches the bond they share.

Howell Book House was established in 1961 by Mr. Elsworth S. Howell, an active and proactive dog fancier who showed English Setters and judged at the prestigious Westminster Kennel Club show in New York. Mr. Howell based his publishing program on strength of content, and his passion for books written by experienced and knowledgeable owners defined Howell Book House and has remained true over the years. Howell's reputation as the premier pet book publisher is supported by the distinction of having won more awards from the Dog Writers Association of America than any other publisher. Howell Book House/Wiley has over 400 titles in publication, including such classics as The American Kennel Club's Complete Dog Book, the Dog Owner's Home Veterinary Handbook, Blessed Are the Brood Mares, and Mother Knows Best: The Natural Way to Train Your Dog.

When you need answers to questions you have about any aspect of raising or training your companion animals, trust that Howell Book House/Wiley has the answers. We welcome your comments and suggestions, and we look forward to helping you maximize your relationships with your pets throughout the years.

The Howell Book House Staff

Dedication

For Penny (RC Ottabea Peney, February 20, 1994–September 25, 1999), who raced into our lives and filled our world with joy. She may have been last place on the track, but she was first place in our hearts.

And for all the retired racers out there waiting to race into our hearts and homes.

Author's Acknowledgments

I didn't write this book. Well, at least I didn't write it alone. Many people played important roles in bringing this book to life and I thank each and every one of them.

With very special thanks to Ben, my husband and best friend, who supports me in everything I do. Thanks to my own needlenose crew plus two, who have waited patiently while my time and attention have been directed at completing these pages.

For nearly two decades, Dr. Calvin Clements has kept our canine and feline family happy and healthy and has comforted us when that was no longer possible. He graciously gave his time to review the health care sections of this book and share his knowledge. For that I am most grateful.

Not only does Dr. Suzanne Stack treat hundreds of racing Greyhounds in her veterinary practice, she lives with retired racers and volunteers her time and expertise freely to adoption groups. She contributed generously of her extensive knowledge of racing Greyhounds as well.

Bonnie Stoner, a Harrisburg pet photographer volunteered her time and talents to take many of the photographs that appear in these pages.

Many Greyhound owners jumped in to help me assemble photographs of retired racers and other Greyhounds for this project. Thanks especially to Peggy Levin, Laurel Drew, Rob and Elaine Summerhill, Nancy Beach, Kathy Johnson, Bruce Skinner, M.J. Barkley, Dee Dee Colella, Close Encounters of the Furry Kind, Rick Dodd, and The Greyhound Hall of Fame for the use of photos from their collections. Thanks also to Marcia Herman for the use of her photo for the book's cover.

Colleen Dauphine at the Greyhound Hall of Fame responded quickly and cheerfully to every request I made of her. Tim Horan with the National Greyhound Association offered excellent technical assistance.

Brent Burns, President of Country Roads Kennel, contributed to the information on puppyhood and racing. He and his family and the staff at Country Roads are committed to finding good homes for their racers at the ends of their careers.

Thanks also to Dani Weinberg for her friendship and counsel and encouragement.

My deep appreciation to Dr. Ian Dunbar for his confidence in me and for the doors he opened. A whole generation of dog trainers owes him a debt of thanks for what he has done to make dog training a gentle art.

Thanks also to my technical editor, Peggy F. Levin, president and founder of Personalized Greyhounds, Inc. Her commitment to the welfare of retired racers is unceasing and her activities on their behalf is inspiring.

Thanks to Dominique De Vito, Publisher at Wiley Publishing, Inc., for encouraging me and helping me to bring this special project to life; Scott Prentzas, Senior Editor, for jumping in and guiding me through; and the Production team, who took care of the details.

Thanks especially to Elizabeth Kuball, my Project Editor, who kept everything on track — including me — and held my hand through the process.

Barbara Frake added her talents to produce the illustrations and did so with amazing efficiency.

And to all my animal companions who, for more than half a century, have so enriched my soul and brightened my days and contributed greatly to my education. But especially to Murphy and Penny who are waiting at the Bridge.

Publisher's Acknowledgments

We're proud of this book; please send us your comments through our online registration form located at www.dummies.com/register.

Some of the people who helped bring this book to market include the following:

Acquisitions, Editorial, and Media Development

Project Editor: Elizabeth Netedu Kuball

Acquisitions Editor: Scott Prentzas

Technical Editor: Peggy F. Levin

Editorial Director: Kristin A. Cocks

Editorial Manager: Pamela Mourouzis

Cover Photo: © Stefano Lonardi / iStock

Composition Services

Project Coordinator: Maridee Ennis

Layout and Graphics: Jason Guy, Tracy K. Oliver, Jill Piscitelli, Rashell Smith, Jeremey Unger, Erin Zeltner

Proofreaders: Vickie Broyles, John Greenough, Carl Pierce, Marianne Santy, Charles Spencer, Nancy Reinhardt

Indexer: Becky Hornyak

Illustrator: Barbara Frake

Publishing and Editorial for Consumer Dummies

   Kathleen Nebenhaus, Vice President and Executive Publisher

   David Palmer, Associate Publisher

   Kristin Ferguson-Wagstaffe, Product Development Director

Publishing for Technology Dummies

   Andy Cummings, Vice President and Publisher

Composition Services

   Debbie Stailey, Director of Composition Services

Contents at a Glance

Cartoons at a Glance

By Rich Tennant

page 5

page 25

page 147

page 211

page 63

Fax: 978-546-7747
E-mail: richtennant@the5thwave.com
World Wide Web: www.the5thwave.com

Table of Contents

Introduction

· ·

So you're thinking about adopting a retired racing Greyhound? Or maybe you already own one and are looking for some information to guide you through the coming months? You've turned to the right place! Retired Racing Greyhounds For Dummies is a reference for anyone wanting all the basics on these fantastic dogs — all in one place. Whether you're looking for information on how to adopt a retired racer, what to do to prepare for the homecoming of your new best friend, or how to train him after he arrives, this book has it all. Most of all, you'll find great suggestions for ways to build a strong relationship with your retired racing Greyhound — and having that kind of bond with one of these gentle creatures is the greatest reward in the world. So get comfortable and dive right in. Whether you read from cover to cover or skip around to the chapters you need most right away, I've got you covered.

About This Book

Let me first tell you what this book isn't. This isn't a general book about dog training and dog care. This is a book about living with retired racing Greyhounds. It goes beyond simple basics that are in any good book on dog care or training and delves into the issues and topics that are important to someone who lives with a retired racing Greyhound or is considering adopting one.

I love dogs. I love all kinds of dogs. But retired racers are something very special to me. From the day I met our first retired racer, I knew I was hooked. Most of us who live with Greyhounds talk about how their eyes seem to touch our very souls. My family's experience has been no different. I love the gentle sensitivity blended with the raw speed and power. To me they are a perfect blend of form and function. I can't imagine not sharing my life and my heart with them.

I wrote this book for three reasons. The first is to share with you some of what I've learned about living with, caring for, and being owned by retired racing Greyhounds. The second reason is to share with you my perspective on training and living with my best friends. I want your life with your retired racer to be a long and happy one. Lastly, I want you to have the resources you need to go beyond what I can offer within these pages.

Why You Need This Book

Sharing your life with a retired racer is great fun. But making a decision to share your life with any dog is a serious responsibility. The better you understand your retired racing Greyhound, the more you'll enjoy your years together.

So why should you read this book? There are some things I've learned from training companion animals that I want to share. So I wanted this book to be different. This isn't a general book about dogs disguised as a book on retired racers. This isn't a book about breed history or the history of racing or the political issues related to dog racing. This is a book about deciding whether a retired racer is right for you, about the issues of taking a retired racer into your family, and about getting the most out of your relationship with your retired racer. So this book focuses heavily on the training and behavioral aspects of living with a retired racer. And just as important, it's about finding new and creative ways to interact with your hound and teach him about the world around him.

I provide information on grooming, care, and training. But I've tried to give you the inside track on those issues as they relate to retired racing Greyhounds and show you ways to keep your life with your hound safe and stress-free.

I introduce fun and easy ways to train your dog that not only help you have a well-mannered dog but deepen the bond between you and your retired racer. I offer specific techniques I've found most ideally suited to the retired racer's personality and particular needs.

How This Book Is Organized

Retired Racing Greyhounds For Dummies is divided into five sections. If you're trying to decide whether a retired racer is right for you, you may want to start with the first part and work your way forward. If you already have a retired racer, turn to whichever section interests you most and go from there.

Part 1: Getting to Know Greyhounds

If you don't really have much knowledge of Greyhounds as a breed, this is a great place to start. In this part, I give you a quick history of Greyhounds. I also tell you about facets of your racer's past life and his personality and how that affects his life in your living room.

Part II: Finding Your Soul Mate

Turn to this section to do some serious soul-searching. You'll discover whether a retired racing Greyhound is the right dog for you. And if you come to the conclusion that he is, you can find information on where to go to adopt and what to do when you first bring your Greyhound home.

Part III: Training Your Greyhound for Life after the Racetrack

Whatever your training question, you'll find the answer in this part. I cover everything from the basics — how to help your retired racer adapt to his new world — to the more advanced, such as teaching your retired racer to do more complex behaviors. And if you already have a retired racer whose manners need some fine-tuning, there's a chapter in this part to guide you through the process of ridding him of those not-so-appealing habits. Finally, I finish the part up with an important chapter on helping the Greyhound who is fearful of his new world. This chapter helps you help your dog, so before you know it, he'll be right at home.

Part IV: Keeping Your Retired Racing Greyhound Healthy

Turn to the chapters in this part for everything from nutrition to grooming to the prevention of health problems. And if your retired racer does get sick, I let you know which illnesses you can handle at home (and how), and which ones require the help of a veterinarian. I also devote an entire chapter to keeping your retired racer safe and healthy at home and away. Whatever your dog's health situation, you'll find useful information in this part.

Part V: The Part of Tens

In this part, I cover Greyhounds from A to Z — all in a few short pages. I give you ten great reasons to adopt a retired racer, ten things to do before your Greyhound arrives, ten great training tips, and ten ways to have fun with your dog. If you're in a hurry but still want some useful information, this is the place to turn.

Icons Used in This Book

Icons are those little symbols you'll find in the margins of this book, and they're meant to grab your attention when you're reading on the run. In this book, you'll find the following six icons:

This icon grabs your attention and points you to a useful tip, something you can do to make your life, and your Greyhound's life, easier.

This icon reminds you of information so important that it's worth repeating — and storing away in your long-term memory.

This icon highlights information that provides a background for why things work the way they work. If you're in a hurry, this is the information you can safely skip. But if you have the time, check them out. The paragraphs marked with this icon contain some fascinating information.

Any time you see this icon, pay close attention, because these paragraphs let you know about things you should or shouldn't do to make sure your dog stays safe.

This icon points you to information that's fun to know, but not necessarily essential.

When you see this wagging tail, you'll find information highlighting great products or services for Greyhound owners.

Part I

Getting to Know Greyhounds

The 5th Wave   By Rich Tennant

GREYHOUND

RETIRED GREYHOUND

In this part . . .

In this part, I give you the lowdown on the history of
Greyhounds and how your dog's history is a part of
who he is today. I also let you know all the basics you
need on Greyhounds as a breed, including information on
racing. If you're wanting a primer on Greyhounds, whether
you have one already or are thinking of adopting one, this
is a great place to start.

Chapter 1

The History of Greyhounds

In This Chapter

▶ Understanding your Greyhound's ancient roots

▶ Knowing what Greyhounds were bred for

*I*f you're considering adopting a retired racer or you already share your home with one, understanding your best friend's lineage provides great insight into his personality and behavior.

Cave paintings in France show that dogs have been part of our lives for perhaps as long as 15,000 years, with the earliest known bones of dogs dated to 12,000 B.C. Greyhounds, or at least Greyhound-like dogs, have been part of that history almost from the beginning.

The Greyhound evolved to hunt on the open, flat plains of the Middle East perhaps as long as 8,000 years ago and became an important part of ancient life in that region. Greyhounds are one of a group of dogs referred to as *sighthounds* or *gazehounds* because they rely on keen sight and blazing speed to hunt prey.

JUST FOR FUN

Do I know you from somewhere?

Many breeds of dogs are barely recognizable from drawings or paintings of their early ancestors. However, the Greyhound's appearance has changed little since he first appeared on coins in 500 B.C. The reason is simple: The Greyhound's purpose remains the same. He was, and always has been, bred for speed.

What's in a name?

The origin of the name *Greyhound* is unknown, but it could be derived from the Saxon words *Grech* or *Greg*, meaning "Greek," because they thought the breed originated in Greece. The name could also be derived from the term *gazehound*, used to describe a dog who hunts by sight.

Regardless of its origin, the name has nothing to do with the Greyhound's color. Gray is actually *not* a common color among Greyhounds.

Of Coursers and Kings

Greyhounds were treated with almost god-like reverence by ancient Egyptians and highly regarded by other cultures in the Middle East. As time passed, the Greyhound became both a hunter and a sporting dog. A favorite pastime of nobility almost from the moment the first sighthounds were bred was a sport called *coursing*, in which dogs compete against each other in the pursuit of a lure. Coursing existed in Rome by at least the first century A.D. For centuries, only royalty were allowed to own Greyhounds.

The modern Greyhound is a product of late-eighteenth-century England. During this time, the Earl of Orford was obsessed with the breed and set about to produce the "perfect" Greyhound. He created the first public coursing club in 1776. The Greyhound as we know him today was the work of careful breeding in England and the eventual practice of keeping careful pedigree records called *studbooks*.

On to the New World

Greyhounds have been in the New World since Christopher Columbus first landed here. But Greyhounds weren't established in the United States until settlers in the Midwest discovered that, just as the jackrabbits were fond of their crops, Greyhounds were fond of jackrabbits. The Midwest became the seat of Greyhound coursing and eventually of Greyhound racing. In many areas of the Midwest and West, Greyhounds are still bred by backyard breeders to hunt and kill jackrabbits and coyotes.

Guinefort and the Cult of the Greyhound

A legend dating back to at least the eleventh century tells of a duke in France who left his faithful Greyhound Guinefort to watch over his young child. When the duke returned, he found the nursery covered in blood, the cradle turned over, and the baby missing, but Guinefort remained. The duke assumed that Guinefort had killed the missing baby, so he drew his sword and killed the dog.

Just as Guinefort made his last dying cry, the duke heard a wail and found the baby safe beneath the cradle and the body of a poisonous serpent nearby. Guinefort had attacked the snake and protected the infant from harm.

When the duke realized his error, he buried his faithful dog in a well.

Guinefort was made a national martyr in France and a saint. The well in which St. Guinefort is buried was thought to hold healing powers for sick infants. The feast day of St. Guinefort was celebrated on August 22.

Over several centuries, the legend of Guinefort gave rise to a cult. The Catholic Church was not amused and viewed the cult as a sacrilege. Sporadic inquisitions were held for hundreds of years to eradicate the "Cult of the Greyhound."

The Racing Greyhound

Greyhound racing as we know it today developed in the early 1900s. Today there are 47 Greyhound tracks operating in 16 states. Greyhound racing is regulated by the individual states that host tracks and by the National Greyhound Association (NGA).

Racing Greyhounds, like the ones shown in Figure 1-1, are registered with the National Greyhound Association (NGA). The NGA is responsible for registering racing Greyhounds in the United States. The NGA keeps careful ownership records of all registered racing puppies and detailed records about a racer's bloodlines.

Not all Greyhounds are racing Greyhounds. Some Greyhounds are bred for dog shows. Others compete in lure coursing, in which two dogs race after a lure (usually a white plastic bag) to see which dog is fastest.

Photograph courtesy of Greyhound Hall of Fame

Figure 1-1:
Greyhound racing is the sixth most popular spectator sport in the United States.

Chapter 2

Retired Racing Greyhounds 101: The Basics of the Breed

*R*etired racing Greyhounds are delightful, charming, and easy to live with. But I don't want you to adopt one for the wrong reasons. Any time you consider bringing a dog into your family, you need to understand the benefits and drawbacks to sharing your home with an animal. Retired racing Greyhounds are no different. So in this chapter I give you the lowdown on the breed, covering everything from how racing Greyhounds are prepared for life on the track to how they adapt to your home.

The ex-racer is the perfect companion . . . for some of us. No breed of dog is perfect (although you would have a tough time convincing owners of retired racers of that). Not all Greyhounds are alike. They share many traits. But individuals, whether human or canine, are just that: *individuals.* So as you read this chapter, keep in mind that every Greyhound is unique.

In this chapter, I help you understand your responsibilities as an adopter, and I point out the pros and cons of adopting a retired racer. But I don't (and can't) guarantee that a retired racer is the right dog for you.

Understanding What Sets Greyhounds Apart

Few athletes are as ideally suited for their chosen sport as the Greyhound is for racing. Arguments about using dogs (or any animals, for that matter) for the entertainment of humans will probably continue forever. But regardless of your position on racing as an industry, you can't argue with one reality: Greyhounds love to run and they do it superbly. After all, they've been doing it for thousands of years.

Faster than a speeding bullet

Why are Greyhounds so fast? For many reasons. But here's the short explanation. Not only do Greyhounds have long legs and long spines, but their spines are extremely flexible. This flexibility increases the Greyhound's speed by lengthening his stride and by allowing him to place his paws on the ground where they will provide the most thrust. Greyhounds also have developed strong muscles in their hindquarters, which provide tremendous forward thrust when they run. The racing Greyhound's leg length compared to the depth of his chest, called his *legginess ratio,* also contributes to his speed. When most dogs run, all their paws leave the ground only once in each full cycle of steps. But the faster a dog is capable of running, the more likely it is he will have all his feet off the ground twice in each full cycle of steps. This is called a *double-suspension gait.* The double-suspension gait is a very demanding style of running. Animals who run this way can only do so for short distances. And this is the way Greyhounds run. Check out the fourth and eighth sketches in Figure 2-1 to see how all four paws leave the ground twice in each full cycle.

Figure 2-1: In the double-suspension gait, the Greyhound leaves the ground twice in each full cycle of steps.

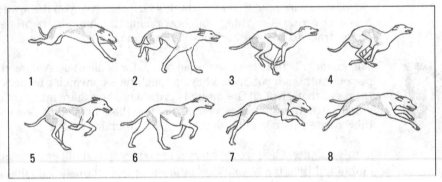

1   2   3   4

5   6   7   8

More powerful than a locomotive

In addition to the Greyhound's gait, other anatomical differences set the breed apart from other dogs, making him more powerful overall:

✔ The Greyhound's heart is slightly bigger than the hearts of other dogs, and it has a thicker left wall.

✔ The cardiac output of a Greyhound increases by five times during a race, which means that, in just one minute, a Greyhound pumps his own body weight in blood.

✔ The Greyhound's blood pressure is higher than that of other breeds.

✔ In other breeds, 7.2 percent of their body weight is blood. But in a Greyhound, 11.4 percent of the body weight is blood.

✔ The Greyhound has more red blood cells than other breeds.

✔ Greyhounds have thinner skin, a shorter coat, and an aerodynamic design that reduces wind resistance.

✔ The Greyhound's body weight is only 16 percent fat, less than half the amount of dogs of a similar weight in other breeds.

✔ Greyhounds gallop and hunt using their sight (60 percent), their sense of smell (20 percent), and their hearing (20 percent). Other dogs use their senses differently, depending upon what they were bred to do.

Check out Figure 2-2 for an illustration of the Greyhound's external features.

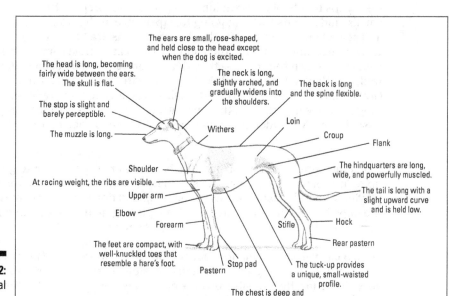

Figure 2-2:
The external features of a Greyhound.

Greyhounds: The odor-free dogs

Greyhounds' short, thin fur with no undercoat is easy to maintain. It produces no oil, which means you'll smell no doggy odor as long as you brush it regularly and keep your hound healthy.

Growing Up in the Fast Lane: The Puppyhood of Future Racers

Puppies are adorable, and Greyhound puppies are no exception. Looking at a litter of pudgy pups, usually six or seven in number, you may have a hard time believing that they will grow into sleek speed machines.

Early puppyhood for most racers from good farms is much like puppyhood for other dogs who are bred by responsible breeders. Good breeders recognize that handling and nurturing is critical. They take the time to introduce their pups to lots of different kinds of people and prepare them for the sights, smells, and sounds they are going to experience at the track. These owners and kennel operators believe that happy hounds are better racers. Greyhounds who aren't handled and nurtured as puppies are problematic when they reach the track — they don't train easily, they usually don't run well, and they're just plain difficult to deal with. Unlike most other pups, Greyhound puppies are kept with their littermates for several months. Before they are three months old, they are tattooed with their National Greyhound Association (NGA) identification numbers. These tattoos uniquely identify each dog.

When the pups are about six months old, they are separated into groups of up to four pups. These pairs will spend the next six to eight months together, playing with old plastic bottles, running up and down the fence lines racing the pups in adjacent runs, digging holes, playing hide-and-seek, and hanging out in a wading pool in the summer heat. They are taught manners like leash walking, and they get their noses bumped for jumping on people. The pups learn basic verbal commands that will become important in their racing lives. They are introduced to muzzles, and occasionally they go to the racetrack for very slow runs. Responsible owners encourage these kinds of activities, which promote good behavior and personality. Sound temperament and training is as important in racing as it is in the living room.

No two racers have the same ear tattoos. The tattoo in a Greyhound's left ear is his litter registration number, which is assigned by the NGA. The tattoo in his right ear identifies a specific puppy in that litter. The tattoo in your retired racer's right ear identifies the month and year of his birth and the order in his litter in which he was tattooed. The first number refers to the month he was born, the second number is the last digit of the year he was born, and the last digit is the order in which he was tattooed (which may or may not be his birth order in his litter). So if your retired racer's right ear tattoo reads 24C, it means he was born in February (2) of 1994 (4) and he was the third pup in his litter to be tattooed (C). These numbers are sometimes difficult to read. If you can't read them, try shining a flashlight behind your hound's ear.

At 12 to 14 months of age, the dogs' training begins in earnest. They are moved to a kennel room along with their littermates and the dogs from two or three other litters. In the kennel room, they are housed in wire crates stacked one row above another (with the females usually housed in the upper row). A radio plays around the clock to help block out noises from other kennel rooms, arriving and departing vehicles, and other noises that may disturb the Greyhounds. Four times a day, the Greyhounds are *turned out* (let out into a fenced area for about an hour each time). When they are out of their crates, they have a chance to eliminate and to play with the other racers from their kennel room. During this time, the crates are cleaned and bedding is refreshed. They return to their crates and get some ear rubs, treats, and petting before the crate doors are closed.

Between the ages of 12 and 14 months, the Greyhounds are taken to the training track once a week. From the age of 14 months until they move to the track permanently (at about 18 months of age), they are taken to the training track twice a week.

When the pups arrive at the track, their early experiences with handling and exposure to new people and situations again play an important role. If a racer wasn't handled extensively as a puppy and exposed to lots of new people and situations in positive ways, the transition to life at the track can be stressful.

The Bertillon Card

Each registered racing Greyhound has an identification card called a *Bertillon Card,* which lists 56 identifying points on that registered Greyhound. The card even includes the color of the dog's toenails. This precise means of identifying an individual dog serves as a control point for the integrity of racing. It assures that the dog who is entered in a race is actually the dog who runs.

Every time an NGA Greyhound changes owners, she is formally registered to the new owner. When you adopt a retired racer, you can contact the NGA and get your own certificate of registration for your dog. The reverse side of this certificate has the Bertillon Card for your dog.

See Appendix A for information about how to obtain a pet certificate for your dog and to see a sample NGA Certificate and Bertillon Card.

When the Greyhounds have permanently moved to the racetrack, they race about twice a week, competing against other dogs who are also novices. Greyhounds who don't do well are retired, even though they may only be about two years old. If a Greyhound wins, he begins to climb in grade and race against better and better dogs. As a dog ages, he begins to lose and moves down in grade. He may also move down in grade when he returns to racing after he recovers from an injury. Eventually, he will be retired from racing. Some exceptional dogs will be used for breeding. The lucky ones, when they're retired, will be adopted into homes like yours. The unlucky ones are killed.

REMEMBER

Many adopters want to know what the people in the racing industry are like. Although not all adoption groups will agree with me, my experience has been that the people who breed or own racing Greyhounds, train racers, or operate racing kennels are as diverse as any other group of people. That means they are as good, bad, or indifferent as any group of people. Some owners don't remember their dogs unless the dogs make money and have no interest in their dogs' futures when their careers end. Other breeders or owners take pictures of each dog before they send him off to the track to begin his career. They say goodbye with a hug and kiss and include a note to the kennel owner or trainer with information on each individual dog. Our newest girl just received a birthday card from the folks at her racing kennel.

Before the 1980s, nearly all racing Greyhounds were killed at the end of their careers. In the early 1980s, reputable industry people and public attention combined to focus attention on this problem. At that time, some conscientious breeders were already placing their Greyhounds in good homes at the ends of their careers, but there was no organized effort to do so. At one time, it was estimated that 60,000 Greyhounds were being destroyed each year. By the early 1990s, the industry began to provide estimates of the numbers of adoptions based on their records. In 1991, approximately 52,000 Greyhounds were born, but only 7,000 were adopted.

In the past ten years, thanks to the efforts of people in the industry and the work of more than 200 dedicated adoption groups, there has been a dramatic change in the fate of retired racing Greyhounds. By 1999, the number of racing Greyhound puppies born had dropped to about 33,000. The estimated number actually available for adoption each year is about 25,000. For the past several years, the number of retired racers adopted has leveled off at about 18,000 annually. Although the racing industry is doing a great deal to reduce the numbers of racers being bred and encourages breeders and trainers to make retired racers available for adoption, the number of racers born is still higher than the number being adopted. A lot of work still needs to be done to ensure that racers are placed in loving homes like yours at the end of their careers.

JUST FOR FUN

The half-million hound

The most money ever paid for a racing Greyhound was $500,000 in 1986. The dog's name was P's Rambling.

Sizing Up the Greyhound's Physical Needs

Retired racers are large dogs and vary considerably in size. The smallest retired racing Greyhound can weigh as little as 40 pounds, and the largest may tip the scales at more than 90 pounds and still be at a normal weight. In the following sections, I guide you through the basics of a Greyhound's body — letting you know what physical traits and basic physical needs you can expect from a retired racer, and what that means to you.

Regular exercise

All dogs need *some* regular exercise, and retired racers are no exception. Walking a Greyhound one or two times each day should be sufficient exercise. You don't have to go on long hikes; a good leg stretch for ten minutes or so will work for most retired racers.

At a minimum, your Greyhound also needs a few minutes each day for a good romp. If you don't have a fenced yard, he's likely to turn an area of your home into his own little racetrack for a minute or two each day.

Avoidance of injuries

Like all athletes, Greyhounds are prone to injuries — it's the nature of their job and their breed. Greyhounds have a light coat, very thin skin, and long thin bones, all of which means that they are more injury-prone than other breeds. What would be a simple scratch to a Labrador Retriever may be a nasty tear requiring several stitches for a Greyhound. For this reason, Greyhounds are muzzled when they run together, even if they're just running for fun or exercise.

Like other athletes, the dings and bumps your retired racer received in his professional career may flare up as arthritis as he ages.

Fenced-in play areas

Greyhounds are part of a group of dog breeds called *sighthounds* (sometimes called *gazehounds*). The sighthound has keen eyesight to detect movement, instant reaction times, and incredible speed and agility to close in on prey.

What does this mean to you? Whether your hound had a successful racing career, he can go from a dead stop to speeds in excess of 40 miles per hour in three strides. When he takes off after a rabbit that you can't even see or startles and bolts at some strange noise, he'll be in the next town before you can even get the word "come" out of your mouth.

Unlike the sporting breeds, which were bred to work side by side with their human companions, sighthounds were bred to find and chase down

game, with little or no guidance from their human partners. Sighthounds are rather independent dogs. When they are involved in their life's work — chasing prey — they're aren't likely to pay much attention to your requests to come or sit.

From the day a Greyhound comes into your home, you must remain committed to never letting him off his lead, except in an enclosed area or other safe setting. Yards surrounded by electronic fences don't qualify. If you want to let your Greyhound run free, you can only do so in a yard surrounded by a real fence. If you expect the dog of your dreams to follow off a leash and look up at you adoringly from your side, a Greyhound is *not* the dog for you.

Health issues

Compared to other breeds, Greyhounds are nearly free of serious health problems, and they usually live to about 12 to 14 years of age.

Greyhounds have thin skin, a very light coat, and little body fat to provide insulation. As a result, they must be protected against extreme weather. Although they may enjoy outdoor activities, they are not suited for outdoor living.

For more information on specific health issues, check out the chapters in Part IV of this book.

Cleanliness

Greyhounds are clean almost to the point of being vain. They have a short, light coat that doesn't shed excessively and doesn't need much care. Many Greyhounds groom themselves like cats do, helping to make retired racers generally low-maintenance dogs.

Greyhounds do have notoriously bad teeth. Whether it's genetics, the track diet, or chewing at the crate out of boredom, the results are the same: Greyhounds' teeth require regular daily cleaning.

Watch that tail!

The long thin tails of Greyhounds break easily. Watch for closing doors. And try to keep an eye on your hound so that he doesn't wag his tail into a wall. Greyhounds' tails can get to wagging hard enough that they'll break if they come into contact with a wall during play.

Retired racers are not housebroken, but they are crate-trained. When you bring a retired racer into your home, you have to teach him to treat your whole house as part of his crate. If you follow the guidelines in Chapter 6, this is generally a simple task.

Answering Some Common Questions about Retired Racers

What is the personality of the retired racer really like? Are they gentle, docile dogs or high-strung and aloof? What can you expect of this former athlete when he moves into your home? Check out the following sections for answers to these common questions on the breed.

How social are they?

Some people think of Greyhounds as aloof and unsociable. Although Greyhounds aren't as demanding of attention as some more gregarious breeds, most are friendly even with strangers. And some are real social butterflies.

In general, Greyhounds are not boisterous dogs who are constantly on the move and demanding attention, but they *can* play the clown with the best of them. We nicknamed our first retired racer the Clown Princess because of her antics. One minute, she had all the refinement and dignity of Grace Kelly, and the next she was acting like Lucille Ball at her nuttiest.

Racing Greyhounds are not accustomed to being alone, because they are housed with other racers throughout their lives. Moving into a house without other dogs can be a big adjustment for a retired racer. That's why alone training is so important. I tell you all about alone training in Chapter 6.

Spooks: Extremely shy dogs

A *spook* is an extremely shy dog who reacts fearfully to many normal situations. His usual response will be to hide and avoid any person or situation that he views as frightening. Unfortunately, he views almost *everything* as frightening. This behavior may be partly genetic, or it may be related to a lack of handling and positive exposures when he was a pup. Turning a spook into a well-adjusted member of your pack is *not* a task for an inexperienced owner. Look for a reasonably social racer for your first adoption.

How do they respond to other animals?

One of the biggest myths about retired racers is that they are not safe to have around cats, small animals, or even toy breeds of dogs. A Greyhound with a *high* prey drive may never be safe around cats or other small animals, including toy breeds of dogs. On the other hand, Greyhounds with a low to medium prey drive can adjust well to life with smaller animals. I discuss this more in Chapter 5.

Many retired racers go into homes with cats or other small animals and decide Fluffy is a great friend. But others decide that Fluffy is lunch. If you have cats, small animals, or a toy breed of dog, work with your adoption group to find a retired racer who will fit best in your home. The adoption group will use a technique called *profiling* to match a retired racer to a prospective family. Some groups are able to expose retired racers to a variety of situations to get a sense of how he will react to cats or children, for example.

You're tempting fate if you try to get a retired racer to make friends with a rabbit or other small animal or a bird. These creatures should never be left alone or unprotected with a Greyhound. Although many Greyhounds live successfully in homes with small animals, these matches are best left to experienced Greyhound owners.

Are they good with children?

Children and dogs are the stuff movies are made of. But is that truth or just more fiction? Greyhounds don't come with training wheels like a bicycle. If you haven't taught your child how to interact properly with dogs, a Greyhound isn't the dog to use to further your child's education.

Many, many retired racers live happily in homes with children. Although most retired racers generally respond well to older, quiet, considerate children, many retired racers have had *no* experience with small children or infants.

Expecting a retired racer to interact with children in the same way as a dog who was properly introduced to children as a young puppy is unfair. If you have young children or are expecting to have children, don't adopt *any* dog, especially a retired racer, unless you are absolutely certain you have the patience required to deal successfully with a dog and a child.

If you have children, keep in mind that Greyhounds weren't built for the rough-and-tumble world of boisterous children. Greyhounds lack the padding that protects most other breeds from the roughness and harshness that a playful or improperly supervised child can wreak. Although children may prefer to play with a dog by wrestling or rolling around on the floor, Greyhounds like to chase things and run. And they generally don't care if you join in or not.

Dogs and children are *not* a match made in heaven. Most people have inaccurate and unrealistic expectations about child/dog interactions. If you have a dog and a child, you have a tremendous responsibility to keep both the child *and* the dog safe.

Many retired racers are returned or surrendered because they have growled or snapped at a child. Because of this, many Greyhound adoption groups now refuse to adopt to families with children under the age of four. Some groups won't adopt to anyone with a child under six. Other groups have established required education programs for adopters with young children.

Before you adopt a retired racer, take a realistic look at your ability to manage your children and a dog and decide if you're being fair to yourself, your kids, and the dog.

How well will a Greyhound adapt to my home?

A retired racer's former world was routine and structured. Most have never been inside a house or taken a walk in the park. Greyhounds have extremely acute senses of smell, hearing, and sight. They tend to startle easily, and their reaction time is so quick that they've usually reacted to something before the average dog has even had time to notice it. With appropriate tutoring and plenty of positive exposure to new people and situations, he'll quickly learn about his new world and not feel the need to react to every new thing he hears.

Guard dogs they are not

Retired racers are not guard dogs. In fact, most aren't even good watch dogs. Greyhounds are quiet dogs who generally don't bark much.

Adopters are fond of saying that the only way a Greyhound will hurt a burglar is if the burglar trips over the dog in the dark.

Your retired racer's keen sight, hearing, and sensitivity to his surroundings can easily distract him from what you had in mind. Keep in mind that he doesn't know that windows are solid or that swimming pools aren't. He has never seen stairs (and he won't like them when he does) or walked on slippery floors. Although Greyhounds learn to deal with these things, you need to be patient with your hound as he adjusts to this whole new world.

How smart are retired racers?

Greyhounds are not always responsive to commands. But that isn't the same as being dumb; they just aren't convinced it's important. Greyhounds are bright dogs. If you doubt your Greyhound's intelligence, see how long it takes him to recognize the sound of his food bin opening or his leash being picked up in preparation for a jaunt in the park. Some Greyhounds really challenge you by learning to open doors and cupboards. In general, retired racers just aren't convinced that obedience has much relevance. Many are easily distracted by strange sights, smells, and sounds — and that makes training both interesting and challenging.

After they've become accustomed to all the strange new things we throw at them in their lives beyond the racetrack, retired racers can be taught to do a wide variety of behaviors. They won't dwell on your every word as if it came from the Mount on two stone tablets, but they are certainly capable of learning the behaviors and skills that make them welcome members of the family. They learn best when training is gentle, interesting, and fun.

Are Greyhounds aggressive?

Absolutely not. Retired racers are seldom aggressive toward people. If they do growl or snap, they do so most often out of fear. Retired racing Greyhounds generally accept human handling very well. As racers, they were routinely handled far more than most dogs. They often tolerate medical procedures that would require sedation or anesthesia in other dogs.

Most Greyhounds are not aggressive toward other dogs. If there is a fight, the other dog usually starts it.

Where'd my other sock go?

Don't be surprised if your Greyhound is a pack-rat. Everything that catches his attention may end up in his crate or favorite resting place. He may get to be better at picking up his toys than your kids are. Of course, you can also expect him to carry off things from the laundry basket, the kids' toys, and anything else that seems appealing and fits in his mouth. Most Greyhounds don't take things to chew. They just like to collect things. So if one of your blue socks is missing, check your Greyhound's bed.

Part II
Finding Your
Soul Mate

The 5th Wave   By Rich Tennant

"I made up a bed for the Greyhound. I threw in a bunch of my old track shoes to make him feel at home."

In this part . . .

If you're thinking about adopting a retired racer, the chapters in this part are the place to start. Here you'll find great information that will help you figure out whether a Greyhound is the right dog for you. When you're ready to adopt a retired racer, you can find lots of helpful tips and suggestions for getting your house ready for your new friend. And you'll also find practical information on bringing your new dog home the very first day.

Chapter 3

Determining Whether a Retired Racing Greyhound Is Right for You

- -

In This Chapter

▶ Debunking some common myths about dogs

▶ Asking yourself the right questions before you commit to caring for a dog

- -

*B*efore you adopt any dog, including a retired racing Greyhound, be realistic about your lifestyle and what you're willing and able to accommodate. Dogs require a huge commitment, and although I believe wholeheartedly that they're worth it, that commitment isn't one every family can — or should — make.

In this chapter, I start out by highlighting some common descriptions of the mythical "perfect dog" and let you know what you should expect instead. I also guide you through a series of questions you should ask yourself — and your family members — before you bring any breed of dog into your home. This is the place to get serious about yourself. If you're honest with your responses and you still end the chapter ready to take on a retired racer, you'll be all the more confident that you're making the right decision.

Dispelling the Myth of the "Perfect Dog"

When I conduct seminars on choosing a puppy or on dog behavior, I ask my audience to define the ideal dog. The list they come up with usually looks something like this:

- ✔ Doesn't shed

- ✔ Doesn't bark except when the owner wants him to

- ✔ Doesn't jump up

- ✔ Doesn't pull on the leash

- ✔ Doesn't chew anything except his own toys

- Doesn't chase cars, cats, kids, bicycles, or joggers
- Doesn't lick your face
- Doesn't need much attention
- Doesn't mind being alone all day and most evenings

If you're expecting me to tell you that this list is the perfect description of the retired racer, you're mistaken. As far as I'm concerned, this list is the perfect description of a pet *rock,* not a dog of any breed.

But just because retired racers don't meet all the qualifications on this list doesn't mean they don't make wonderful pets. If you pick a retired racer whose character and personality are suited to your lifestyle, you can fashion the perfect dog for your family. All it takes is appropriate training and ample doses of patience and attention.

No amount of training will keep your hound from shedding. There is no such thing as a dog with fur who doesn't shed, and Greyhounds are no exception. Real dogs with real fur shed. If shedding is a major problem for you, consider buying a stuffed animal instead. Some groups recommend Greyhounds as hypoallergenic because they don't shed heavily. Although the low-shedding breeds may be less troublesome for some allergic people, no dog is hypoallergenic.

Because most of us don't understand what dogs are really like, we often define our best friend in terms of what he *shouldn't* do or be, instead of what he really *is.* Dispelling the myths of what a dog is and what kind of relationship you can expect to have with him can go a long way toward ensuring that you find the right match for you and your lifestyle.

Unfortunately, many of us get our ideas of how dogs behave from television and movies. But Hollywood's version of man's best friend is usually far from the truth. Unless the film is a comedy, no Hollywood dog ever jumps on Aunt Gertrude or does his business on the Persian rug in the foyer. Hollywood dogs never turn the backyard into an archeological dig or steal dinner off the kitchen counter. And they wouldn't dream of chasing the cat.

All Hollywood dogs have some important things in common, especially the fact that they are all pure fiction. Perfect dogs do not exist — except on TV and in the movies. Keep in mind that the dogs you see in the movies behave well for a living. And just like a race car driver or a concert pianist, they are highly trained professionals.

We can't expect our dogs to be perfect any more than we can expect our children to be perfect. We make mistakes. We forget. And we need to allow our dogs the same latitude.

JUST FOR FUN

> ## Rooing for you
>
> Most Greyhounds don't bark much. In fact, some don't bark at all. But some do like to *roo*. Rooing is like a cross between a bark and a whine and happens when Greyhounds get excited.

Getting Serious about Adopting a Greyhound

Before you commit yourself to taking care of any dog, but especially a retired racer, ask yourself some very important questions — and be honest with your responses.

Does a dog fit your lifestyle?

Think about your present and anticipated future lifestyle. What will happen to your dog if you get married, get divorced, relocate, have a baby, or experience other significant lifestyle changes?

If you think owning a retired racer could pose a problem with any changes in your lifestyle — not to mention your lifestyle as it currently is — this isn't the time to add a retired racer or any dog. Wait until a better time to add a dog to your family.

Are you committed to caring for your retired racer for ten or more years?

Most racers end their careers when they are between two and five years old. Because their life span is about twelve to fourteen years, you can expect to have your friend with you for ten years or more. Dogs of any breed are not disposable items when they misbehave, get old, or outlive their entertainment or fashion value.

Just as a very young child is totally dependent on you for all of her needs and her emotional well-being, so is your dog. Children grow up, become independent, and leave home (at least we hope they do). But your dog will be completely dependent on you for his entire life. If you can't say without any doubt that you can commit yourself to caring for your dog for the next ten or more years, don't adopt.

Can you afford a dog?

The cost of caring for your Greyhound doesn't stop with the adoption fee and the cost of food. The initial cost of adopting a retired racing Greyhound varies greatly, but expect to spend between $100 and $300. Some dogs are adopted with all the trimmings — a physical exam, spay/neuter, heartworm test and preventive, worming, dental cleaning, vaccinations, a bath and flea/tick check, some introductory training on stairs and house-training, a leash, a collar, and microchip identification. Other groups supply a hound with a pulse, a collar, and an ID tag.

Be sure you know specifically what is included in the fee, because any retired racer will require certain basics, and if they haven't been provided for your dog by the adoption group or kennel, you'll have to provide them yourself. An adoption fee can sound very reasonable until you realize what wasn't included. The lowest fees I've seen are around $100. Most fees are in the $150 to $250 range. Adoption fees usually include spay/neuter surgery, because owners of racing Greyhounds usually require this as a condition of allowing the racer to be placed for adoption and because responsible kennels and adoption groups know there are too many unwanted dogs already. Most adoption fees also include a physical exam and up-to-date vaccinations.

Keep in mind that if your Greyhound's vaccinations are "up-to-date," that doesn't mean the vaccinations aren't due again in a month or two. It just means he doesn't need them today.

Look for a group or kennel that provides a dental cleaning, along with the spay/neuter. Most Greyhounds need to have their teeth cleaned. If it is done when the other surgery is performed, you save money and, more importantly, keep your hound from having to be anesthetized a second time. Because some Greyhounds have awful teeth, you may not be able to tell by looking in his mouth whether he's had his teeth cleaned recently.

Expect to spend at least $500 to $700 when you initially adopt your retired racer. This amount should cover the adoption fee, spaying or neutering, a basic bed, a crate, coat, toys, food, an initial veterinary exam, and grooming supplies. I'm not talking about anything fancy, just the bare-bones stuff you'll need to properly care for your racer the day he walks through your front door.

The American Humane Association estimates the first year of acquiring and owning a puppy will cost about $1,500. Expect something similar when you adopt a retired racer.

After you get your racer home, you'll need to pay for annual vaccinations, heartworm prevention, flea and tick control, a license, and food. For a 65-pound dog, count on spending at least $750 each year. This estimate assumes you'll do your own training and grooming, that you'll encounter no illnesses or accidents, and that you aren't going to spoil him with new toys and other goodies. And always budget a little extra in case your dog does get sick, because even a minor illness can mean medical bills of more than $100. A major illness can run into the thousands of dollars.

Prepare yourself for the financial costs of getting a retired racer. Some groups provide the initial health care your retired racer will need. Others can barely afford to provide a collar and leash. If you have to provide them yourself, the initial health care expenses listed here could cost a few hundred dollars in even a small urban area. If these weren't done by the group or kennel, you'll need to take care of them within the first week or so.

At the very least your Greyhound is likely to need:

- A physical exam
- A heartworm test and a supply of preventive
- A fecal exam and de-worming
- Current vaccinations/immunizations
- Spay/neuter

And it doesn't stop there. When you're hooked, there is no end to the things you'll do for your hound. One adopter quipped when asked what it costs to adopt a Greyhound, "Ninety dollars for my hound plus $25,000 dollars for the minivan to get him to the vet." Another adopter I know replaced all her smooth flooring with carpeting because her Greyhound fell and became frightened of slippery floors. One adopter recently admitted to buying a waterbed just for her hounds. We're a crazy bunch.

Do you have children or are you planning to have them?

A retired racer can be the ideal companion for the right child, and most live in homes with children. Because of their gentle nature and their preference for a calm environment, they do best in homes with quiet, well-mannered children who are school age or older, like the girl shown in Figure 3-1.

Adopting a dog or puppy requires more time, commitment, and experience than most families realize. Keeping both young children and a dog safe and happy takes a lot of work. Wait until your children are grade school age before you add an adult dog to your family.

Figure 3-1:
Greyhounds
prefer quiet
and
considerate
children.

Photograph courtesy of Bonnie Stoner

Are you prepared to care for your aging racer?

Although the retired racer you bring home may be an active and playful young dog, you have to think ten years down the road and be prepared for the changes that may take place. Consider whether you're prepared for the responsibility of caring for an aging Greyhound in five or ten years. If you work all day, how will you address the needs of an animal who may no longer have the bowel and bladder control that he once did? As most dogs age, they develop arthritis. How are you going to deal with a 60-pound or 80-pound Greyhound that can no longer manage stairs on his own? If your hound becomes ill as he ages, are you prepared emotionally and financially for the challenge? *Remember:* A prolonged illness can strain even a well-padded budget. And will you be ready emotionally for his increased dependence on you and the behavioral changes that often accompany aging?

More than 20 percent of the animals that are abandoned to shelters are abandoned because of the problems of aging. They deserve better than that, and unless you're committed to giving your retired racer a home for life, don't adopt.

Will you consider your pet one of the family?

A recent survey of twelve shelters in the United States indicated that more than half of the dogs surrendered to shelters were given up because of human lifestyle and housing issues. If you cannot make a lifetime commitment, please don't consider adopting a retired racer or any other dog. Dogs are social creatures, and they need your attention and company.

If you choose to make a Greyhound a member of your human pack (otherwise known as your family), you need to be prepared to treat him as a member of that family for the rest of his natural life.

I can't remember what our home was like before our first retired racer adopted us. We adore almost everything about our retired racers. But I know they aren't the right dogs for every family. Take the time to consider whether a Greyhound is right for yours before you make the commitment to care for one.

Chapter 4

Getting Ready to Adopt
a Retired Racer

In This Chapter

▶ Knowing what characteristics you're looking for in a retired racer

▶ Deciding whether to adopt through a racetrack or a private adoption group

▶ Understanding the adoption process

▶ Choosing the Greyhound that's right for you

*I*n this chapter, I make the assumption that you understand the ups and downs of owning a retired racer and you're ready to move on. You've decided to make a retired racer a part of your family. Now what?

You still have lots of decisions to make. Where do you get a retired racing Greyhound? What's involved in the adoption process? Do you get to choose your own retired racer or is one chosen for you? Should you get a male or a female? Should you get a young Greyhound or an older one? Here I answer all those questions and more. So if you've decided a retired racer is for you, read on!

Determining What You Want in a Retired Racer

If you're certain you can provide a loving, lifelong home for a retired racer, think about what kind of retired racer you want before you contact an adoption group or a track kennel. If you take the time to list the characteristics you want in your retired racer and any lifestyle issues you need to address, you're much more likely to find one who will soon become a valued part of your family.

Consider the issues that matter in your home, like the following:

- ✔ The Greyhound's size
- ✔ How he interacts with children, including those who may come to visit
- ✔ How he interacts with other animals in your home
- ✔ How much time you have to spend playing with and training him

As you consider these issues, be sure to make clear distinctions between wants and needs. You may *need* a hound who deals well with children. And you may *want* a smaller dog but would welcome a larger dog into your home as well. Only *you* know what your wants and needs are, so be honest with yourself.

The right Greyhound can adapt to almost any lifestyle. But that doesn't mean that asking him to adapt to dramatic changes is always fair. Look at what the Greyhound was bred for. You may be happier if you looked elsewhere for a training buddy for that marathon. And he may be happier in front of the fireplace or the campfire than blazing a trail through a thicket of blackberry bushes.

In short, look at your lifestyle, consider the Greyhound's temperament, and think of the individual personality of the retired racer you're considering. Then worry about things like sex, age, size, and color, all covered in the following sections.

Sex

Each dog is an individual, just as each sibling within a family is unique. Look at each individual dog and how he or she fits into your lifestyle. Unless there is a very specific reason why you must have a male or a female, let the personality of the dog be your guide.

Many Greyhound owners swear that males are better with children. Personally, I think your child's behavior around your retired racer is more likely to influence your hound's response than his gender is.

If you already have a dog in your family, choose a dog of the opposite sex. They're less likely to argue over who's top dog.

One or two?

Only bring one retired racer into your home at a time. Your retired racer will bond more quickly if you can spend quality time with him alone.

Age

Most Greyhounds end their racing careers between the ages of two and four. Some racers who are particularly good may run until they are five years old, and then they may be used for breeding. Those used for breeding may not be retired until they are as old as eight.

Because Greyhounds don't mature until they are about three years of age, a two-year-old retired racer may still be very much a puppy and quite full of himself. He may need more exercise and more supervision than a dog who is just a few months or a year older.

An older dog — one over six or seven years of age — is a delightful addition to any family. The only downside of adopting an older hound is that he may not be with you as long. Naturally, a senior hound is more likely to need ongoing medical treatment as he gets older. But if you have the financial resources to deal with a problem if one does develop, they have more love to give than money can buy.

Many older hounds are returned to adoption groups or surrendered to animal shelters because they no longer fit a family's lifestyle. The family may be moving to a big new house and doesn't want the lawn ruined by a dog that loves to run. Or maybe they've had a baby and have found owning a dog to be too inconvenient. The reasons are endless and often ridiculous, but the result is an abandoned racer who needs a loving family. Because Greyhounds have an average life expectancy of 12 or more years, even a seven-year-old dog is likely to spend another five to seven years with you. That's a lot of love left to give, so don't dismiss older guys.

Size

Racing Greyhounds range from 24 to 30 inches tall at the shoulders, and active racers weigh between 40 and 80 pounds (see Figure 4-1 for an illustration of the size differences in adult Greyhounds). Because of their early training, retired racers don't tend to pull on their leashes. This makes them easier to manage than other untrained large dogs.

Greyhounds are the smallest large dog I've ever encountered. Although they are very tall dogs and can sprawl over an entire queen-size bed, they are also like a furry folding table. They can tuck in their legs and curl up into the most amazingly small spaces. They also tend to back up rather than try to turn and scurry when they are in the way, which is a real blessing when your arms are full and you can't see that the dog is in the way. Greyhounds just don't seem to get underfoot, even in small spaces.

So unless you have serious physical limitations or a really tiny bed, size doesn't need to be a factor in your decision-making process. Just keep in mind that even a medium-size Greyhound is still a large dog.

Figure 4-1:
This small
female and
large male
represent
the
extremes in
Greyhound
size.

Photograph courtesy of Bonnie Stoner

Color and physical appearance

Greyhounds are found in virtually every color or combination you can imagine. If color ranks anywhere other than last on your wish list, you should be asking yourself why it is so important. If you have an absolute phobia of white dogs because you were bitten by a white dog when you were a child, that makes sense. With so many dogs available, you should be able to find a retired racer in the color you'd prefer. Just keep in mind that a satisfactory, long-term relationship is a function of temperament and personality, not physical appearance.

Even Greyhounds who weren't the fastest racers on the track still have the hearts of champions. Don't count on finding a racer free of *any* physical imperfections. These dogs are retired athletes. Like all athletes, they've spent years working very hard — and they have the scars to prove it. Your retired racer may have nicks, dings, and scars. He may even be missing a toe or walk with a limp. He may have a crimp in his tail because he wags it too hard or caught it in a door and broke it. None of these things make him a less perfect dog. I like to think these imperfections add character.

Getting more than you wished for

Sometimes, what you get is better than what you thought you wanted.

When we decided to add a retired racer to our family, we contacted a local adoption group. At the time, we already had two other dogs — an 11-year-old and a 5-year-old, each weighing about 20 pounds. We also had a 7-year-old cat. Out of respect for the old man (our 11-year-old dog, not my husband), we didn't want to bring in a younger male. We didn't care about color or injuries. Any age up to about five years old was fine, but even that wasn't set in stone. And our retired racer had to be friendly with cats, small dogs, and our grandchildren.

The only issue we felt strongly about was size. Because we lived in a small townhouse with two small dogs and a cat, we wanted a smaller

Greyhound — less than 50 pounds, or as close to that as possible. Peggy F. Levin, the founder and president of Personalized Greyhounds, Inc., got a call from one of her contacts. Would a 2-year-old, 53-pound female be okay? She adored kids, was safe with cats, and had a great temperament. We decided to take her, figuring that three pounds over our weight limit was something we could easily live with.

Well, when Penny (RC Ottabea Peney) climbed out of the hold of that truck, she just kept coming and coming and coming. She only weighed 51 pounds (two pounds less than we anticipated), but she was nearly 28 inches high at the shoulders! And it took all of a nanosecond for her to race her way into our hearts.

Naturally, the more restrictive your wish list is, the more time you may need to find the right retired racer. If you have your heart set on a blue female who is cat- and kid-friendly, weighs less than 45 pounds, stands less than 24 inches at the shoulder, and is less than two years old, you'll likely have a very long wait. If you have specific, real reasons for narrowing your choices, that's fine. But don't shut yourself off from finding a new best friend for the wrong reasons.

Before you get your heart set on a certain color, sex, or age, think about what's really important — how this particular retired racer will fit into your lifestyle. Leave the fashion statements for the New York runways.

Deciding Whether to Go Factory Direct or through a Dealer

Retired racers usually find their way into homes either through independent adoption groups or through direct adoption from owners or track adoption kennels. Each way of placing retired racers with loving families has its positive and negative aspects. Some owners and tracks take responsibility for placing all adoptable racers when their racing careers are over. Virtually all tracks have their own adoption kennels and/or have a relationship with one or more adoption groups.

The adoption process varies so much from group to group that describing a typical adoption is nearly impossible. About the only thing they all have in common is that you'll be asked to fill out an application. You should also be asked to provide personal and veterinary references. (Some groups check these very carefully, but others barely notice them.) You may have to wait for a call when the right dog is available or you may get to pick your retired racer and leave with him that day. When you contact a group or kennel, ask them to describe their adoption process. If you have very specific needs, work with a groups whose application fee includes profiling. *Profiling* means the adoption group asks specific questions about your situation and tries to find the right retired racer for your needs.

The advantage of adopting directly from the track is fairly obvious: You usually get to pick the Greyhound you want. But this is also a disadvantage if you don't know anything about evaluating an adult dog. The costs of adopting directly from the track are generally lower because you aren't paying for transportation costs or for follow-up care. Some track adoption kennels spay or neuter their dogs before they are released for adoption, but some don't. Adopting directly from the track kennels has disadvantages as well. Not all track kennels have the time or the resources to profile their racers. However, chances are good the racetrack kennel personnel knows each dog's personality well — at least within the environment of the kennel — so be sure to ask lots of questions about the dogs you're considering for adoption.

Private adoption groups also have advantages. The largest adoption groups may have their own kennel facilities and veterinary staff. They often have the ability to house a number of racers who aren't reserved for a particular adopter. Here you can meet several available racers and find the match that is best for both you and the dog. Some organizations place each of their racers in a foster home so they can evaluate him before placing him with a family.

Smaller adoption groups generally depend on a track adoption kennel contact person to profile the racers for them and choose the right dog based on what they know of his personality and behavior as well as what they know about the needs of the adopter. Except for rescue situations where, for instance, Greyhounds have been abandoned or a track is closing and a large number of racers need to be placed in homes quickly, these groups tend to bring in only those dogs for which they have adopters waiting.

Any reputable adoption group or kennel screens prospective applicants. Some groups have more restrictive standards than others. For example, some groups won't adopt to people unless they have fenced yards. Other groups won't adopt to people with young children. Reputable groups should have a screening process to ensure the potential adopter understands the responsibilities of adopting a dog. They should also have a policy for dealing with any dog who is no longer welcome in his adopted home.

Exercising caution when introducing your new hound to your children

A retired racer may respond appropriately to small animals or children in a test situation and still react poorly to a child or small animal in your home. Always keep in mind that the test environment isn't the same as your home. The child or animal involved in the test may behave very differently from your child or animal at home. A racer that tests safe still needs careful supervision.

Most adoption groups allow you to specify the age, size, color, and sex of the retired racer you want. Some groups feel that if any of those issues are that important to you, perhaps an animal with fewer social needs would be a better choice than a dog.

Each group has its own personality and philosophy. Some are vehemently opposed to Greyhound racing. Other groups are directly involved with the racing industry. And still others take no position on the issue of racing. But all work to help retired racers find homes. The attitude of the adoption group toward the sport of racing won't affect the kind of retired racer you get, but it may affect *your* perception of the dog-racing industry and the people who are involved in it.

Not every match is made in heaven

Both large and small adoption groups sometimes have to find homes for racers who are returned to the adoption group from an adopting family. These dogs are called *bouncebacks* or *bounces,* and they may have been returned for what you would consider minor reasons. Although any group should be absolutely honest and tell you why the racer was returned, don't assume that there is something wrong with a dog who has been returned by his original adopter.

Recently, an adoption group was trying to find a home for a Greyhound who had been bounced because he had gas. Other Greyhounds are bounced when owners divorce. Some are returned because the owner decides the landscaping at the new house is more important than the dog. So don't rule out a bounced dog without taking a closer look.

Choosing between adoption groups

How do you decide which adoption group to choose? If you live in a small town or a remote area, you may not have a wide range of choices.

But don't let price be the determining factor. When you look for your new best friend, it isn't the time to shop for bonus buys or coupon savings. The fees charged by most groups are often at or below their actual costs of preparing the retired racer for adoption.

If you're new to Greyhounds, work with a group that offers some pre-adoption education, conducts thorough profiling, and provides at least minimum support after the adoption. Many groups assign each new adopter an adviser who is there to answer questions and provide support.

Picking the Perfect Hound

As you set about to choose the right retired racer for you, look inside yourself and be sure you don't expect a turnkey dog. Just because your retired racer is grown, and just because he has a gentle and loving personality, it doesn't mean you can expect him to walk into your home and into your life and settle in with no work on your part. Every dog requires grooming, housekeeping, training, and attention.

If you work directly with a track adoption kennel, rely on the advice of the kennel workers. They generally know their racers well. But trust your heart, too. You may arrive absolutely convinced that you must have a small, fawn female that looks like Bambi, but there may be something about that large, black male that tells you he's the one who will bond with your family.

If you have a cat, a bird, a toy breed of dog, or another small animal, work only with a kennel or group that can test a racer's reaction to these kinds of small animals. This is a job that should be conducted only by people knowledgeable about and experienced with Greyhounds. The safety of your other pets depends largely on choosing the right retired racer and your commitment to management and training. A special word of caution if your cat, toy dog, or other small animal is all white — many Greyhounds seem to react differently to all-white animals than they do to animals of similar size but different colors.

If you have children, be sure you bring them with you when you choose your retired racer. This is especially important if your children are under the age of five, boys between the ages of six and nine, or children with special needs, all of whom are the most likely victims of dog bites. At the very least, be sure the racer you're considering isn't afraid of your children when they're first introduced.

If you have children, I recommend that you work only with a group or kennel that can test the racer with children beforehand. You can also try to find a racer who has been raised with children. Many trainers have young children who frequently accompany them to work at the kennel or track. The racers from these environments are usually quite accustomed to children.

Few Greyhounds are aggressive to people. The chances that an aggressive Greyhound will be placed for adoption are slim, but mistakes do happen. If the racer is being placed in a home for the second time, because his first placement didn't work out, find out why it didn't work. If there is an obvious problem, you want to know about it before you decide to adopt him.

Why can't I have a puppy?

Little more than a decade ago, more than 60,000 racing Greyhounds were bred each year. Virtually all were killed when their careers were over. The adoption groups, American Kennel Club (AKC) breeders, the Greyhound Club of America, and the racing industry have all worked hard to bring this senseless slaughter to an end. The racing industry has made a commitment to decrease the number of dogs bred — breeding for quality rather than quantity. Racing puppies are rarely available. Only spayed or neutered retired racers are supposed to be adopted.

Greyhound puppies are nothing like their mature counterparts. They have high levels of energy, need lots of exercise, and require a lot of work and training. They are furry little terrors, just like any other puppy.

If you have your heart set on a Greyhound puppy, contact the Greyhound Club of America, listed in Appendix B, to find a reputable breeder. But be prepared for a long wait. Only 146 non-racing Greyhound puppies were born in 1999.

Adult non-racing Greyhounds sometimes need new homes, too. The Greyhound Club of America conducts breed rescue to help place these non-racing hounds.

Chapter 5

Welcoming a Retired Racer into Your Family

In This Chapter

▶ Buying all the equipment you need to make the transition easy

▶ Reading up on training ahead of time

▶ Being prepared for your first days and weeks with a retired racer

▶ Introducing your retired racer to all creatures great and small

Think of the first weeks and months with a retired racer as your own version of the movie *E.T.* Your home is as much an alien planet to a newly retired racer as Elliot's was to E.T. Your retired racer needs time to learn your language, your customs, and your culture. He needs to learn what is safe and what is dangerous in his new world. This won't happen in the span of a couple of hours like it does in a darkened movie theater, however. Your retired racer may need weeks or even months before he learns everything he needs to know to function as a member of your family. And he needs *you* to lead the way.

You can make the transition easier for you and your retired racer by being prepared for his arrival. His basic physical needs include food, water, exercise, play, elimination, and sleep. Be ready to meet these needs as soon as your retired racer arrives. This chapter guides you through the process of preparing your home for your retired racing Greyhound — everything from dog-proofing your home and yard to introducing your retired racer to your other furry friends. Whatever you need to prepare for a happy homecoming, this chapter has the goods.

Looking around Your Home for Potential Dog Hazards

Most of us realize we have to make our homes safe for young children, but many of us don't realize there are common things in our homes and yards that can harm our furry friends. Greyhounds are easy to live with. But like all dogs, they need to be protected from potential danger. Because your retired racer has most likely never been inside a house, he may try to explore in ways you don't expect.

Common appliances, TV sets, vacuum cleaners, and other conveniences of your daily life are as foreign to him as they would be to an alien. Seriously think about what things could present a danger to a Greyhound who has never encountered them and take precautions so that he doesn't get hurt while he learns about life in your world. For example, he needs to learn that windows are solid objects and swimming pools are not.

Look in Chapter 15 for lots more information on keeping your hound safe.

Don't think that hiding forbidden items in a closed cupboard will be any more effective in keeping out a Greyhound than it is in keeping out a toddler; some Greyhounds excel at figuring out how to open doors. If you've adopted a skinny, furry Houdini, you'll figure out how to be very creative.

Getting Your Hands on the Equipment You Need

We all know there are some things we'll need even before our retired racer arrives. Some things are obvious like food and dishes or a collar and leash. But knowing just which items are right for your Greyhound is a bit more complicated.

Being prepared with the basics

As the future owner of a retired racing Greyhound, you'll need to have on hand certain tools of the trade — items you and your new best friend just can't live without.

Be sure to have all of these on hand before you welcome your new pet into your home.

Collar and leash

Your adoption group will probably provide you with a leash and a special type of collar, designed especially for sighthounds. These collars won't allow your hound to back out of them if they are adjusted properly and used correctly. If your adoption group doesn't provide these or doesn't sell them, any 4-foot or 6-foot nylon, cotton, or leather leash will do. If you have to buy a collar, look for collars called , *Martingale collars* (see Figure 5-1), *Greyhound collars, combination* (or *combo*) *collars,* or *Promise collars.* If you can't find one in your local pet store, check out the resources in Appendix B.

Don't use an adjustable-length leash (one that allows your Greyhound to run out ahead and then come back closer to you) until your dog has been trained not to bolt after backyard critters. (I talk about how to do that in Chapter 6.) If you do buy an adjustable leash, make sure it is all tape, not tape and nylon cord and that it is designed for use with a dog the size of yours. The nylon cord versions are more likely to cause injury to you or your hound.

I don't like to hurt my dogs while I train them. So I never use slip collars, choke collars, or pinch or prong collars. And don't allow your local pet store to convince you that a nylon choke collar is more humane than a metal one. Being choked is being choked, regardless of the material.

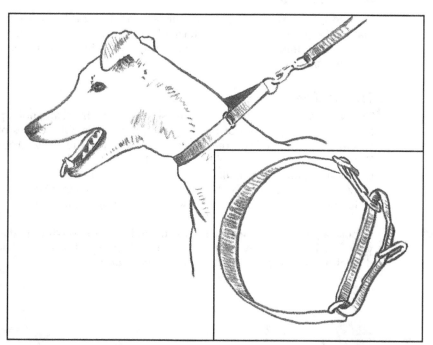

Figure 5-1:
A Martingale collar is geared specifically toward sighthounds.

Fun runs

Fun runs are unorganized or loosely organized events that give Greyhounds a chance to run free in a fenced area. Greyhounds should be muzzled while they're running together. Greyhounds seem incredibly mellow in your living room, but when they're running with other dogs, they're entirely different creatures. If they bump into each other, they might snap or nip, and muzzles help protect their delicate skin from injury.

Ask if a leash and Greyhound collar are provided when you adopt your retired racer and if the cost is included in the adoption fee.

Muzzle

If you are planning to let your hound run with other dogs, or if you are introducing your retired racer to small children, dogs, or other pets for the first time, you need to have a *turn-out muzzle*. Turn-out muzzles are a plastic, basket style muzzle like the ones used by the racing kennels when the dogs are turned out for exercise. If one isn't provided or you can't purchase one from your group, check out the resources in Appendix B.

Identification tags

Your adoption group will probably provide an ID tag with their contact information. Consider this a backup form of identification. As soon as you know what you'll name your retired racer, get him an ID tag with your personal contact information.

Crate and pad

The crate you choose for your home should be a wire crate, not a plastic travel crate designed for airline transport of animals. Wire crates offer better air circulation and allow your hound to see more of the world around him. The crate should measure about one and a half times the length of your Greyhound (not counting his tail) and should be tall enough for him to stand comfortably. For most Greyhounds, a crate that measures 30 inches wide by 48 inches deep by 36 inches high will give the dog enough room.

Choose a pad that can be hosed down and is thick enough to pad and protect your Greyhound's bony joints. Check out Chapter 15 for more advice on bedding choices if you travel with or board your dog.

If you live in a cold climate, add a washable blanket made of a tightly woven material or fleece to your retired racer's crate. You may want to add an additional blanket as a drape over the crate if your home is particularly drafty or if your hound prefers a more den-like atmosphere.

Dog bed

Look for bean bag or shredded foam beds with sturdy washable covers and washable and/or replaceable parts. Or consider a cushion and cot arrangement. The cushion can double as a crate pad and the cover is waterproof. Avoid beds with cedar mixed in the filling. Cedar can be very irritating to some dogs including Greyhounds. Whatever bed you choose, be sure it has lots of padding and will hold up to the digging that Greyhounds like to do before they lie down. Machine washable beds and pads sound like a great idea but they rarely fit into the average washing machine. Turn to Chapter 15 for more information about good bedding options.

My favorite bed for home is the Orvis Dog's Nest. The bed is filled with beads like a bean bag. The cover and filling can be replaced, and it has an optional waterproof inner cover for dogs who get wet or may be incontinent. My first two Orvis beds have held up for nine years and counting. (You can order the bed by calling Orvis at 540-345-4606 or toll-free at 800-541-3541. Or hop online and visit www.orvis.com

Avoid the egg crate style of beds unless you have a very sedate retired racer. Most Greyhounds love to dig around in their beds before they lie down. Those expensive egg crate beds get shredded into packing foam — and they can finish the job in just a few days.

Coat

Greyhounds have very little body fat, so if your retired racer will be exposed to cold weather, he should have a coat to ward off the elements. Because Greyhounds are so long and thin for their size, the coats you'll find in pet stores often won't fit correctly. They tend to be too short or too loose.

Many adoption groups have coats for sale. Check with your adoption group or ask them for the names of suppliers that make custom-fitted coats for Greyhounds. You can also look in Appendix B for sources.

My favorites for really cold weather are the ones that include an attached *snood,* which is a kind of hood that covers your racer's neck and part of his head.

Ultrex/Polartec combination coats are a good choice — warm, wind-resistant, water-resistant, and easy to care for. Call Montana Dogware at 406-388-6593 or hop over to their Web site at www.montanadogware.com. Check out Toastie Coats and Paws online at www.toastiecoats.com or call 914-361-3843 for a catalog.

Grooming supplies

From the first day your new friend comes home, you need to be sure that you keep him clean and well groomed. That means brushing his teeth, giving him baths, brushing his coat, cleaning his ears, and trimming his nails. See Chapter 13 for more information on the wonderful world of grooming your Greyhound.

My favorite new grooming tool is a microfiber cloth. They're called Miracle Cloths, Wonder Cloths, or High Performance Polishing cloths. I use a wet one to give a quick dry bath when real bathing isn't possible. I use a dry one as grooming cloth instead of a brush. I use a wet one as a toothbrush. They're also great for cleaning ears. These can be found in houseware and kitchen-ware stores at outlet malls, the housewares sections of many department stores, and with the cleaning supplies in grocery and discount stores. Do yourself a favor and buy several. After you have them, you'll find hundreds of uses. And not just for grooming your hound.

Baby gates and/or exercise pens

Baby gates are one of the world's best management tools for pets as well as for small children. You can use a baby gate to limit your retired racer to a small room without having to confine your hound to his crate. An exercise pen (often referred to as an X-pen) can be used in place of a crate for most hounds. And it has the advantage of being portable so you can easily move it from room to room or even into your backyard. Look for exercise pens in the pet supply catalogs and Web sites listed in Appendix B.

Don't use a baby gate or X-pen if your racer is still recovering from spaying/neutering surgery. Your dog may try to jump over it and can cause an injury. Instead use his leash to confine the dog to certain areas of your house. But keep him safe by never tethering him if you aren't there to watch him carefully.

A dog harness

Using a dog harness is the only safe way to tie your dog if he's outside. It's also good if you're using a tether for some kinds of training. But Greyhounds are almost as good at slipping regular harnesses as they are at slipping regular collars. Contact Premiere Pet Products to find a retailer who carries the Premiere Sure-Fit Harness. You can reach them at 800-933-5595 or look for them online at www.gentleleader.com. Sure-Fit harnesses can also be purchased online at www.sitstay.com.

Taking Advantage of the Calm before the Storm

Use the time before your retired racer arrives to learn the basics about training and behavior. Decide which house manners are important to you and how you plan to teach them to your retired racer. The training methods outlined in this book are gentle and ideally suited to the retired racer's personality. Check out the chapters in Part III, which provide techniques and tools designed to be used as soon as your racer arrives home.

Call a veterinarian and arrange to have your racer examined within the first week of his arrival in your home.

When you adopt a retired racer, you're getting a dog who has spent little time without the company of either other dogs or humans. But he is unlikely to have ever seen the inside of a home. This combination can make for a difficult adjustment, even with a lot of patience and understanding from his new family.

Knowing What to Expect on the Big Day

If you can, spend a couple of days at home with your new family member as soon as he arrives. If work or other commitments make taking time off impossible, arrange to pick your new friend up on a Friday, so that he will have the entire weekend to get adjusted.

All family members should be present when you choose your new pal or when you pick him up from the adoption group or kennel.

Taking a look at first impressions

When you first see your new best friend, his appearance may be a little rough. Some common problems among retired racers are bald thighs and bare bellies; dings, scrapes, and cuts, which may happen during transport or through encounters with canine traveling companions; a vaginal discharge in females, as a result of testosterone therapy; or inflamed elbows, from rubbing against a hard crate. Expect an assortment of scars or perhaps a crooked tail — all signs of her former career.

Your retired racer will probably greet you as though you are a long lost friend, but that isn't the case with *every* racer. If he has just been transported, your new pal may be stressed and exhibit symptoms such as yawning, panting, nose dripping, or sniffing the ground. If you have a large family or active children, don't overwhelm him with too many people at once. Introduce yourselves one at a time — starting with the grownups. If he seems uncertain or downright frightened, keep all movements slow and gentle and greet him properly. A slower, gentler introduction may be necessary.

If your retired racer seems a bit shy, keep in mind the following suggestions:

- ✔ **Allow him to approach you instead of approaching him.**
- ✔ **Turn slightly to the side as he approaches, instead of facing him head-on.**
- ✔ **Don't stare at him or lean over him. Crouch down to his level if you can.**
- ✔ **As your new pal approaches you, offer your hand slowly, bringing it up toward his lower jaw rather than down toward his head.**
- ✔ **Keep your voice happy but quiet.**
- ✔ **Offer him a tasty treat.** Food has a calming effect.

If your retired racer doesn't want to approach you right away, sit down on the floor, be quiet, and wait. Gently toss bits of food toward him until he gets a bit closer. Then put a few treats on and around you, and let him come take them. Don't move. Let him call the shots. Allow him to approach each member of your family in the same way.

Take special care when introducing your retired racer to your young children. Any strange dog should be introduced to children with a muzzle in place. But warn your child not to hug her new pal — those muzzles will hurt like heck if he gets excited when he greets her and accidentally hits her in the face with it.

Before you leave the kennel or adoption group location, make sure your retired racer is securely leashed and has his ID tags firmly attached. Figure out how to use his sighthound collar correctly *before* you get out the door.

Bringing your retired racer home

Give him ample time to take care of bodily functions before you take him into your house. He may have loose bowels or diarrhea for the first few days he's with you, especially if you're changing his food. Check out Chapters 12 and 16 to learn more about preventing and treating diarrhea.

Feed your retired racer lightly and keep the food simple. Save the fancy treats for another time. Keep the first few days calm and low-key. Save visits from family and curious neighbors for another day. Let him learn where he will sleep, eat, and eliminate. Give him time to absorb all the normal sights and sounds and smells of his new home and his new family.

Surviving the first night

If your new friend won't be allowed to share your bedroom, plan on a rough night or two. He has probably never been alone before. All the things you've heard about using warm water bottles, playing radios softly, or setting ticking alarm clocks in the room with him to comfort him are a waste of your time. If you follow the tips on alone training in Chapter 6, your retired racer's adjustment will be much easier.

If he's whining or barking in his crate, don't give in and open his crate unless he has been quiet for at least two or three minutes. If you reward the whining by letting him out of his crate, it will never end. Although some dogs respond to a simple, "hush," if what he wants is attention, even hushing him can be a reward. If saying "hush" works, fine. But don't reward him for whining or crying by calling his name or talking to him.

If you allow your dog in your bedroom the first night, he'll probably settle right down. Allowing him to share your bedroom is a good way to increase the bond between you and your dog. If you let your retired racer sleep in your bedroom with you, you can use a tether to let him be close but still keep him confined to prevent a house soiling problem. Put his bed in your bedroom, preferably near your bed. Tie his leash to something solid that is near his bed and attach it to his harness. Give him enough leash to stand up, turn around, and lie down, but don't give him enough to allow him to freely roam around the room. Make sure he can't get the leash entangled in something or climb up on something and fall.

Retired racers often show some signs of *sleep aggression* when they first arrive, which means they may respond to being disturbed from sleep with a growl or a restrained snap that clearly isn't intended to make contact with a person. Although this is a form of aggression, it usually goes away in about a month, after they have adjusted to sharing their sleeping space. The first time you encounter this in your hound let him know immediately it's unacceptable. Give him a harsh *aah-aah* or *no* in a tone that says, "Don't even dream it, bucko." While he's adjusting, use his name, or a sharp handclap to wake him and give him time to awaken fully before you touch him or try to move him. Sleep aggression isn't a serious behavior problem unless it involves more than a simple growl, continues beyond a month or two, or worsens with time.

Getting up and at 'em on Day 2

On the track, your Greyhound's daily routine may have begun as early as 4:00 a.m., and the first morning he wakes up in your house may be just as early. You can gradually adjust his morning routine, however, so it is more in sync with yours. Every few days, simply take him out about ten minutes later, until you get to a schedule more in tune with yours.

Make new experiences fun for your Greyhound. Use lots of gentle laughter and calm, normal behavior so he understands that the new experience is no big deal. If he's hesitant about a new experience gently reassure him. But don't coddle him or baby him.

Helping Your Retired Racer Adjust to His New Family

Many racers are returned because of conflicts with children or resident pets. These conflicts have nothing to do with the character of Greyhounds specifically. The statistic is true of adult adoptions of *any* breed. Generally, the conflicts occur when parents expect dogs and children to be something they're not.

Whether you're blending dogs and kids or dogs and small animals or all three, two simple rules will keep you out of trouble:

✔ Supervise all interactions, and separate your child or the smaller animals from your hound when you can't supervise.

✔ Whenever the child or small animal is in the room or in sight, be sure your retired racer's experience is a good one, full of rewards.

Check out the following sections for more tips on helping these relationships go smoothly.

A child's best friend

From short stories to novels, from TV series to movies, from *Lassie* to *Old Yeller*, the theme of a boy and his dog has been a popular thread in all forms of fiction. Somehow, children and dogs just go together. What could be more natural, right?

Don't patronize me. . . .

Many adults teach their children to pat a dog on his head. But most dogs really hate being patted on the head. Have someone pat *you* on the head for several seconds. It's really annoying, isn't it?

Dogs *do* make great playmates for children. And they *have* done heroic things to save the lives of their young companions. But just the same, dog bites are the fourth leading cause of death among children, and 70 percent of those fatalities occur in children younger than ten. (Biting a child is also the leading cause of death for dogs because dogs who bite children are usually put to death.)

Most Greyhounds like or are at least very tolerant of children. But liking the kid down the block isn't the same as living with one. Greyhounds usually aren't a pet-me-hug-me-play-with-me kind of dog. And kids spend a lot of their time petting, hugging, romping, running, squealing, jerking, and falling over. So the match isn't necessarily one made in heaven.

If you have dogs and young children, adopt this as your mantra: *I will never leave my dog and my child alone. Never.* Use crates, baby gates, or whatever it takes to keep your dog and child far enough apart that they can't touch each other when you're not supervising or when your racer is more than an arm's length away from you. Take your child or your hound into the bathroom with you, if necessary. Just never leave them alone together.

Any dog who is going to live with children must be reliable. If you say "sit," the dog should sit instantly, regardless of what is happening around him. Not sometimes. Not usually. Always. Your hound needs to be trained to respond reliably. And I show you just how to do that in the next three chapters.

Teach your retired racer to accept child-like handling. Gradually get him accustomed to hugs, light grabs, and sudden movements. Add squeals, shrieks, and child-like yells. Start slowly and gently, and reward positive responses. Don't move ahead until your retired racer is comfortable and clearly ready to enjoy being in a home with children.

Every parent who wants to include a dog in the family should read *Child-proofing Your Dog* by Brian Kilcommons and Sarah Wilson (published by Warner Books). In fact, you should read it twice.

Teach your child how to interact with her new pal. Don't let your child hug her hound until you have taught your dog to accept and enjoy this. Use a muzzle until you are *sure* it's safe.

Even when you're comfortable that your retired racer and your child are comfortable with one another, your work is still not done. Keep in mind the following tips for daily living with children and pets:

- **Although you should teach your hound to accept humans of all sizes near his dish or food, you should also teach your child to never approach any dog while he's eating.**

- **Children should never be allowed to hurt their furry pals.** If you won't let your three-year-old hit or pinch your infant, why would you allow her to do it to your Greyhound?

- **Give your hound a crate, a room, or another safe haven to which he can retreat when he is feeling overwhelmed and teach your children that when he goes to his safe haven, they are not allowed to bother him.**

- **Instruct your children to never pet a sleeping Greyhound.**

- **Be sure your children's friends or any other children visiting your home also know and understand these rules.**

- **Take the time to teach your racer basic house manners and to properly socialize him to the world he lives in.** Give him the skills he needs to be your child's best friend, and he will be.

Life with dogs and children may not always be as idyllic as it is in the movies, but common sense, solid training, and close supervision will make it a great experience for the whole family.

Retired racers and other dogs

Greyhounds get along well with most dogs. The preparations I suggest in this section may seem overly cautious, but preparing your retired racer for interactions with other dogs is a lot less trouble than taking him to the veterinarian for emergency repairs.

If you already have another dog with existing behavior problems, fix those problems *before* you bring home your retired racer. Working through behavior problems can take a couple of months or more, so allow plenty of time for this and don't expect it to happen overnight. If your resident dog is a dominant or territorial breed, don't even think about bringing any new dog into your home until you have a balanced relationship with your existing dog and reliable control of her behavior.

Greyhounds don't have the kind of skin that tolerates teeth. Even a minor skirmish can require stitches — or worse. Dogs notice the amount and the kind of attention they get. Before your new racer comes home, reduce the amount of attention you are giving the resident dog to a level *below* where it will be when your new hound joins the pack. This way, your current dog will think he's actually getting *more* attention when your new hound arrives.

If possible, introduce the dogs in an enclosed area on neutral territory. A fenced yard is ideal but other possible choices are a garage, an apartment hallway, a little-used basement, an enclosed porch, or a friend's home. Bring your resident hound outside or into the neutral area to greet the newcomer. Follow these steps:

1. **Leash and muzzle both dogs, but do not hold onto the leash of either dog.** The leash is only there in case you need a way to intervene safely. If you are not in an area where you can safely drop the leashes, you'll need a helper to hold the other leash. Don't pull tightly on their leashes. Try to keep the leashes loose and dragging.

2. **If possible, let the dogs meet on opposite sides of a fence or closed gate so they can see each other, meet, and sniff for a moment before they interact.**

3. **Then let them interact.** Laugh and talk happily but calmly to the dogs as they greet each other.

4. **Reward all positive responses by both dogs.**

5. **Keep the initial meeting short — just a few minutes at most.**

After you have them inside, keep them on opposite sides of a baby gate until you've had the opportunity to observe them. Again, keep laughing and chatting — even if you're the only one in the house. Keep interactions short for the first few days. And avoid having the dogs together in a small space like a car or narrow hallway. Keep feeding areas separate, and avoid giving your dogs toys or chewies that they may guard. Whenever possible, show more happy attention to the resident dog. Let him see that the presence of the new dog means fun. Make the association a pleasant one.

As they continue to get acquainted, remove the gate. Later remove the muzzles. Watch both dogs carefully for the first several weeks. Keep them separated unless you are there to supervise.

Aggression is most likely to be related to food, possessions, space, or the arrival home of a particular family member. Whenever the dogs are in sight of one another, laugh, chat, and be happy.

If you have more than one dog at home, introducing the dogs can get trickier. Adding a third dog may heighten aspects of pack dynamics that were unnoticeable or irrelevant with only two dogs. The amount of prime sleeping and eating space, or lack of it, can also affect the pack dynamics. If you're introducing more than one dog to your new hound, simply follow the advice above. But introduce your new dog to each resident dog separately outside your house or apartment or other neutral area. And remember, if your resident dog isn't a Greyhound, your new dog may be hesitant or uncertain about this strange creature. After all, he may have never seen a dog that wasn't a Greyhound before and may not be sure what to think. To learn more about handling sibling rivalry, turn to Chapter 10.

If you are introducing your Greyhound to a toy breed of dog, combine the tips for introducing your Greyhound to your cat (see the following section) with the instructions for introducing your Greyhound to other dogs. In some ways, introducing a Greyhound to a toy dog can be the most dangerous kind of introduction. The Greyhound may see your toy dog as prey, but the toy dog will react to the Greyhound as a dog. A cat will likely run, but even a tiny dog may decide to guard his food or space. If he's a terrier or another dominant breed, he may actually start a fight with your Greyhound. So exercise special caution with toy dogs.

How to avoid fighting like cats and dogs

Before you bring your retired racer home, create a safe environment for your cat, toy dog, or small animals. Create a safe room where you can confine your small animal. That way she'll have a place where she can be safe if you don't want to keep your needlenose crated all the time when you can't supervise.

Don't even think about trying to create your version of the peaceable kingdom by combining a high-prey Greyhound who overreacts to cats or other small animals. Question your motives, if not your sanity, if you try to mix an active breed of cat, like an Abyssinian or one of the oriental breeds, with even a medium-prey Greyhound until you've had more experience.

Cat testing conducted by adoption groups isn't foolproof, because it usually happens in an artificial environment and may not involve a real cat, so always exercise caution when introducing your retired racer to a cat.

When you're ready to introduce your cat to your retired racer, find a helper if possible and follow these steps:

1. **Muzzle your hound and put him on his leash. Keep a firm hold on his collar.**

2. **Have your helper carry your cat into the room, getting only close enough that your racer can see your cat.**

   Don't dangle the cat above your racer's head. Keep your cat at a distance, and as long as your hound is paying little or no attention to the cat, reward him with small treats and quiet praise. If your hound is behaving reasonably, let go of his collar but keep a firm grip on his leash.

3. **Gradually bring the cat closer, but not so close that the cat gets frightened and makes a run for it.**

   Gradually let your hound get closer to your cat, if your cat will allow it. If things are progressing safely, drop your hound's leash. Be prepared to grab it if you have to.

4. Watch the dog's reaction, and discourage any response toward the cat that goes beyond idle curiosity.

If your hound begins to overreact, use a harsh noise to interrupt his behavior. The key is to interrupt the behavior just as it is beginning. Don't wait until your Greyhound is overly excited to step in. Interrupt him as he's *thinking* about chasing the cat.

What danger signs should you look for? If your Greyhound's ears are pricked, his body is quivering, he's whining, and his tongue is flicking from side to side, that's not good. If he's also smacking his lips, blowing puffs of air from the sides of his cheeks, freezing in place, and intently staring at the cat, he's a high-prey dog. And if he can't be called away or distracted even with exciting food under his nose or exciting sounds like squeaky toys, and/or he lunges toward the cat, chances are he may never be safe with cats.

After you've seen your cat's and your racer's initial reactions, you'll have a sense of how much work you'll have to do. If your hound tries to chase the cat, respond to each and every incident with a harsh sound or a well-placed blast from a squirt gun. If you ignore even one episode, the reward of chasing the cat may be just too great for your Greyhound to overcome. If you respond consistently and on every occasion over several days and your retired racer is still reacting inappropriately to the cat, you may *never* be able to trust them alone.

In the meantime, reward your Greyhound for calmness and disinterest in the cat (see Figure 5-2), and you're more likely to increase this behavior. Teach him basic manners so he has better things to do than chase the cat. (I show you how in Chapter 8.)

Whenever your cat is present, make good things happen for your hound. He should begin to associate the presence of your cat and the absence of a negative response to her with some very good things. If he pays more attention to you than he does to her, reward him heavily. Make his calmness in her presence a *very* good thing.

When you feel like the introduction is going well, try it without the muzzle, but with a long leash so you always have a way to get control. When this is going well, remove your hound's leash. After several weeks of close supervision (and crating your hound or confining your cat to a safe room when you can't observe), use a tall baby gate to give the cat an escape route. Set it up in the doorway to her safe area, but elevate it several inches off the floor so she can get under it but your Greyhound can't.

Unless your cat is particularly friendly with dogs, expect her to hiss for about a month, until she settles down and accepts the new member of the family. If your cat is accustomed to dogs, you may have the opposite problem. She may try to initiate games with your racer, just as she does with the slower dogs in your house. Your cat will be in for a surprise, because your Greyhound can outrun them all. So keep your guard up.

Figure 5-2: Reward your dog for good behavior around your cat, and they can become the best of friends.

Your Greyhound and your cat may get along quite well inside, but that may change when they're outside. When they're outside, your hound may act as though he has never seen your cat before and decide that Tabby looks a lot like lunch. You may also find you have to do some minor reintroductions if the cat was boarded or hospitalized for any length of time.

A new member of the pack can throw everything out of balance. One dog may be quite willing to get along with the cat. Add a second dog and suddenly the dogs may start to behave like a pack and Tabby becomes a great chew toy. The same applies if your dogs get along just fine with your resident cats and you add a new one. Be especially cautious about adding a kitten. The activity level and sounds of kittens are far too prey-like for high-prey dogs of many breeds.

JUST FOR FUN

Finger lickin' good

My Greyhound, Chaco, showed no interest in our cat, not much interest in the backyard squirrels, and some interest in the local rabbits. He had no interest in the ducks and geese at the park along the river. But the first time he saw a white chicken, he went berserk. So don't jump to conclusions about prey drive based on one experience.

Birds of a feather

Introducing your hound to small animals takes patience and time. Rushing the process is likely to be a deadly error for one or more of the participants. The techniques you use to introduce your hound to cats are the same techniques you should use with birds, ferrets, or any other furred, feathered, or scaled creatures you may have around the house. But with these smaller animals, you have to be even *more* careful.

Cage all the birds or critters and put them in a room where the door can be closed and latched. Leash and muzzle your dog and take him into the room. Gradually let the dog approach closer and closer to the cage. Reward your Greyhound's disinterest in the small animals. Always correct inappropriate attention. If he gets too close to a cage, firmly tell him "No," and gently use the leash to move him back. If he's too insistent, use a squirt gun to emphasize your position. Your retired racer needs to understand that these critters are *always* off limits.

After you've made your introductions with the small creatures in their cages, you can introduce them outside of the cages. Crate or tether your Greyhound and bring the bird or other creature into the room where he's crated. Reassure your small animals that your retired racer is safe.

One Greyhound adopter says that she believes seeing the dog in his crate makes her birds think he's one of *them*. Figure 5-3 illustrates just how close a bird and a retired racer can be, under the best of circumstances.

Later, with all the critters caged, let your racer roam freely around the house while you supervise. If he wanders into the critter room, follow him with the squirt gun. Be certain you respond to each and every approach to the cage with a squirt.

Never trust your dog alone with your small animals, and never make the mistake of leaving animals alone with an unconfined dog. Even if the animals are caged, they can be killed if their cage is overturned. Some hounds have been known to exist peacefully with small animals for a very long time and then, one day, they go after the cage with no apparent cause. Keep small animals in a separate room with the door closed and latched when you can't supervise them.

Redirecting your dog's attention

I prefer to interrupt my dog and redirect his behavior before he misbehaves rather than punish him after the fact. However, noises are frightening to small critters, so this is one of the rare times I use punishment to make sure my dog understands I mean *never*. Many groups recommend using a spray bottle to squirt your hound. I don't use spray bottles because so many things we have to use on our dogs now come in spray bottles, and I don't want him to associate spray bottles with bad stuff. A squirt gun has a slightly different appearance and sound, so using it instead may help prevent your Greyhound from becoming frightened of spray bottles.

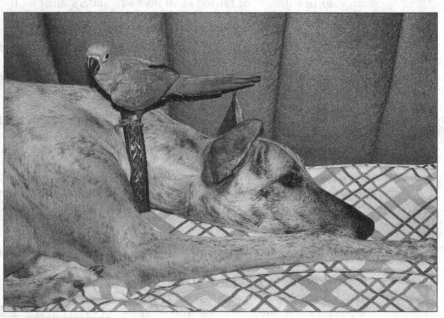

Figure 5-3: Greyhounds can learn to live with birds and other small animals, but you should always be just an arm's length away, like the photographer of this picture was.

Photograph courtesy of Kathy Johnson

Part III
Training Your Greyhound for Life after the Racetrack

The 5th Wave   By Rich Tennant

"Look, call me crazy, but I think I've found a way to exercise the Greyhound without leaving the house."

In this part . . .

Your retired racer is sure to race her way into your heart. But that doesn't mean she's prepared for life in the new world of your home. Retired racers aren't familiar with life beyond the track, so your job is to help your new friend adjust by training her well. The chapters in this part guide you through training, from the basics of dog behavior to more advanced steps. You also figure out what to do if your Greyhound is exhibiting some typical behavior problems, and you'll find the information you need to help a frightened Greyhound overcome her fears.

Chapter 6

Living with a Retired Racing Greyhound

In This Chapter

▶ Making it through house-training with flying colors

▶ Guiding your dog through the experience of staying home alone

▶ Introducing your dog to his neighborhood and the outside world

▶ Helping your pet conquer the more difficult household challenges

*P*art of living with any dog is training him to be a well-behaved member of your family and forming a bond with him that turns him into your best pal. You can start to form this natural bond by teaching him some basic behaviors that will help him live in your home comfortably and happily. These basics include house-training, teaching him the dangers and joys of living in a home, helping him learn to be home alone, and acclimating him to foreign objects, like the stairs.

The first days your retired racer spends in your home are all about overcoming culture shock and forming a bond with your family. So don't be afraid to begin these lessons on the very first day. When your Greyhound has mastered the behaviors I explain in this chapter, he'll be a happier hound — and you'll be happier, too.

Part of training is managing your retired racer so he can't get in trouble while he learns the rules. Some of your management tools will be a crate, a safe area (an X-pen or a part of your house, a room, or part of a room that you've carefully dog-proofed), and a harness and tether (a leash or line fastened to your belt or an immovable object). I tell you more about safely managing your hound's environment throughout this chapter and the rest of Part III.

Helping Your Retired Racer Get to Know You

Most retired racers are very good about people approaching them while they eat. Many are equally tolerant if a dog approaches. But be certain your hound learns that hands and people near his food bowl mean good stuff by taking the time to train him. Try these food bowl exercises in order. Add a different one each day. Don't move ahead until your hound is happy at each step.

Pick up his bowl. Measure your hound's meal into a separate container. Put his empty bowl on the floor. He'll sniff the bowl and look confused. He now wants you to approach his bowl. Drop one piece of kibble in the bowl and retreat. When he looks for more, approach and put in another piece. After several repetitions, drop in a handful of kibble and offer a tasty treat with the other. Don't move on until you've successfully done this ten times. Take everything one slow, careful step at a time.

Approach your needlenose and his empty dish. Remove his bowl to add a handful of food. On some occasions add something extra and delicious like cooked chicken breast or lean roast beef. Put his bowl back down. Retreat. Move on when you have ten successful repetitions.

Sit next to your hound and his empty bowl. Put one of your hands on his bowl and keep it there. Use your other hand to feed him his meal in installments. Repeat several times.

Sit next to your hound and his bowl. Put your hand on his bowl. Stroke your hound and talk to him while he eats his kibble. Occasionally add something really tasty with the other hand. Repeat several times.

If there is a problem, find professional help. Ask your veterinarian for a referral.

Retired racers have been handled extensively and are usually very compliant about being handled. But accepting handling and enjoying it aren't the same thing. When one of our dogs first came to us, he was very frightened of having an arm over his shoulders and being restrained. Now he happily accepts that even from strange children and readily allows me to brush his teeth with an electric toothbrush and trim his nails with an electric grinder. Here are some ways to make handling fun and to build your bond with your new friend. If you take the time to do these exercises, you'll make things like nail trimming and tooth brushing easier and more pleasant for everyone. You don't have to set aside any special time. Just use some of the time over the next days or weeks that you'd be busy petting him and spoiling him anyway. Move as quickly or as slowly as you need to so every experience is fun.

Gently stroke your boy from head to toe. Note if he tenses at having any part of his body touched. Areas that are most likely to be "touchy" are his muzzle, chest, paws, shoulders (especially if you reach over them), belly, and the tail area. Speak to him in a calm happy tone while you do this. Give a treat when you move to a new part of his body. At the end of each session, feed him a taste of yogurt from a metal spoon.

When he's comfortable and enjoys your touch everywhere on his body, make your handling a little more intrusive. Touch the outside of his ear. Give him a treat. Look into the ear. Give him a treat. Lightly and gently groom him with a soft brush or a cloth, and give him a treat as you move to each new area. Touch the outside of his mouth. Give him a treat. End your session with giving him yogurt from a spoon.

Gently brush him. Touch the inside of his ear. Give him a treat. Touch the inside of the other ear. Give him a treat. Lift his lip on each side and treat. Touch each toe. Give him a treat after each. Give him some yogurt.

Gently massage his body. Wipe each ear with cotton and give him a treat. Apply a bit of pressure to each toe with your fingernails and give him a treat after each. Open his mouth and look inside. Give him a treat with yogurt.

Groom or massage, whichever he likes best. Put the nail grinder or clippers right in front of him. Apply pressure to each of his toes and nails and touch with clippers or grinder, but do not try to file or cut. Give him a treat after each toe. Touch the empty spoon to the teeth then give him his yogurt.

Groom or massage him. Touch a toothbrush or finger brush (or dampened microfiber cloth) to his teeth with a tiny bit of peanut butter or poultry-flavored dog toothpaste on it. Gently clean one small spot by moving the brush or your finger in a circle one or two times. Give him some yogurt. Put a small amount of ear cleaning solution on some cotton or a cloth and gently wipe each ear. Give him a treat after each. Run the nail file lightly against each nail or barely touch the trimmer to the nail and pretend to clip while you gently squeeze the nail between your fingertips. Don't even try to take any of the nail off the first time. Give him a treat after each nail. Even if you aren't going to do his nails, someone else will have to. Make it as stress-free for him as possible.

TIP

Feeding from your hand

For at least the first week your retired racer spends in your home, feed him from your hand. You can measure the food into his dish, but feed it to him a few pieces at a time, by hand. Hand-feeding helps your retired racer bond to you and view you as his new leader. Feeding your Greyhound by hand teaches him to trust you to take care of him. Finally, hand-feeding helps your retired racer learn that hands *give,* they don't take. Everyone in the family can take turns feeding, but children should be carefully supervised. If he's one of those hounds who won't take food from your hand, just drop his food on the floor at his feet a bite at a time.

Groom or massage him. Increase the number of teeth you can brush while still keeping the encounter positive. Treat generously. Try to file or clip just the very tip of a nail. Give him a treat. If he stays cool, try a second, and so on. Alternate teeth and nail days until you can brush all teeth and trim all nails in a single session.

If your dog is going to be around young children, gently and slowly get him used to even more intrusive handling. Teach him to tolerate pinches and hugs and the inadvertent bangs and bumps that an uncoordinated toddler may accidentally inflict.

House-Training 101

House-training is primarily a matter of managing your dog's environment and rewarding his good behavior until he figures out what you want. The following sections provide some proven house-training tips.

Helping your retired racer identify his den

Most dogs naturally want to keep their living areas clean just as their wild relatives keep their dens clean. So it is your job to teach your retired racer to view the entire house as his den. Some hounds catch on quickly. Others have to be taught room by room.

If you allow your new Greyhound to share your bedroom, he'll likely recognize that room as part of his den very easily. But just because he can go all night without messing in your bedroom, doesn't mean he's house-trained. Teach him the behavior you want one room at a time.

Giving him food and water on a regular schedule

If your needlenose eats on schedule, he'll likely eliminate on schedule. Don't give your retired racer free access to his food. Put his food down for no more than 30 minutes. Then remove his food dish, even if he hasn't finished eating. Eventually, he'll understand that he only has a set period of time to eat, and he'll finish within his time limit.

Feed him his last meal at least four hours before his bedtime. Remove his water about two hours before bedtime, to ensure that he won't have to urinate in the middle of the night.

If you're going to be gone more than two hours, or if you live in a warm climate and do not have air-conditioning, teach your retired racer to drink from a water bottle and attach it to something accessible to him. Or simply leave several ice cubes in his water dish. You aren't restricting his fluid intake. You're just controlling how fast he drinks.

Keeping track of your dog's schedule

Start house-training by taking your Greyhound out about every two hours during the day, so you can learn his patterns. Plan to stay out 15 to 20 minutes each time. Most hounds hate the rain, so be prepared to wait him out if the weather is bad and you're absolutely certain he has to go. Take him out about 15 minutes after every meal. And take him out within ten minutes or so of a vigorous playtime and when he's awakened from a long nap. But don't get into the habit of popping in and out every few minutes, or he'll never learn to adapt to a reasonable schedule.

If you take your retired racer out and he doesn't do anything, but you're convinced he has to go, wait 10 or 15 minutes and try again.

Get a small notebook or a magnetic board you can put on the refrigerator, and keep a journal for at least seven to ten days, recording when your Greyhound eats, when he drinks, when he plays, and sleeps, and how long after each of these activities he needs to eliminate. At the end of this period, see what patterns have emerged. Schedule your trips accordingly or rearrange his feeding and watering schedule to accommodate yours.

Defining the elimination area

When you're house-training your Greyhound, always take him out to a specific area. Don't just open the door and let him out into a fenced yard or put him on a tie out. You can't reinforce good behavior if you aren't there to see it. Define a small, specific area that your retired racer can use for elimination. As he assumes the position to do his business, calmly say a few words that tell him what you want him to do (such as "hurry up," "go on," or "potty").

When he's begun to eliminate, let him know this is what you want. Immediately tell him he's a good dog and offer him a treat as soon as he has finished. Delivering a treat immediately is important, so carry your treats into the yard with you. If you wait until you bring your Greyhound inside, he may not associate the treat with eliminating outside, but may instead think he'll get a treat for coming inside.

Encouraging your Greyhound to do his business

Keep his area of the yard clean. Otherwise, he won't want to use it. Pick up after him daily. Clean the area frequently — especially in warm weather. Simply add two tablespoons of dish washing liquid (not dishwasher detergent) to a sprayer attachment on your garden hose and spray your lawn liberally. Wash the lawn down with the soapy spray and then rinse until all the suds are gone. This will take care of a smaller yard. Adjust the amounts or the number of applications to fit your needs.

Don't take your hound for a walk to take care of business. Let him learn to use a portion of your property or some other specified area. If you take him for a walk to allow him to do his business, he may quickly figure out that he can extend the walk by not getting down to business right away. And if you're in a hurry, chances are you'll bring him in before he accomplishes what you had in mind. So treat him, and then make a walk part of the reward.

Preventing accidents

Preventing accidents is the management part of house-training, but you don't need an MBA to do it well. If your retired racer can't be trusted out of sight or out of reach, you need to manage his environment. You can't crate him 24 hours a day. Crates are for short-term confinement.

No dog should be crated for more than a few hours at a time (except overnight while you're house-training).

Because your Greyhound was accustomed to being let out several times during the day, he may not have the control to wait all day when you first bring him home. Use a pet-sitter or a neighbor to help, if you can't be there to take him out about every three to four hours. If you can, come home at lunchtime for a while. Gradually extend the number of hours you ask your Greyhound to wait between potty breaks.

Separation anxiety

If soiling accidents occur only when you're away, and you're sure you aren't expecting your Greyhound to wait too long to do his business, the accidents may be related to separation anxiety. Ask your veterinarian for guidance or for a referral to a trainer who can help.

TECHNICAL STUFF

Marking his territory

When any dog marks his territory, he's not having an accident. He's intentionally leaving his scent behind. Territory marking usually involves an upright object, like a wall or the side of a chair.

Although most Greyhounds don't tend to mark indoors, even neutered male dogs and female dogs may occasionally try to mark. I offer some suggestions for addressing this in Chapter 10.

When you're home, crate your Greyhound, confine him to his safe area or X-pen, or fasten him to your waist by simply attaching his leash to your belt or belt loop. He can't get out of sight or out of reach if he's tethered. If you crate him or use a safe area, keep his crate or safe area in full view of where you and your family generally spend most of your time.

If your hound does have an accident, use an enzyme-based cleaner specifically developed to clean pet messes. Use it on the soiled area even if there is no stain or if the spot isn't on a carpeted area. Enzyme-based products neutralize the odors that may attract him back to the same spot. Follow the directions on the product label carefully. After you've used the enzyme cleaner to neutralize the odor and the spot has dried completely, you can use other products to remove any remaining stains.

Being sure you don't punish mistakes

When you punish your Greyhound's house-training accidents, you tend only to make him afraid to go when you are watching. And that can make the task of house-training even more difficult. If you see your retired racer start to squat or lift his leg in the house, take him by the collar and calmly say "outside," as you escort him to the appropriate place. Shouting only tells him you're upset. It doesn't tell him *anything* about what you want him to learn. If he finishes doing his business outside, reward him even though he started on the carpet. Immediately clean the surface where he had his accident by using an enzyme cleaner.

Accidents after house-training

If your Greyhound suddenly begins to eliminate in the house after weeks or months without any accidents, consult your veterinarian. He's more likely to have a medical problem than a house-training problem.

If you are managing your retired racer, he won't have the opportunity to have an accident. Whenever he's eaten, awakened from a nap, played, had a training session, or otherwise gotten excited, he needs to be taken out. After a week or so of observation, you'll know what his triggers are. *Until you've gone three months without an incident, do not leave him unattended or unconfined.*

If you eliminate free feeding, manage your hound to prevent accidents, and use lots of rewards for doing it right, you should expect to see significant progress in just a few days. But remember to go slowly to give him time to learn what's expected of him.

Helping Your Hound Stay Home Alone

Your retired racer has most likely spent all his time with other Greyhounds or humans. Help him learn to stay home alone by following the suggestions in this section. You can get started the very first day he arrives. Just because you've already left him home alone with no problem doesn't mean separation anxiety can't develop as he becomes more attached to your family. So back up a bit and do some alone training. It's much easier than trying to treat separation anxiety.

If your retired racer has been in your home for a while and has separation problems, start over as though he just moved in today.

The biggest mistake you can make the first few days you have your Greyhound is to be constantly in his sight and to shower him with company and attention. As exciting as it is to have a new Greyhound in your home, don't overdo the attention in the first few days. Let him get used to the fact that he'll be spending at least some time alone.

If he's destructive (see Figure 6-1) or having accidents only in your absence, he's probably stressed and fearful. Take a look at Chapter 10 for more information on handling this common problem. A crate may protect your furniture, but it doesn't do anything to make your hound feel safe and secure. Alone training is about letting him feel secure in your absence. See the difference?

Check out the following sections for specific suggestions on how to train your dog to spend time alone.

You can condense and speed up your hound's alone training if he responds well, but at least go through the motions to be sure your retired racer is comfortable at each level.

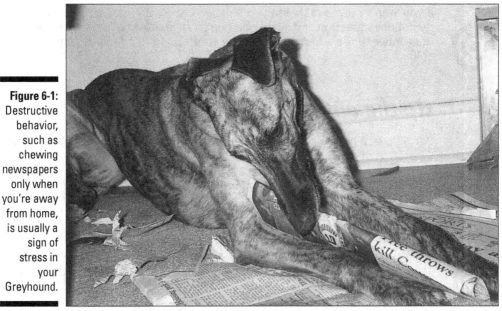

Photograph courtesy of Personalized Greyhounds, Inc.

Make it interesting

From the moment you bring your Greyhound home, begin throwing interesting new toys and food tidbits into his crate, X-pen, or safe area so that he always has something new to discover. Stand near the entrance to the area or crate and say the word *crate* (or some other appropriate word) and then throw in a really tasty tidbit. Don't attempt to close the door or gate to the area just yet. After your retired racer enters the crate and gets his treat, call him out. You can encourage him to come toward you by making enthusiastic sounds with your voice, by clapping your hands excitedly, or even by making squeaky noises. Don't reward his exit from the crate in any other way.

After he successfully enters and exits his crate or safe area about ten times, change things around a bit. Stand at the entrance and gesture, just as if you still had a treat in your hand, as you say *crate.* Then wait for him to enter. If he doesn't respond, end the session and try again a little later. Go back to luring him into the crate with food for another ten tries.

When your hound does go into his crate or safe area on request, without the lure or a treat, make a very big deal out of it. Give him really neat toys or great treats while he's still in his crate. Rewarding this kind of behavior is like putting money in the bank.

If you aren't using a crate but you still need to do alone training, start with the following section and simply tie him to an immovable object instead. Remember to use a harness. Never tie your hound to an object using his collar.

Up the ante

Use a *Kong,* a hollow rubber toy that can be found at most pet supply stores, to make your absence less noticeable.

Stuff the Kong with peanut butter, bits of dog biscuit, and maybe even some leftover chicken. Do the same with a second Kong, but put it in the freezer — that way you'll always have one ready to go. And if you give him a frozen Kong, it'll take him longer to empty it.

Remember to clean each Kong thoroughly after use. After you've removed any remaining food scraps, you can run them through the dishwasher on the top rack.

Ask your hound to enter his crate or area. Close the door, gate the area, or tether him. At first, stay in the room and in your Greyhound's sight, but just out of his reach. Vary the amount of time you keep the crate or safe area door closed (or the time he's tethered to an immovable object). Initially, try doing it for just one minute. Gradually build the time you are out of reach.

When your frozen Kong is ready, you're ready to move ahead. It's time for your first absence. Confine or tether him, give him his Kong, and then pop out of the room and right back in. Remove the Kong as soon as you reappear. Then disappear for one minute, then three, then eight, then three. Get a cold drink or make a cup of tea and then return. Make some popcorn and then come back. Throw in a load of laundry or put a letter in the mailbox. Fit in whatever other chores or at-home activities you want or need to do during that first day. Just return every few minutes. Don't forget to give him his Kong as you're about to leave and to remove it as soon as you return.

Tether cautions

Do not leave your Greyhound tethered and alone in the house for more than a minute or so. Do not leave him tethered and alone if you can't hear him. Build up the amount of time he spends alone in the house by leaving the room. When you're ready to try leaving the house, leave him loose in the house or a small part of the house and start with very short absences.

Don't forget to practice leaving him alone after dark. As you get into evening, turn the lights on and off when you enter or leave the room. Make sure he has plenty of fun toys in his crate or area to keep him occupied. Believe it or not, a soft stuffed toy that he can use the way a child uses a teddy bear actually helps many retired racers overcome their fear of being alone. And don't forget to keep that Kong stuffed with tasty treats.

If your retired racer shows any sign of stress, you're moving too fast. Slow down and go back a few steps until he's comfortable again.

Leave the house

When you can leave your retired racer alone in the house, his crate, or his safe area for 15 minutes without causing him any stress, you're both ready to test the waters a bit more. Now it's time to leave the house.

Make no issue of leaving. Don't say good-byes. Don't tell him to watch the house. Just give him several stuffed Kongs, pick up your keys, and go. Get in the car and leave for about 30 minutes. If your Greyhound is going to have a problem, it usually happens in the first 30 minutes that he's alone.

If your Greyhound seems more anxious at night, try leaving the lights on for him. If leaving the lights on helps, install a timer or leave the lights on if you're going to be away at night.

Making Friends

Most dogs are cautious or even frightened of things they've never experienced, and retired racers are no exception. Greyhounds who have a good basic temperament and who were raised by responsible breeders are sociable with people and other Greyhounds. But there's a whole world of new experiences you can introduce them to.

Your retired racer has most likely never seen the inside of a house. Everything is likely to be a little scary at first. But in the following sections, I provide some exercises that will help.

Making your Greyhound feel at home

Consider what may be frightening or dangerous for a dog who hasn't set foot in a house before. And expose your hound to as many household items and experiences as possible.

Put any particularly noisy appliances, like vacuum cleaners or lawn mowers, in plain sight for several days before you use them. If he's hesitant about approaching something, move him away to a comfortable distance and let him decide when he is ready to approach. Reward any movement forward with gentle praise or treats.

Create new experiences without having to leave your home. Family members can put on hats and hooded jackets or other unusual items of clothing, to let your Greyhound learn that people come in lots of sizes and shapes. Ask your family and friends to make weird noises and play the TV or stereo at different volumes and on different kinds of stations. Expose your hound to at least one new sound, item, and person every day for several weeks.

Giving your hound the tour of the neighborhood

When you go out with your retired racer, always carry plenty of treats to reward his appropriate behavior and to give to children and strangers so they can treat your Greyhound. He'll learn to like and trust them. If he is already fearful of strangers, try feeding him really great treats as soon as a stranger appears and continue feeding him treats until the stranger disappears from view. Or turn to Chapter 11 for more help.

If he's leery of strangers or children, take it slow. Walk through your neighborhood and arrange for your new friend to meet and greet your neighbors, particularly any neighborhood children. Instruct the kids to greet him properly by letting your Greyhound approach them instead of allowing them to crowd around him and hug him. If you know the neighbors well, you may even consider visiting them before your new hound arrives and offering to teach their children how to respond to your retired racer in a way that will ensure he'll become their new best friend. If your dog is hesitant to approach your neighbors, ask them to stand still at an angle and gently toss a treat or two toward your hound. Ask them not to reach for him from above his head, and ask them not to bend over him. Ask adults and children to wait until he approaches them, and then reach gently up under his chin. They can gently scratch his neck and the underside of his chin. But they should only continue this if he is having a good time and responding well. And be sure to remind children not to hug your retired racer.

After your retired racer has met your neighbors, you can introduce him to other common neighborhood situations by walking him near school bus stops and letting him greet larger groups of children. Start at a distance so he isn't rushed by lots of giggling, screaming kids. Move closer only if he's clearly having a good time and is ready for the experience. And always reward him for good behavior.

And don't just limit his larger-group experiences to children. Walk him near public transportation stops if there are any in your neighborhood, so he can see and politely greet a variety of strangers of all ages.

Finally, if any well-mannered dogs reside in your neighborhood, let your hound meet them with their owners present. Start with the dogs on opposite sides of a fence if possible. Offer lots of rewards and praise for friendly behavior from either dog. If that goes well, proceed to closer greetings.

Going out on the town

New experiences are as important for your retired racer's social development as they are for your child. So try to find ways to increase his worldview every day. Always keep your mood calm and happy when you're interacting with him, especially in new situations. When you go to new places, make it fun with lots of treats and praise.

Here are some things you can do to turn your hound into a social butterfly who'll be comfortable in any situation:

- ✓ **Take your Greyhound for walks near nursing homes.** This will allow him to meet people using walkers and wheelchairs.

- ✓ **Lead him on walks near schools and day care centers.** This exposes him to the sights and sounds of large groups of children.

- ✓ **Take your retired racer to the veterinarian's office** *before* **you go for an exam.** You can let the staff make a fuss over him and give him treats without having any other purpose in mind. This way he won't associate the vet's office only with scary experiences. Do the same with the groomer, if you use one.

- ✓ **Go for walks with your Greyhound near places where large groups of people congregate.** This will teach your Greyhound to tolerate crowds without getting stressed. Lines at movie theaters are a great place for your Greyhound to meet lots of kids and practice his people-greeting skills. Move on to outdoor cafes or flea markets. Walk him at outdoor malls and shopping centers where he'll encounter shopping carts and kids on skates and skateboards.

- ✓ **Visit your local high school's football stadium when there is no game being played.** There you can teach your retired racer to climb bleachers. Later, when he's ready for it, take him to a small soccer match or a Little League game.

> ✔ **Take your Greyhound to a local hotel that allows dogs, just to walk around for an afternoon.** Here you can expose him to elevators.
>
> ✔ **Make a weekly trip to a nearby pet store.** Most pet stores welcome leashed pets. Look for friendly, calm dogs for your boy to meet. Pet stores are also great places to work on distraction training. Start with trips when the store is unlikely to be crowded, like just after the store opens in the morning or just before it closes at night.

Exposing your retired racer to many different experiences helps prepare him for the real world, the world outside your home. The more pleasant experiences he has, the more excited he'll be about his new world.

Whether you are at home or out on the town, always clean up after your hound.

Facing Challenges with Your Greyhound

You and your retired racer can look forward to numerous adventures together. Some will be more pleasant than others. In this section, I cover some of the more frightening experiences for retired racers — everything from stairs to windows. Just approach each new experience with patience, and in no time your Greyhound will be a very happy pup.

Tackling the stairs

Stairs are never fun for retired racers. They've never seen them before and their bodies just aren't built for doing stairs. If you're lucky, he's been introduced to stairs by your adoption group, but this is a rarity. If you don't have stairs in your home, consider borrowing a friend's home. Life will be easier for both you and your hound if he learns to use stairs.

Introducing him to stairs is much easier if you have the help of an assistant whom he already knows. Work slowly. Also consider that not all stairs are the same. Your retired racer may readily go up or down carpeted stairs but have difficulty negotiating wooden or steep ones, so be patient. Work him through each situation as though he's seeing it for the first time.

Carry some really tasty treats, like dime-size pieces of leftover chicken or steak. Use a fanny pack to hold the treats, or keep a plastic bag in your pocket so you can keep your hands relatively free to work with the hound. And follow these steps:

1. **Take hold of your Greyhound's collar at the bottom of the stairs.**

   Let him lean against your leg if he needs to.

2. **Hold a piece of food in front of his nose.**

3. **Encourage him with the food and with the sound of your voice to put his front paws on the first step.**

   If you have to, physically place his front paws on the step, but avoid doing that if you can. Coercion may only make him more hesitant.

   Keep your tone of voice happy, reassuring, and encouraging. View this experience as an adventure. Keep the food treats and verbal praise coming.

4. **Encourage him to bring his rear legs up to the first step.**

   If you absolutely have to, put his rear legs on the steps for him.

5. **Slowly alternate his front and rear legs up the stairs.**

   Take it one step at a time, praising and rewarding frequently as you go.

6. **When you reach the top of the stairs, take a break.**

7. **Start back down the stairs, with his head behind your legs so it doesn't look so scary.**

   Coming down stairs is more difficult for your hound than going up. Be even more patient and enthusiastic on the way down than you were on the way up. Continue to chat happily as you reward and praise him. When you get to the bottom, rest again.

Repeat this process at least one more time, and work on this a few times in the first few days, as needed. Associate the stairs with good things, like food, a favorite toy, or something he values, and he'll be flying up and down the stairs in no time. Retired racers usually stop being frightened of stairs when something they really want is waiting for them at the top or bottom.

If your stairs are open, steep, or uncarpeted, make sure your Greyhound's nails are short enough to give him plenty of traction. Allow plenty of extra time to do this training.

When your retired racer first starts coming down the stairs on his own, hold your breath. He may take them two or three at a time. You may also find that, early on, if anything stops his progress while he's on the stairs, your Greyhound will get stuck. He may need a moment to figure out which foot to put where in order to get himself straightened out. You may even need to help.

Avoiding the great escape

When you open or close any outside door, be absolutely certain you or someone large enough to control your dog has a firm, proper hold on his collar. Almost every adoption group has a story of a retired racer that bolted through an open door before anyone could stop him.

If your retired racer has a high prey drive, take him by the collar and hold him carefully before you open the door. If he's out at the end of his leash, he can back out of even a sighthound collar.

The first time you have your needlenose on a leash and he spots a critter in the backyard, both of you are likely to go flying. Pay very close attention so you're prepared. The instant he spots the critter and as he's about to or is beginning to lunge, let out the loudest "no" or "ah-ah" you can manage. Scare the bejeezus out of him if you have to. His life depends on learning this lesson well and quickly. It usually only takes one or two adventures for him to get the picture. And don't forget to reward him when he sees a critter and doesn't try to lunge. See Chapter 8 for techniques to teach him not to bolt through open doors and for walking nicely on a leash.

Slip slidin' away

Many Greyhounds are afraid of shiny or slippery floors. Those long skinny legs can fly in six directions at once. And after he's had a bad experience on a slippery floor, getting him to try it again can be difficult. You can help him get his footing by applying to his feet a small amount of the stuff office workers use on their fingers to sort documents. Ask for it at an office supply store.

Working on windows

Introduce your retired racer to windows and glass doors by taking him to each window and tapping on it. Take his paw and put it against the window. Watch him carefully for a while. Greyhounds have been known to try to chase squirrels through a second story window. Put decals or other objects on windows or doors until he understands they are solid objects.

Chapter 7

Learning to Speak Dog

*W*hen I first began training dogs in the early 1960s, it was quite an adventure. My job was to issue commands, praise my dog for doing it right, and correct my dog with a sharp jerk on his choke collar if he did it wrong. The entire approach was about showing your dog who was in charge. *Do it because I said so and I'm the boss* was the underlying message. It wasn't much fun for me. And I can't imagine it was much fun for my dog.

In this chapter, I ask you to take a leap of faith with me and learn to look at dog training in a whole new way. Instead of looking at training as something you do *to* your retired racer, I want you to learn to look at training as a mutual learning process. This is the chapter where I lay the foundation skills you need to communicate with your hound. I use analogies that may not be technically accurate, but I want to keep this easy. And I teach you how to use tools that help you build the behaviors you want and ways to make training fun and easy for you and your retired racer. In fact, it's so easy I call it *couch potato training* because our hounds aren't always the only couch potatoes in the house.

Aren't Dogs Just Wolves with Manicures?

No one can agree on how dogs evolved. We can't agree on how long they've been domesticated or on their ability to experience emotions or to think. But we almost all agree that we can't live without them.

Between alpha theories, which suggest that all dogs are looking for a chance to take over the world, and the myths created by the Hollywood hound that all dogs are like Lassie, separating truth from fiction can be difficult. In the following sections, I give you my take on the domestic dog.

Waiting for alpha

For many years, most dog-training books were based on some variation of the alpha theory. In short, the alpha theory says that dogs are wolves with very nice manicures.

The simplified version of that theory goes something like this: Wolf packs have a hierarchy, a pack order. Only one wolf is at the top of that pack. He is the alpha wolf, and everyone submits and defers to the alpha. If they don't, alpha gets ticked. And when alpha ain't happy, nobody's happy. The other member of the pack who controlled behavior was Mom. Mom didn't have to be the alpha wolf. She just had to be Mom. Alpha shows his dominance by doing things like rolling the offender onto his back and pinning him there. Mom shows junior who's boss by grabbing his neck or muzzle.

According to this approach, when we bring a dog into our home, we have to be constantly on guard. Because if we don't show Rover who's boss, pretty soon he'll be wearing the pants in the family.

We have gathered a lot of valuable information about our dogs by observing their wild cousins, the wolves. But some of our interpretation about what that means and how to use it to communicate with our dogs is faulty. We *can and should* use canine body language to understand our dogs and to communicate with them. We just have to make sure the messages we're sending or receiving are the messages that are intended.

Rescuing Timmy from the well

Another common image of dogs is based on the Hollywood hound. But what do Lassie, Benji, and Old Yeller have in common? They're all fiction.

In the movies, dogs are moral, loyal creatures, capable of knowing right from wrong. They have the full range of human emotions, from greed to guilt. They plot and plan and premeditate. And their power to reason would challenge even a rocket scientist. After all, Lassie not only comes running home, she tells Mr. Martin where to find Timmy and shows him he needs a rope to rescue the boy from the well.

My way or the highway?

There may be as many training methods and styles as there are trainers. There's a T-shirt that summed it up nicely: "The only thing you can get two trainers to agree upon is that the third trainer is doing it all wrong."

So we expect the same thing from our dogs. We assume they know when they've done something wrong, because we think they look guilty. And it's not much of a leap to assume that your pal did it to spite you. "He did it to get even with me, because I left him alone. . . ." It's fiction, folks, pure and simple.

Einstein or Idiot?

Retired racers do best when training sessions are short and fun. Short means no more than ten minutes — less when you're first starting or doing something difficult. And don't repeat things over and over. If he got it the first time, do it once more for good measure and then move on.

Understanding your retired racer's five senses

We all know that dogs have some physical senses that are more sensitive than ours. What we rarely think about, however, is how their senses affect learning. But if you understand how your dog's natural abilities work for and against you when you train, you'll be able to be more successful in reaching your goal.

Dogs can hear sounds at four times the distance we can, and they can detect sounds at higher frequency ranges and more precisely than we do. And how does that affect how our hounds learn?

Just as we soon stop noticing the sounds of cars going by if we live near a busy highway, our dogs begin to block out noises that don't have any meaning for them. That's why your retired racer can hear the sound of his leash being picked up if he's a floor away, but ignores you when you say his name if he's watching a squirrel.

JUST FOR FUN

A Greyhound's vision

No evidence shows that Greyhounds have better vision than other dogs. What sets them apart is their *peripheral vision* — how well they see to the sides. Some sources say they can see movement in a range of 270 degrees — that's almost a full circle. And they *do* have remarkable reaction time, incredible speed, and a high prey drive.

If you keep saying "sit," and he doesn't know what you mean, he either stops paying attention or begins to think sit, *sit,* **SIT** is the way you tell him, "Put your butt on the floor." If you keep raising your voice, sooner or later he won't notice anything you say unless you yell. So keep your voice quiet and calm. You don't need to bark orders. In fact, whisper sometimes. That way he'll learn to pay more attention in order to hear you.

Greyhounds see movement that is off to the side or even partially behind them much better than most dog breeds and about ten times better than we do. The better a dog sees to the side, the less well he sees straight ahead. Dogs have poor vision up close but reasonably good vision at a distance. Their eyes are more sensitive to light and movement than ours, but their power to focus isn't as good. They see best at twilight. And contrary to popular belief, they *can* see in color, but this ability is very limited.

So at night your hound may be able to spot the slightest movement of an animal in the bushes. Because his vision doesn't focus as well as a human's does, he probably doesn't recognize your face. But he relies more on your scent and your movement to identify you than he relies on your appearance. His ability to see slight movement even when it is well off to the side is one of the reasons it can be difficult to keep his attention focused when he's in a distracting environment.

Although Greyhounds may be called sighthounds and rely on their sight more than other dog breeds, they also have a strong sense of smell. Their sense of smell is their most powerful tool for examining their environment.

JUST FOR FUN

Smells like home

Smell memories last for life and affect almost every canine behavior. Dogs prefer odors of animal origin to all other odors.

Our retired racer's senses make him exquisitely good at discriminating even minor changes in his physical environment.

Making sense of the strong silent type

Dogs don't use language to communicate, so we have no reason to believe they think using language or words. In fact, he will learn to respond to the nonverbal signals in his world long before he learns the words you use to communicate with him.

The best way to describe how dogs view the world is to realize that everything that happens to them is captured in their minds like a photograph. But this "photograph" includes all the sights, sounds, tastes, feelings, and smells that are occurring the instant the shutter on their mental camera is snapped. Good and bad experiences are recorded this way.

When you snap a photograph, if you move slightly to get a different angle or different lighting, you understand that it is still the same picture, even though it is a slightly different photograph. Our dogs don't make this same connection. When anything in the photograph changes, they see it as a completely different picture. That's why he may sit in the kitchen but act as though he doesn't have a clue what you're talking about in the living room or the backyard. Or he may sit quickly if you're standing in front of him, but ignore you if you say sit when you're lying on the floor or even standing beside him instead of in front of him. His photo album doesn't have those pictures yet. If I remind you that your hound doesn't generalize, that's what I mean. Some hounds generalize better than others — but none generalize as well as humans expect them to.

Dogs are really tuned in to their physical environment. That means your hound picks out all the sights, sounds, smells, routines, and experiences that are important to him. They become photographs in his album. If he gets upset when you leave, it won't be long before you swear he knows you're going to leave the house before you know it. It may be something as unimportant to you as where in your morning schedule you brush your teeth on weekdays as opposed to weekends. Something you do that you may not even think about may have snapped a picture for his album. Your hound doesn't *generalize* well. But he *discriminates* wonderfully.

Getting Past the Alpha Theory: Looking at Training in a New Light

Now that you know about some of the things that affect how your hound learns, you can figure out how to educate your hound. I call my approach to training *win/win learning*. Win/win learning is based on mutual learning, not just training. What's the difference? Training has traditionally been something we do *to* our dogs rather than something we do *with* or *for* our hounds. Win/win learning is about understanding your hound's language so you can teach him yours. Learning is about setting him up to succeed and removing the fear of failure. Win/win learning is about catching your hound doing something *right* so you can reward him. It's about understanding what is and isn't realistic in his world. And most importantly, it's about having fun while you and your hound work on the behaviors that are important in your home.

Humans and dogs everywhere owe a tremendous debt to some very special people who have worked to take the hurt out of dog training and put the fun into learning and problem solving. Those leading the way have been Ian Dunbar, Terry Ryan, John Fisher, Karen Pryor, Gary Wilkes, Sue Sternberg, Ted Turner, Patty Russo, Leslie Nelson, Marian and Bob Bailey, Patricia McConnell, William Campbell, Suzanne Hetts, and Karen Overall. Most of my techniques and methods have evolved from the works of those individuals. If you want to learn more about their work, turn to the resources in Appendix B.

Everything you need to know about training your hound boils down to these simple truths — that dogs work for the following reasons:

- To get good things to happen
- To prevent good things from ending
- To prevent bad things from starting
- To get bad things to end

Almost every aspect of my approach revolves around getting the good things to start and teaching my hounds how to keep the good things from ending — good behavior and positive rewards.

Working within the Training Triangle

The Training Triangle provides the framework for win/win learning. The parts of the triangle are:

- ✔ **Establish your relationship with your hound.** Your relationship drives all your other interactions.

- ✔ **Find a way to communicate with and educate your hound.**

- ✔ **Manage his environment so he always wins.** Throughout your hound's life, you'll constantly shift the balance of those factors to fit the situation at hand.

Establishing a good relationship with your retired racer

If you want your hound to follow, he must have unquestioning faith in the behavior and actions of you, his leader. If you want him to walk calmly near a snarling, aggressive dog when he's leashed and defenseless, he has to believe you will take care of him and not let him get hurt. If you ask him to walk down an open flight of stairs, he has to believe that you won't let anything bad happen to him. Your hound has to focus on you and trust whatever you ask him to do. If and only if he has this kind of trust in you, you have assumed the role of leader.

Your job is to be a kind and benevolent leader. His job is to pay attention and to follow your lead. If you become this kind of leader, he isn't likely to question or challenge you. But how do you get to be that kind of leader?

Leadership starts with trust. Develop a pattern of kindness, fairness, and ample rewards. Every positive thing you do in your relationship with your dog is an investment in your future together. In the beginning, you may have to put far more into the relationship than you get back. But always keep in mind that today's actions earn interest in the future.

Using food to reinforce positive behaviors

Many people object to using food for training. If I use food, the thinking goes, my dog will only work if I have food on hand. But I believe that if your dog only works if you have food, you're using it incorrectly.

So how should you use food to train? First and most importantly, never use food as a bribe. Unless you're teaching something new and using the food as a lure or a learning tool, the food shouldn't appear until the behavior has been performed. If it's in sight before or when you ask for the behavior, you're using it as a bribe, not a reward. Don't use food to get your dog's attention. *His* job is to accept you as his leader and to pay attention. *Your* job is to make paying attention rewarding and to be a good leader.

Helping your hound to view you as his leader

Because your relationship with your hound is about being his leader, make it fun for him to follow. Encourage and reward submissive behaviors. For example, if your Greyhound rolls over onto his back, rub his belly and give him a treat. Give it a name so he learns to do it on cue.

Teach him to move from your bed or the sofa or to simply get out of the way. My dogs know what *move* means because I trained them to move. I toss them a tidbit and say "move" as they begin to go after it. If your hound is on the floor, shuffle your feet toward him. As he begins to move, mark that behavior with a clicking sound. Later I add a verbal cue (the word *move*) and fade away the shuffling so that my dogs move any time I say the word.

Teach him to work for a living. Instead of giving him things for free, expect him to earn them. Get him to sit or pay attention before he gets that treat or a neck scratch or a ride in the car.

Never use pain to train. Collars or leashes aren't necessary for training unless the specific exercise or your hound's safety requires it. When I'm training my dogs, I try not to use my hands on them, except to pet or praise. I also don't force my dogs into physical positions, like sits or downs. Instead, I use targeting and lures and reward markers (which I explain shortly) to communicate. And I use lots of food, rewards, praise, love, and attention, to pay my dogs for a job well done.

Rewards are whatever your dog will work for. What's rewarding to one dog may not be rewarding to another. What I think is rewarding may not be what my dog values.

Establishing a good relationship with your dog is also about learning what's important to him, not just teaching him what's important to you.

Finding a way to communicate with your Greyhound

If you're going to teach your dog, you have to figure out how to communicate in a way that your dog understands. In the following sections, I explain how dogs respond to the environment around them and how you can use those responses to communicate.

The sound of the shutter snapping

Making a sound that your dog can associate with doing the right thing isn't the same as praise. Praise is a reward. This is the sound of the shutter snapping and a new picture being taken for his album. Think of it this way: If your dog loves to ride in the car, chances are he gets really excited when he hears the sound of your car keys. But it's not your keys that he wants. He wants what he now associates with the *sound* of the keys. If we don't use a reward marker, we must deliver the reward within ½ to one second of when he performs the behavior we want or he won't understand why he's being rewarded. See why a reward marker is so important?

Teaching English as a second language

Teach your retired racer to speak English. Give names to everything in his world. Let him learn to associate sounds with actions or objects. Say *downstairs* as he's about to start down the stairs. Say *car* as he's about to get into the car. Say *hurry up* as his speed increases when he's coming toward you. In no time, with almost no work from you, your hound will learn that those words — sounds — mean, "Do that behavior." I told you this would be easy.

Helping your dog make associations

Your hound views his world as one big photo album. To make some of the technical stuff simpler, I use taking photos as a way of explaining some basics.

If you want to put pictures in your hound's album, you have to help him put film in his camera and teach him how to make the shutter click.

Teach your dog a specific sound that means, "Yes, that's it. That's exactly the picture I want in your album. Now come and get your reward." That way, it doesn't matter if your dog is on the other side of the room or what he does after he hears the sound. He'll quickly learn that whatever he was doing the moment he heard that sound is something that earns him a reward and that it's something you want him to do again. When he learns its value, he'll start working to get you to make that sound. This sound is his *reward marker*. It is the shutter on his camera.

Choosing the right kind of treat

If your dog has dietary problems, use a different brand of appropriate kibble as a treat instead of using human food or high-calorie dog treats. If your dog has a weight problem, decrease his daily rations to make up for the use of treats. Better yet, use his daily rations for training instead of just giving it to him for free.

For your reward marker, choose a sound that is quick, precise, and absolutely distinct. The best choice is a mechanical sound like a *clicker* (a small device like a child's toy called a *cricket* that makes a clicking sound — see Appendix B for sources) or even a whistle. I also teach a verbal sound so if my hands are occupied or I can't get to the mechanical clicker quickly enough, I can still snap the shutter on my hound's camera. This sound could be a tongue click or a really quick, sharp "yes" or "yip," or any other word or sound that is sharp and crisp. You can teach your dog either or both kinds of click. From now on, when I say *click* I mean make this sound. When I say *treat*, I mean reward your dog.

Start teaching your hound the sound of the shutter clicking in a quiet area of the house. Follow these steps:

1. **Gather up some really yummy treats.** The treats should be small enough and soft enough to eat quickly — roughly half the size of a dime — and soft, so your dog doesn't have to think about chewing. Put the treats out of your hound's sight.

2. **Put a treat in your hand and put your hand behind your back.**

3. **Pause for about one second. Click. Pause for another second. Now deliver the treat.** The pause between the click and the delivery of the treat helps to settle you and to keep you from moving your hand and delivering the treat before you've clicked.

4. **Do lots of repetitions — try 15 or 20.** Be sure you're rewarding your hound when his body is in different positions so he doesn't think the shutter only snaps if he's lying down. Sometimes deliver the treat from your hand. Sometimes drop it on the floor.

5. **After you've tried a lot of repetitions, let your dog wander off.** Wait a moment, and click again. If his ears perk or his head spins in your direction, you'll know he's beginning to catch on. If he isn't there yet, wait a while and try again later.

6. **After he begins to respond to the click, change locations — do the repetitions in lots of rooms and outside.** And change positions (stand, sit, lie down, turn your back) so he gets lots of different pictures.

You don't have to save your click for formal training sessions — because everything in life is a training session. Use it whenever you see your dog do something you want to see again — as long as you have a reward available.

The purpose of reward markers

Reward markers are not recall devices. Don't use them to get your dog's attention or to get him to come to you. You'll ruin their effect.

Getting the Behavior You Want from Your Greyhound

Training is really a matter of figuring out how to communicate with your dog about what you want. You can use a combination of several different techniques to get the behavior you want, and I cover these in the following sections.

Using rewards in training

I use lots of *rewards* when I train. A reward is anything my hound will work for. It can be a food treat or a favorite toy or a run in the park. Use lots of kinds of rewards to make training interesting. And include lots of *life rewards*. Life rewards are the things your hound wants now. If he's all excited about going for a walk, he wants that more than any treat you have to offer. So use that life reward instead of a treat.

When I say *treat* that's shorthand for reward. It doesn't have to be food. Remember a reward is anything your dog will work for.

Create lots of life rewards. Give names to anything your Greyhound likes, and then you can use them as rewards: playtime, Ben's home, go for a ride, treat. You'll begin to see that the words for which he has the best associations (the best photos in his album) are the ones he responds to most quickly. Some day if you need to distract him from something or interrupt an inappropriate reaction, you'll have all kinds of ways to divert his attention by using one of his favorite words.

The trick to using rewards when you train is to make them unpredictable. Our hounds are hunters. And hunters are gamblers by nature. That's why they keep going hunting even though they don't always catch anything. When you first start teaching a new behavior to your hound, you click every time he gets it right. But after he's done it right several times, you start clicking only the best or the fastest behaviors. Can you ever stop rewarding behavior? Sure. After you've taught a behavior really, really well. But I still use occasional rewards for behaviors my dogs know well because I like to treat my dogs and because I want them to keep gambling.

Sometimes you use a *lure* to get your hound to do something you want him to do. That means you hold a treat or toy in your hand to get him to follow your hand or you toss the lure to get him to follow it. You then reward your hound with the lure when he's done what you wanted. If you use the lure too much, it becomes a bribe. I use teaching him to go in his crate as an example. You stood at the entrance to his crate, tossed the treat in his crate, and he followed it. You did several repetitions. Now you use exactly the same hand motion but there is no food in your hand. This is called *fading* the lure. If he still goes into his crate in response to the position or movement of your hand, he's figured it out. I call this position or movement a *lure signal*. Get the food out of your hand. If you're using a lure, you don't have to click if you don't want to, because the reward (the lure) can always be delivered immediately.

Targeting

Targeting means your hound learns to touch his body, his nose, or his paw to a particular object or put his body or part of his body in a particular place. This is one of the first behaviors you teach because when your hound understands it, you can teach all kinds of marvelous things. If you teach your hound to target, you don't need to use a lure. I show you how to teach targeting in Chapter 8.

Shaping

Another way we get a behavior we want is to *shape* it. That means we take something and break it into tiny steps. Pretend you want to train your hound to spin in a circle. You wait until he turns his head in whichever direction you want him to spin. Then click. When he figures out he's being clicked for turning his head, he'll start repeating it to get you to click some more. Now you wait to click until he turns his head a bit more. After a few more tries you wait until he turns even more. Before long, he's completed a circle. Now you wait until he starts a second circle before you click. See how shaping works?

Nothing says you have to lure, target, or shape a behavior in order to click it and treat it. If you want to be a couch potato trainer, you can simply watch your hound and click what you like when he does it on his own. If you want to teach him down, just wait for him to lie down and then click.

Releasing your hound when the behavior is performed

Each stationary behavior like sit or down has two parts — a cue and a release. If the dog is deciding when to release, he doesn't know the behavior. End of discussion.

When you use a clicker, the click tells your hound, "The behavior is over, come get your treat." As you begin to fade out the click, you need another way to tell your dog his job is finished. Simply pick a release word that tells him he's done *(thank you, all done, finished)* immediately before you click. If you aren't clicking, say your release word in a neutral tone of voice and remove eye contact. Make releases boring so he won't want training to end. Remember when you were a kid and Mom said time for bed? And you said, "Aw, Mom, just five more minutes, please." That's how you want your hound to view being released.

A release means he can do something else. It doesn't mean he *has* to. It's a release, not a command to get up or move.

Dogs respond to physical cues easier than they respond to verbal cues. If you want to replace a physical cue with a verbal cue, add the verbal cue immediately before you use the physical cue.

Only give the cue once. Don't keep repeating it. And after you've given the behavior a name, don't pay him for it if you didn't ask for it. Each cue, whether physical of verbal, must be distinct. You can't use the word *down* to mean "lie down," "get down off the sofa," and "get your paws off me."

What's in a name?

We call the names we give to the behaviors we're training *cues*. In traditional training, these are called *commands*. Don't worry about naming the behaviors you're teaching right away. Names get in the way when your dog doesn't know what you're talking about. Because we humans use words all the time, as soon as we give something a name we tend to think our hound knows what that word means, and we tend to get frustrated or angry if he doesn't respond. Your dog won't really know the word you use until he hears it associated with the behavior countless times, in all kinds of situations.

At first, your lure signal is a cue. Sometimes it's exaggerated and we fade it. For instance, when you first teach your hound to lie down using a lure, you may have to put your hand the whole way to the floor or even get down on the floor. It sure wouldn't be convenient to do that every time you want your hound to lie down. In time,

the exaggerated motion is faded so that simply pointing at the floor becomes the only cue you need to use.

Even though we haven't given a name to a behavior, that doesn't mean we aren't giving cues. Your body postures and hand movements are very powerful cues, and you may not even realize you're giving them. You may think he understands what *sit* means when you use a word, but he may be responding to the way you inadvertently move your foot as you say *sit*.

When you want to change to a verbal cue or add a verbal cue, simply add the new cue immediately before you give the old cue.

Using cues correctly is important if you want your hound to respond reliably. Name the behavior when you're willing to bet real money that he'll do it again within several seconds.

Avoiding Punishment

What is punishment? Punishment is the other half of the four things dogs work for — to prevent bad things from starting and to get bad things to end. Punishment is anything your hound will work to avoid. For some hounds, even a gentle "no" sends them into hiding for several minutes. Greyhounds are sensitive and don't like it when you are upset with them.

I avoid punishments for several reasons. First, punishments drag down your relationship with your dog. Second, punishments frequently don't work or they teach the dog only that it isn't safe to do something if you're watching. Most importantly, if you're communicating with your dog, teaching your dog, and managing your dog, you shouldn't have much need for punishments. If your dog is misbehaving, you have failed in one of those key areas.

Why doesn't punishment work? Because it is so difficult to do it right and so easy to do it wrong. To be effective, punishment has to have *all* these traits:

- ✔ **It has to be immediate.** Punishment must happen as the misbehavior is about to begin or as early into the misbehavior as possible. So when you come home and find that your dog has urinated on your new living room carpeting, punishing him for that behavior doesn't do any good, because it isn't immediate.

- ✔ **It has to be something your dog doesn't like and it has to be strong enough to stop the behavior.** But punishment can't be too strong, or else you risk physically or psychologically harming your dog.

- ✔ **It has to be associated only with the behavior and nothing else such as a person or a place.**

- ✔ **It has to happen *every* time the behavior occurs.**

- ✔ **You have to provide an alternative behavior for the dog for which he can earn a reward.** It has to be something he can't do if he is doing the behavior you don't want. Sitting instead of jumping up is an example. He can't do both at the same time.

That's an awfully tall order, even for a skilled trainer. Before you look at ways to change a behavior, you have to figure out all the things that may be rewarding the behavior. If you're punishing your dog and he's continuing to do the behavior, something else is rewarding him. Sometimes the behavior itself is the reward. Chasing squirrels, barking, and jumping up are common self-rewarding behaviors.

Every punishment you give your dog is a breach of trust. Look at punishment like spending with a credit card. You may get what you want today, but you're paying exorbitant interest and draining your finances in the long term.

Using crates for short-term confinement

Crates should be tools not prisons. Use them only for short-term confinement. If your dog is destructive when he's alone, work on the underlying problem. Don't forget that even though the furniture is safe when he's in a crate, your dog still needs help with the fear that causes the destructive behavior in the first place.

Unless your hound, another animal, or a person is at risk, ignore bad behavior and reward good behavior. If your retired racer weighs 85 pounds and likes to greet your 80-pound grandma by jumping off the ground and springing at her, manage his environment so he can't do that while you train him what to do instead.

Never use electronic devices or shock collars or other so-called *training tools* or *training devices* that physically hurt your dog. Even in the hands of an experienced trainer, the fallout from these tools can be aggression or serious emotional problems in your dog.

So what should you do? Look at any problem behavior as a management problem. Are there ways you can resolve it by managing your dog or the environment? How would you deal with the same problem if your toddler were doing it? Be creative. Want to know more about management? Read on.

Managing your dog's environment

The more your retired racer gets to practice behaviors you *don't* like, the better he learns how to do them. Put simply, management is what you do to keep your dog from practicing things you *don't* want while you teach him what you *do* want.

Humans use management tools all the time when we work with our children. We can do the same thing with our hounds. The tools are different but the idea is the same. Keep him out of trouble with collars, harnesses, leashes, crates, safe areas, X-pens, and baby gates. And just like any tool, they should be used in addition to teaching, not in place of it.

So how should you use management tools like leashes and crates? If you notice your hound likes to counter surf, for example, use a baby gate to keep him out of the kitchen when you can't supervise and while you teach him to settle in a particular spot. If he likes to jump up on people to greet them, use his leash to control him when visitors arrive so he doesn't get more opportunity to practice. Hold him back or tether him to something solid while you work on teaching him to sit to be greeted.

REMEMBER

The most overlooked management tool is exercise — physical and mental exercise. If your Greyhound gets plenty of exercise, he won't be inclined to look for things to do.

TIP

Look at every problem first as a management problem and think of how you might manage the environment to eliminate the problem altogether. If your Greyhound steals trash in the kitchen, sometimes the easiest solution is simply to put the trash in a container with a lid or move it inside a cupboard.

REMEMBER

No one ever seems to notice when his hound is being good. We ignore good behavior all the time. But we sure do notice and respond to the bad things our hounds do. This approach is absolutely the opposite of what we *should* do with our needlenoses.

Management requires some imagination. Think about any nuisance behavior or problem behavior in terms of management. Always ask yourself what you can do to keep your dog out of trouble while you teach him what you expect of him.

Remembering who owns the can opener

Let's get real. Your dog is your virtual prisoner. He eats when and if you choose. He goes out when and if you choose. He plays or sleeps if you choose. You control everything he does and doesn't have. You literally control your dog's life and death. So using that power to your dog's advantage is all the more critical.

If you develop your relationship with your hound and teach basic manners, you'll avoid most problem behaviors. But sometimes a retired racer may need a reminder that you own the can opener. If he gets a bit pushy and growls, there is nothing wrong with reminding him with a harsh "ah-ah" or a "no" that that kind of behavior is absolutely not acceptable. But if it happens more than once or twice, get professional help immediately.

Talk to your veterinarian. There are many physical causes for aggression and your hound needs a complete physical including thyroid testing to rule out any of those causes. Working through aggression isn't a do-it-yourself project. Don't do anything that might initiate an aggressive response from a problem hound. And the sooner you seek help, the better your chances of bringing the behavior under control will be.

WARNING!

Growling

Don't just punish your hound for growling. Treat the cause, not the symptom. Punishing him for growling is like cutting the rattle off a rattlesnake. You keep him from warning you, but you don't make him any less dangerous.

How treatable is aggression? It depends on the dog. Keep in mind the length of time your Greyhound has been practicing his aggression, the severity of the incidents, the age he was when the aggression began, and the frequency of the incidents.

If your Greyhound snaps at you but doesn't actually get you, he didn't mean to. Keep in mind that these dogs can catch flies out of the air. They know exactly where their teeth are. If he did nip, it wasn't an accident. It was a warning.

Any dog is capable of biting if he's provoked. But what your Greyhound views as provocation may not fit your definition of provocation. Aggression is treatable, but it *isn't* curable. Be aware that even if your Greyhound's aggression has been successfully controlled, it can resurface when he's under stress.

Chapter 8

Elbows off the Table!: Teaching Your Greyhound Basic Household Etiquette

* *

In This Chapter

▶ Getting your retired racer to know his name

▶ Holding your dog's attention

▶ Mastering some simple behaviors with your dog

▶ Asking for the same level of politeness that you ask for from your kids

▶ Working on duration, distance, and distraction

* *

*I*f you want even simple behaviors to be reliable, you have to work on them as a family. Agree on which cues you'll use to get your dog to perform certain behaviors. Each family member has to spend at least a little time practicing with your retired racer so that he views you as his leaders and forms good relationships with each of you. Your hound will learn to respond to cues from everyone from Grandma to your toddler if you help him take lots of pictures.

Training should be fun for you and your dog. If you're doing it right, he won't want the session to end.

Remember the basics. When I use the word *click,* that means that you should use your verbal or mechanical reward marker, such as making a sound with a clicker, and *then* reward your dog. Never click without treating afterward.

Remember win/win learning isn't about commands. It's about catching your dog doing something *right.* All you need is a reward marker like a clicker, some rewards, a sense of humor, and some basic ground rules to set your dog up for success.

Here is a quick review of the steps for teaching a new behavior:

- **Get the desired behavior.** Lure it, target it, shape it, or just wait for it to happen naturally.
- **Click the behavior as close as possible to its beginning.** For example, when you first start clicking a sit, you'll click as soon as his butt is about to hit the floor. It's better to click too early rather than too late.
- **If you're using a lure to help teach a new behavior, get it out of sight as soon as possible.**
- **Follow every click with a treat.**
- **Release stationary behaviors.**
- **Make rewards unpredictable so he learns to gamble.**

Teaching Your Retired Racer His Name

Your Greyhound's name is more than what you use to call him for dinner. It helps to lay the foundation for your relationship. Most dogs don't really know their names very well because their owners haven't taken the time to teach it to them. Retired racers are no exception. If you like his track name, keep it. If not, feel free to change it. Short names (no more than three syllables) are best.

Pick a name you like, and use it when he comes toward you, when you feed him, and at every chance you get. Start feeding your hound by hand. Every time you hand him a bite of food, say his name and *then* deliver the food. Every time you want to pet him, say his name first. If he isn't ready to take food from your hand, just drop a bite at his feet or toss it to him. And every time you use his name, be sure something pleasant happens for your dog — smile, pet him, scratch his ear, take him outside, give him a treat or a toy. Do anything you can think of that would be pleasant for your dog. He will begin to respond to the sound of his name in almost no time. Eventually, he will learn that when he hears his name, he should be ready to pay attention, like the attentive hound shown in Figure 8-1.

Never use your dog's name in connection with the word *no* or with anything negative, like scolding or punishment. The sound of your dog's name should always be followed with something positive. After he is responding to his name, don't use it unless you want a response. When you talk about him in his presence, use a word other than his name. If you overuse his name, it will lose meaning.

Practice saying your Greyhound's name in different tones of voice. Someday you may have to yell over a strong wind or whisper to keep from waking a baby.

Figure 8-1:
When your
Greyhound
knows his
name,
getting his
attention is
easier.

Photograph courtesy of Laurel Drew

Getting Your Retired Racer to Pay Attention

Before you can do any kind of training with your Greyhound, you have to get his full attention (see Figure 8-2). A hound who isn't paying attention isn't listening. The only way your dog will learn is by staying focused on you.

Using doggie Zen to teach attention

If you want to teach eye contact in a formal training session, here's how. First, pick up a treat and let your Greyhound see the treat. Put it in your hand and close your hand. Let him nose around, paw at your hand, or whine. Eventually, he'll stop and look at you. When he does, click.

When he has stopped looking for the treat and directed his attention to you about ten separate times, introduce the cue. As he is about to look at you, say "Watch me," and then click.

After you've tried this another ten times, remove the food from your hand, and try getting him to look at you with just your verbal cue.

Why are you staring at me?

Eye contact and attention are not always the same thing. Some dogs find making eye contact to be very difficult. For them, eye contact is simply too threatening. A pushy dog may view extended eye contact as a challenge. So as long as your Greyhound is paying attention to you, it's okay if he's not staring your way.

Being the couch potato version of a Zen master

The couch potato way to teach him to pay attention is simply to reward your hound's attention whenever you see it. You can reward eye contact with a smile, a scratch behind the ear, or a pat on the head. If you have really good rewards handy, simply click as he looks in your direction. Any time your retired racer makes eye contact and you see it, acknowledge his eye contact and reinforce it. Later, you can begin to say "look" or "watch me" as he looks in your direction.

Figure 8-2:
Teaching your Greyhound to pay attention is the foundation for all other training.

TIP

Shrinking violets

If you have a retired racer who is reluctant to make eye contact with you, try this method instead.

Touch a treat to the tip of your Greyhound's nose. Slowly bring the treat toward *your* face so that it comes to the point just between your eyes. When he makes eye contact, click.

After ten or so repetitions, try this with no food in your hand. When he responds consistently, add a verbal cue just as you begin the hand signal. Gradually fade away the hand signal until he looks at you after hearing the verbal cue.

Warning: Don't try this with a dog who may lunge toward your face to grab the treat.

Getting your hound on target

Targeting is the foundation for all kinds of things. Because it doesn't look like anything you've taught a dog before, you may be tempted to skip over this. Please don't. After your hound understands this, you can use it to teach everything from a retrieve to tricks.

And because this doesn't look like anything your hound already knows, it's a great way to help your dog learn how to learn.

Start with an object that is too large to fit quickly in your hound's mouth so he isn't encouraged to bite at it instead of touch it with his nose if your click is a bit late. Your fist or a large ball is ideal.

Encourage your hound to touch your fist with his nose by extending your fist toward him. Click. Keep repeating with your hand in the same position until he seems to get it. On or about the fifth try, the dog may hesitate. If he does, rub a bit of something interesting on your fist and put your hand back in the same spot. Repeat until your hound is reliably touching your target. See Figure 8-3 for illustrated instructions.

Now move your fist to see if he'll touch it. Keep moving the target around — up down, toward you, away from you — and reward for all successful attempts to touch it. Put the target over your hound's head so he has to jump to touch it. Put it behind you, then move it ahead so he follows it with his nose. Touch the floor. Finally, give it a name (*touch, target,* whatever you like) and keep practicing.

When your hound will target this object consistently on cue, change to another object that isn't part of your body. A sticky note makes a good target because you can move in anywhere. When he's touching this object reliably, give it a different name. You've helped him learn to generalize his targeting behavior to different kinds of objects and objects at different distances.

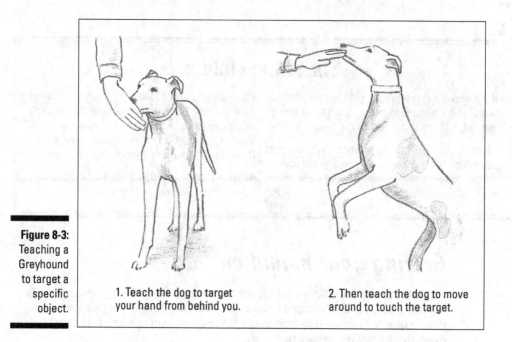

Figure 8-3:
Teaching a
Greyhound
to target a
specific
object.

1. Teach the dog to target
your hand from behind you.

2. Then teach the dog to move
around to touch the target.

Now you're ready to use it to teach him how to walk at your side, settle on his mat, or ring bells to let you know he needs to go out.

Mastering Simple Stationary Behaviors

In this section, I guide you through the behaviors that form the foundation for leadership, self-discipline, and control. If you spend a few minutes a day working with your dog on these behaviors, you'll probably never have to look at Chapter 10, which covers behavior problems.

One important thing to keep in mind as you train your retired racer is that Greyhounds do get bored. So don't try to do too many repetitions. Take a play break and then work some more. Always quit on a positive note, when you and your dog are having fun. Keep your training sessions short. Turn commercial breaks or a few minutes during halftime of Saturday's big game into a training session. Set aside two minutes before you give him his dinner to work on training.

In this section, I show you how to use a lure to teach sit and down. Because the position of your hand when you move the lure becomes a cue, be consistent about how you hold your hand. It doesn't matter if you hold it palm up to teach a sit and palm down to teach a down or vice versa. What matters is that you do it the same way each time, that the cue for sit is different than the cue for down, and that every member of your family does it the same way.

Your dog learns something every time you interact — even if you don't realize you're teaching him anything. Make use of your time together and spend it wisely.

Start your training on carpeted or padded surfaces instead of linoleum or tile floors. Some dogs are so leery of slippery surfaces that they never really get comfortable doing a sit or a down in those places. In time, a dog will do it because you asked . . . even if he doesn't like it.

Down

Down is a submissive and defenseless position. Your retired racer may be reluctant to do it in a strange place or when he feels particularly stressed. Make sure you teach him the down position well in all the places where he's comfortable before you ask him to learn it somewhere else.

The couch potato way to teach down is to wait for him to go into the position on his own. When you see him start to lie down, click as his body is about to hit the floor. Eventually, add the verbal cue, *down*.

You can also lure your Greyhound into the down position from the standing position (as shown in Figure 8-4):

1. **Touch a treat to your dog's nose.**

2. **Slowly lower the treat straight to the floor.**

   Hold it there and let him sniff at it. Be still, be quiet, and wait.

3. **As his front and back legs are about to touch the floor, click.**

4. **Eventually fade the lure away and introduce a verbal cue.**

If your Greyhound won't put his butt the whole way down, shape him into the desired position. Start by clicking as he lowers his head. Then click when his front legs bend a bit. Gradually let him get closer to the down position before you click.

After you've taught your retired racer to sit, teach down over again from the sitting position (see Figure 8-5):

1. **Touch a treat to his nose.**

2. **Slowly move it straight to the ground between his front paws.**

   If his butt is coming up from the floor, be certain you're moving the treat straight to the floor rather than down and away from him.

3. **As his front legs are about to touch the ground, click.**

4. **Fade the lure away and introduce a verbal cue.**

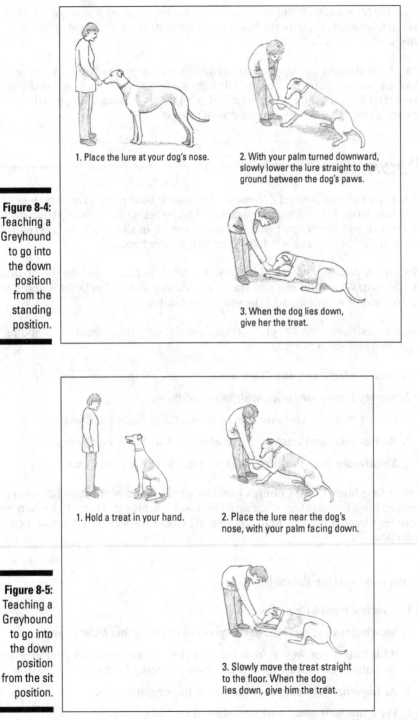

Figure 8-4:
Teaching a Greyhound to go into the down position from the standing position.

1. Place the lure at your dog's nose.

2. With your palm turned downward, slowly lower the lure straight to the ground between the dog's paws.

3. When the dog lies down, give her the treat.

Figure 8-5:
Teaching a Greyhound to go into the down position from the sit position.

1. Hold a treat in your hand.

2. Place the lure near the dog's nose, with your palm facing down.

3. Slowly move the treat straight to the floor. When the dog lies down, give him the treat.

Sit

Most training guides show you how to teach sit from the standing position. But the easiest way to teach a Greyhound to sit is to teach it from the down position. Follow these easy steps (shown also in Figure 8-6):

1. **Hold a treat in the fingers of your upturned hand.**

2. **Hold your fingers at your Greyhound's nose.**

3. **Keep your palm turned upward as you slowly bring your hand up and slightly back, with the treat at his nose the entire time.**

4. **As his front legs come up into a sitting position, click.**

5. **Fade the lure away and introduce a verbal cue.**

 If your dog brings his butt off the floor before you get him into a sitting position, you may need to shape this behavior in small stages. You can begin by clicking as soon as he raises the front of his body even slightly off the floor. Gradually get him closer and closer to a true sitting position before you click.

 If he moves directly into a stand without sitting on the way up, you're probably moving the lure away from his nose or moving it too quickly as you're bringing it up from the floor.

1. With your palm turned upward, place the lure at your dog's nose.

2. Keep the lure close to your dog's muzzle as you move the lure up and back.

3. When your dog is in a sitting position, give him the treat.

Figure 8-6: Teaching a Greyhound to sit from the down position.

If going through all these motions to train your dog to sit seems like a lot of work, try the couch potato way. Most dogs — even Greyhounds — sit on their own at least once in a while. Watch your retired racer to see if he sits to scratch his neck or ear, for example. Does he sit as he lies down or gets up from a down position? If he ever sits naturally, on his own, simply wait for him to do it and click whenever he does. When he figures out that he gets a reward for sitting, you'll have a sitting fool on your hands.

Regardless of whether your dog sits on his own, you probably won't get a nice straight sit the first time you try it with him. You can gradually shape a nicer looking sit, however. Your hand movement becomes the physical cue. Fade the lure away and add the verbal cue when he's reliably following your hand.

When he understands the concept of sit and has had lots of practice doing it from the down position, it's much easier to teach it from the standing position (shown in Figure 8-7):

1. **Hold a treat in the fingers of your upturned hand.**

2. **Keep the treat near his nose and move it straight back between his eyes.**

   As his nose follows the treat, his butt will begin to lower.

3. **As his butt is about to hit the ground, click.**

   If his butt is leaving the floor to reach for the treat, the lure is too far above his head. Put the treat closer to his muzzle.

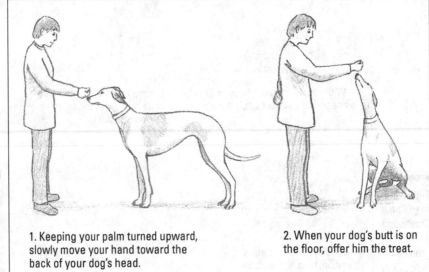

Figure 8-7: Teaching a Greyhound to sit from the standing position.

1. Keeping your palm turned upward, slowly move your hand toward the back of your dog's head.

2. When your dog's butt is on the floor, offer him the treat.

Backing him into a corner

You can increase the odds of getting your Greyhound to sit from a stand by starting with his butt in a corner. This way, he can't back up to follow the lure, because he has nowhere else to go.

REMEMBER

Your retired racer's butt will never be solidly on the floor if his legs are tucked under him. His anatomy doesn't work that way. When he gets into a full Greyhound sit from a standing position, break out the champagne. Reward a first sit from a Greyhound in a huge way.

Come

Teaching your dog to come isn't about a casual "Come 'ere, boy." This is your emergency recall word. This is the word you use if your dog is chasing a rabbit into the path of an oncoming truck. You say *come,* and he turns around and runs right back to you.

Don't hold your breath waiting for this kind of response from a Greyhound, however. Coming when called is the toughest behavior to get from *any* dog. And Greyhounds aren't just any dog. They are bred to run, and they are independent.

REMEMBER

You should *always* keep your Greyhound on a leash or in a fenced yard, but accidents do happen, and even if you have the best of intentions, your retired racer may get out accidentally. So be prepared by training him to come when called . . . and pray you never need it.

Work on *come* regularly. Pick a cue that you haven't misused. And don't use a cue that you've under-rewarded either, or else it won't mean anything to your Greyhound. Check out these sacred rules:

- Never call your dog to you for anything *un*pleasant.
- Never call your dog to you to end anything pleasant.
- Never punish him for failure to respond.

> ✔ *Always* **reward correct responses generously.** This behavior is so
> important that it warrants a regular reward.
>
> ✔ **Make the reward memorable.** How would you reward him if he did turn
> away from the path of that truck? That's how you want to reward your
> hound's recall when you train.

Expect to spend at *least* a full year teaching an adult dog to respond reliably
to a recall cue.

Before you start to work on this behavior, reward your hound anytime he
comes to you, even if you didn't call him. Let him learn that coming toward
you is always rewarding, even if the reward is a simple smile. You want him to
learn that only good things happen when he approaches you.

When you start working on this, use sweet, happy, excited tones. Do anything
you can think of that will get him to move toward you as long as it doesn't
involve a food bribe. Start these excersises with your dog no more than 9 or
10 feet away. Crouch down. When he starts to come toward you, say "come"
and immediately click. Increase the distance slowly. Gradually, fade out the
excited voice and crouching until he clearly associates the behavior with the
verbal cue, when there are no distractions.

When your hound responds to the verbal cue "come," reward it big time.
Offer lots of petting, lots of excitement, neck rubs, ear rubs, lots of praise,
plenty of play, and lots of interesting food. Put great photos in his album.

Red Rover, red Rover . . .

You can use games to help teach your Greyhound recall. Kids love these games, too. Play the games with your dog in a hallway or small room. Encourage the dog to run back and forth between you and other family members. Use the dog's name, noises, and lures. When he starts toward you, say "come" and then click. Only reward his movement toward the person who says "come." Have everyone else ignore him.

At first, you'll click as soon as he turns toward you. Later, as he gets better at the game, you'll click as he's on his way. And eventually, you'll click when he gets to you. Later, you'll ask him to sit before you click. And finally you'll ask him to sit and you'll take hold of his collar before you click.

You can also try playing hide-and-seek with your retired racer. Start out by making it easy. Hide partially in sight. Then call your dog's name, clap, or make other noises. Reward him for a response. Eventually start using the verbal cue "come." Increase the difficulty as the dog learns the game and enjoys playing it.

Only asking for what you know you can get

Never use the come cue in training unless you know your dog will comply. For example, if he's headed in your direction and there is absolutely nothing that is going to distract him before he gets to you, say "come." Or if you've gone into the kitchen to make dinner and you know he'll come from anywhere in the house if you're in the kitchen, that's another good time to say "come." The last thing you want your dog to learn is that come is optional.

Whenever you tell your dog to come and he does as you ask, give him a reward that is delivered quickly, is generous, and is unpredictable.

Remember: A recall is about regaining control and protecting your dog from danger. Many dogs learn how to come just close enough to get their reward and immediately take off again. That isn't control and it doesn't keep him safe. So ask for that sit and get your hand on his collar before you click or reward.

For training purposes, consider the recall cue sacred. Practice each day. But don't overdo it. Always leave him wanting more. Unless you're training, only use the word *come* in a near-emergency situation. If your dog hears the word too often, it will eventually have no meaning for him.

There's a difference between saying, "Come on, here boy," and saying, "Come." If your Greyhound is too busy sniffing and ignores you when you casually ask him to come, you may be frustrated, but you haven't destroyed your work on recall. If you have to groom your dog or do something else he doesn't like, go get him and lead him to your destination. Don't call him to you.

Retrieving a loose hound

What if your retired racer gets loose or takes off and it isn't really an emergency? Try one or all of these suggestions:

- ✔ **Don't run toward him.** If you run toward him, he'll instinctively move away from you.

- ✔ **Run the other way.** His chase instincts will likely swing into action.

- ✔ **If he isn't looking at you,** make some kind of strange sound that will get his attention, and then, when he's looking at you, run away.

- ✔ **If he's watching you,** make strange noises and fall down on the ground or act like you've found something incredibly neat that you don't want him to see or have.

When he comes to you, take his collar and ask him to sit. Now click. Don't pay him until your hand is on his collar and he's sitting. Eventually, *come* will mean "Stop whatever you're doing, come to me, sit, and let me take your collar."

Teaching Your Greyhound to Share

When you're part of a family, you have to learn to share. So make your Greyhound a real member of the family by teaching him how to behave politely when the three-year-old down the block has an ice cream cone in her hand.

Understanding the concepts of "mine" and "yours"

Hold a tasty treat in your open hand. Point to it. When your retired racer goes for the treat, say "mine," and close your hand before he can get it. Wait for him to back off. Open your hand again. Say "yours," and offer him the treat. Repeat until your hound backs off immediately when he hears "mine" and doesn't take it until it is offered with the word "yours."

You can extend this training even further. Place the treat on your knee, point to it, and say "mine." If he goes for it quickly, cover it with your hand. When he backs off, offer it to him with "yours." Gradually move the treat farther and farther away. As you move it farther away, use a helper who can get to it before the dog can. In time, if you do this slowly enough, you'll be able to leave your sandwich on the coffee table while you get yourself a glass of iced tea from the fridge.

Giving up objects

Sharing doesn't come naturally to dogs. But you can prevent food and object guarding and games of keep-away when he has a chicken bone in his mouth by teaching your Greyhound to give up objects that you don't want him to have. This training is also part of the foundation for games of fetch.

Make a list of ten to fifteen objects your dog likes to put in his mouth or at least is willing to put in his mouth. On this list, include only things he's allowed to have. Rank them from the things he likes best to the things he likes least. Be sure the item at the bottom of your list isn't an object he'll guard. Start with the item he likes least.

Training Your Dog to Behave Like He's One of the Family

If you expect your three-year-old to say "please," there is no reason why you can't expect similar behavior from your dog.

Begin working on these exercises as soon as your hound begins to sit in response to a cue. His response doesn't have to be completely reliable. It just has to be solid enough that he understands he gets paid to sit. If your boy has an injury that makes sitting difficult, you can use down instead.

Pass the bread, please

Put some food in your hound's bowl and hold the dish just above his head. If he doesn't sit, ask him to sit. As soon as he sits, begin to lower his dish to the floor. If he starts to move toward it, immediately straighten up. When he stops and sits back, start to lower it to the floor again. Keep this up until you can place his food on the floor and let go. Now say "yours" or "okay," and release the dog to eat.

Gradually increase the length of time you require him to sit before you allow him to eat. Vary the amounts of time, but gradually increase the total time. Then work on distance. Put the dish down farther away from the dog. Start a foot away. Each time you feed, move the dish farther away from the dog.

When your Greyhound has this behavior down, you can move the dish closer to him and add some waiting time. Then add some distance, then some more waiting time, and so on. The point is that your dog learns that he can only eat when you tell him it's okay to eat.

Please and thank you

Hide a large, chewy treat in your hands, cross your arms across your chest, and wait. Eventually, your hound will sit. When he sits, offer him the treat. But only move it toward him if his butt stays on the ground. Continue to hold the treat and let him nibble on it while you get really excited and offer lots of verbal praise. Continue to hold the treat and jog around him as he nibbles. Sing out loud, stomp on the floor, or make weird noises while he nibbles. Eventually he'll learn to sit calmly for everything he wants, no matter what is going on around him. Sitting will become your retired racer's equivalent of saying "please."

Wait your turn

If your Greyhound goes crazy every time you pick up his leash, you can teach him to wait calmly. As soon as he gets crazy, drop the leash and cross your arms. When he stays seated for three or four seconds, calmly reach for the leash. If his butt comes up, straighten up again, cross your arms, and wait. Repeat this so that, eventually, your dog sits calmly until his leash is on and you release him to get up from the sitting position.

You can extend this behavior to teach him not to bolt through open doors by walking to the door, putting your hand on the doorknob, and requesting the sit. As soon as he sits, reach for the doorknob. If his butt comes up off the ground, remove your hand from the doorknob and stand still. Ignore the dog. When he sits, reach for the doorknob again. Repeat this until his butt stays down. Open the door an inch or two. If his butt comes up, slam the door closed. Repeat this until you can open the door the whole way. Then release him from sitting and get outside and have some fun!

Practice this behavior at different doors. Repeat it until he automatically sits at all doors. Train the same behavior coming in. That way he'll always sit and wait until you open the door and release him instead of bolting out — perhaps into the path of a truck. And then teach him to do it in the car so you can load and unload him safely.

Walk this way

Most Greyhounds don't pull on leashes. But if your retired racer is not calm when the door opens, chances are he'll learn to pull on his leash in no time. So training him to wait calmly when you're ready to go out will go a long way toward helping him walk well, too.

If you want to prevent your hound from learning to pull on his leash, you only have to follow two rules. First, allow him to do whatever he likes as long as his leash is loose. What's a loose leash? If you can hold a full cup of coffee without sloshing it in the hand that has the leash, the leash is loose. If you can't possibly hold that cup of coffee in the hand that's holding the leash, you and your hound have some work to do. Secondly, if the leash is tight, you make absolutely no movement in the direction he's pulling. Stand still and wait for him to release the pressure. If pulling doesn't work, he'll learn not to do it.

Chapter 9

More Training: Adding Multitask Behaviors

- -

In This Chapter

▶ Teaching your Greyhound to take the next step

▶ Working on behaviors that keep your Greyhound safe

- -

*I*f you want your Greyhound to do more than a simple sit, you have to make a commitment to pay close attention to him. You can't ask for a sit, then forget to release him because the phone rings. And you can't interrupt a training session because your neighbor stops by, without letting your hound know that the session is over. When you begin a training session with your needlenose, you've entered into a mini-contract. You've agreed to give one another your undivided attention. After all, if you expect your boy's attention not to stray, you have to be willing to give him the same.

The behaviors in this chapter are about strengthening what your hound already knows and teaching him to remain calm and in control. Remember that part of your contract is to be his leader. That means you have to pay attention not just to him but to all the things that are going on around you that may pose a threat to him. This is especially important if he's on a leash, because he feels particularly vulnerable then. Make sure you and your hound have mastered the behaviors in Chapter 8 before you try to tackle the ones in this chapter.

You've probably noticed that sometimes your couch potato doesn't pay any attention to things he "knows." He'll sit in the backyard, but not in the park. Guess what, he doesn't know it. If he did, he'd do it. Here's the scoop.

Keeping in Mind the Degree of Difficulty

The behaviors you teach your hound have varying degrees of difficulty. Each time we change what we ask our hounds to do, we have let them take new pictures. You can't expect your hound to sit when you're in a park full of squirrels and dogs and neat smells if the only picture he has of sit is in a quiet living room. Work on things like *duration* (the length of time you require the behavior to be performed), *distance* (the space between you and your hound when you require the behavior to be performed), and *distraction* (the amount of noise and other activities surrounding your hound when you require the behavior to be performed). But work on each of these three elements separately. Don't expect your retired racer to be able to master them all at once.

If your hound isn't succeeding, you're either changing too many things at once or you're moving ahead too quickly. Be patient. He'll learn what you want if you give him the time he needs. The more places you train and the more experiences you provide, the more your hound will learn how to learn.

Teach your retired racer duration, distance, and distraction separately. Then put them together. Whenever you increase difficulty in one area, make it easier at first in the other areas, use your click, and increase how frequently you reward. Add these degrees of difficulty as early in your training as you can. The longer you and your Greyhound stay stuck in one place, the more difficult it will be for him to generalize the behavior to other situations. Getting him to be reliable — that is, doing something the moment you ask for it, every time you ask for it — means teaching each behavior in lots of situations with lots of practice and lots of rewards. If he isn't doing it, it's because he doesn't have enough photos in his album yet.

Wait

For a variety of reasons, you want your hound to wait when asked. His life is easier if he waits while the vet is examining him or while you or the groomer are trimming his nails, for example. Being able to get your hound to wait is also very handy when you're going down the stairs with your arms full of laundry and you want him to stay at the top of the stairs instead of getting under your feet. And it's a great safety measure while walking when you're reaching an intersection. I think it's easier to teach your hound to respond to a cue to lie down if he's away from you if he has already learned the concept of wait first. His world is much safer if he waits when you tell him to.

Being patient with your pal

When you're teaching your hound to wait, be sure you have plenty of patience or your training will be shot. Wait is a totally pointless and boring exercise from your hound's perspective. So take it slow so he can win. Whenever you increase the difficulty of one element, decrease your expectations and minimize the other elements. Increase your reward pattern. Decide in advance what you are going to work on in each session. How else will you know when you get there?

I use the word *wait* to tell my hound that he can't move from whatever position he's in when I say it. If my boy is lying around in the yard when he sees a rabbit, I can't very well tell him *down*. He's already lying down. That's where wait comes in handy. (You can substitute the words *stay* or *freeze* for wait if you prefer.)

Start with your hound in a standing position. As he to walks toward you, put your hand out in front of his face like a traffic cop, touching your hand against his nose. The instant he stops, click. Do it again. Keep practicing this behavior until he stops the instant your hand is in place. Then work on getting some distance from your hound. Start with your palm about an inch from his nose and gradually increase how far away you can be when you give him the cue. When you can get him to stop immediately about a foot away, begin to build duration. Make him wait for longer periods of time. When you've got a bit of duration and distance, introduce a verbal cue (*freeze, stay, hold,* or *wait,* for example).

When your Greyhound responds well to the verbal cue with no distractions, work on getting the response when he's not facing you. Start with him at your side. Put your hand, palm open and facing backward, to his nose as he moves forward. The instant he stops, click. When he responds immediately to your hand signal, build some duration. Then reintroduce the verbal signal.

Now you're ready to move. Keep your back to the hound. Give your signal (keeping your hand at his nose), then move your foot forward as though you are going to take a step. Immediately bring your foot back into place and click if he's remained in place. If he hasn't, try just lifting your foot like you would if you were marching in place. Now try marching in place with both feet. Then try taking a full step forward. Immediately step back into place and click. Gradually increase the distance. Add distractions.

Eventually, your retired racer will stop advancing toward you when you give him the cue. He'll stay as you move away from him. How do you get him to stop when he's moving away from you? This is the tough part. Start with your hound at your side. As he walks along beside you, stop. As he moves ahead of you, put your hand on his chest to block his forward progress. The instant he stops, click. Repeat this frequently. Increase the distance until your arms run out of reach. Then add the verbal cue. Gradually add distance after that.

Finally, begin to add distractions. With your hound beside you, toss a treat just ahead of you. As he moves forward, give your signal. Put your hand against his chest if you need to. The instant he stops, click and release him to get the treat. Increase distance and distractions very slowly. If necessary, use a helper or a leash so you can control when he gets the treat.

When he's solid with this behavior, you can begin to work on it when he's sitting and lying down. After you are working on wait in the down position, gradually build duration to 30 minutes or more. If he's breaking before you release him, you're pushing him too hard. If you aren't using a clicker and you're going to reward a wait, always reward him while his body is in the correct position, and then release him. You don't want to reward him for breaking; you want to reward him for waiting. And because you always want him to win, help him if he's having trouble. If you know he's good for 10 minutes, but not 11, at 9 minutes give him a reminder: Say "wait" again.

Steady

Wouldn't it be nice if you could get your hound to sit calmly beside you without a word from you when you're in the park or something has him really excited? Guess what? You can.

Choose a specific way you'll hold his collar so he understands what you want. When your boy will sit on cue, get him on your left side. Take hold of his collar using the hand position you decided on and ask for a sit. Click. Repeat until he automatically sits as soon as your hand grasps his collar in that special way, without any verbal cue.

When he has that behavior down fairly well, add eye contact. Grasp his collar. When he sits, say "watch me." As soon as he makes eye contact, click. Gradually fade the verbal cue for attention as well so that all you need to do to get him to sit and look at you is grasp his collar a specific way. Work on adding distractions and duration of eye contact. You want him to sit and make eye contact no matter what's going on around him.

Settle

Teaching your retired racer to settle is your first and best defense against counter surfing. It's also the perfect way to get him to lie down and relax, no matter where he is.

Counter surfing

You can prevent your hound from learning to get up on the kitchen counters to surf for food by keeping food and other things out of reach and out of sight. If your Greyhound never gets rewarded for the behavior, it will disappear.

Never feed your hound in the kitchen (or only feed from his bowl). If he's never rewarded in the kitchen, he won't look for food in the kitchen. It's that simple.

Start by finding a towel, a dog mat, or a small blanket. This will be your target. Cover your hand with part of it and hold it just in front of your Greyhound's nose. Let him move toward it and touch it with his nose. When he touches it, click.

Gradually move your hand closer to the floor. Wait for him to touch the target, and then click. Continue to click touches as you gradually move your hand away from the target. If he happens to put a paw on the target, begin to click that behavior.

When your Greyhound consistently touches the towel on the floor, push him a bit. Wait for him to put a paw on it. The target is large enough that his paw will come in contact with it at some point. Begin clicking only paw touches. Move the towel around so that he learns that wherever it is placed, paws on the towel trigger the click.

If more than one paw is on the towel, all the better. His nose no longer has to touch it. At this point, you're clicking only when his paw is on the target. Wait to move to the next step until he learns that only all four paws on the target get clicked.

When he consistently gets his paws on the target, don't click. Cue the down position. Keep doing this until he begins to drop as soon as he gets on the target. When your hound can't wait to lie down on his towel, give it a name like *settle, place,* or *chill.* Add distance, duration, and distractions.

Take your hound for a good walk or a run. Wear him out. Plan on spending lots of extra time to prepare dinner. Use a helper if you have one. Place the towel in a specific spot in or near the kitchen, where your Greyhound can see you. Tell him to settle on the towel. Begin to work on dinner (or ask your helper to do this). After about ten seconds, walk over with a treat. Randomly walk over and reward him from time to time as long as he stays on the towel.

If he looks like he's going to get up, correct him with a gentle "ah-ah." If he does break, take him back to the towel and start over. He'll quickly learn that lying on his towel gets him paid, but coming into the kitchen doesn't.

The lazy way to settle

Place a towel on the floor and wait for your hound to lie down on the towel. Any time he lies down on it, click. When he figures out that lying on the towel has a payoff, move the towel around so he understands it's the towel that earned the click, not a geographic area. You can speed things up by tossing a treat on the towel at first.

When you've built up distance, duration, and distraction, test him. Send him to his towel. Put something truly appealing on the edge of the counter. Duck around the corner and watch. If he even thinks of moving, rush in and say "ah-ah." You want him to think you're always watching. If he doesn't make any attempt to move, release him and give him a treat. If your hound already counter-surfs and this doesn't help, turn to Chapter 10 for more help.

Close

When your Greyhound is *close,* it means that he's walking nicely on your left side within a defined area — his zone. Start by teaching your Greyhound to think that being on your left side is lots of fun. Pretend you're standing in the middle of a clock face. You're facing noon. Your dog's shoulder can be anywhere from 9:00 to 11:00 and within 18 inches of your left leg. When your hound is in that space, he's in his target zone. Being in the zone is a very good thing. Whenever he's in the zone, click him, talk to him, and praise him. When he wanders out of the zone, ignore him. You can keep walking (as long as the leash is loose), but nothing else exciting is going to happen. When he returns to the zone, say "close." In time he'll respond to *close* as a cue to return to the zone.

As you're about to make left and right turns, simply alert him by saying "this way." You have a leash attached to the hound's collar — you don't want to yank him around. The idea is to advise him with your voice that you're changing direction.

Use close for short distances when control is important. Use it to work your way through a crowd, to cross busy streets, or in other places where you need more control and focus than a loose leash provides. Walks are supposed to be fun, so don't overuse it.

Though adorable, racing puppies are rarely available to the public. If you have your heart set on a puppy, contact a reputable AKC breeder. And prepare for a long wait.

Good nutrition and plenty of time with his mother and litter-mates are important factors in a Greyhound's future good health and emotional development.

Don't let these angelic faces fool you. Greyhound puppies are nothing like their quiet, calm, adult relatives.

Greyhounds show a remarkable range of colors and patterns. Even puppies in the same litter can look quite different from one another.

This Greyhound has dug a hole in the sand to cool off on a warm summer day. Your Greyhound may do the same in your backyard if he gets too hot. Always be sure to offer your dog plenty of shade, and don't allow him to stay out too long in extreme temperatures.

Most adopters of retired racing Greyhounds find it impossible to have only one.

This brindle Greyhound enjoys the company of a well-mannered, considerate child. Be sure to teach children the correct way to treat dogs.

Greyhounds quickly learn to sit if you use gentle, reward-based techniques.

If you learn to speak Greyhound, you'll soon be able to tell that these two dogs are only play-fighting.

Photograph by Nancy Beach

Greyhounds have delicate skin, so they should always be muzzled when they get together for a run.

Photograph by Bonnie Stoner

Photograph by Nancy Beach

This 7-year-old male has no trouble keeping up with this 2-year-old female. Most Greyhounds love the company of other Greyhounds.

Although Greyhounds enjoy the warmth of a cozy fire, they are sturdy enough to welcome a romp in freshly fallen snow.

Although most Greyhounds love the outdoors, they do need to be able to escape the summer heat and sun, like these hounds who are enjoying a dip in the water.

Even in large wooded areas like this one, responsible owners keep their Greyhounds leashed.

Photograph by Bonnie Stoner

Very few Greyhounds are actually gray (a color that breeders refer to as blue). The name Greyhound has nothing to do with the dog's color. Blue dogs like this one are hard to find.

Photograph by Bonnie Stoner

Running is as natural as breathing for Greyhounds. This courser doesn't care that the lure he's chasing is only a white plastic bag.

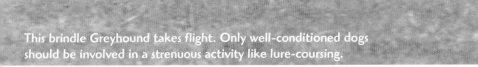

This brindle Greyhound takes flight. Only well-conditioned dogs should be involved in a strenuous activity like lure-coursing.

Chapter 10

Dealing with Behavioral Problems

In This Chapter
▶ Figuring out how to treat behavior problems without punishment
▶ Working on common behavior problems with patience
▶ Helping your dog overcome serious behavior problems, including aggression

G reyhounds are pretty easy to live with. But like all dogs, sometimes problem behaviors occur. When it comes to dealing with your Greyhound's behavioral problems, unfortunately there are no magic wands to make the problems go away. If there were, you could buy one at the nearest pet store and folks like me would be out of business. Instead of looking for quick fixes, look at increasing your hound's physical and mental exercise and spending more time on training. It always takes more time to fix a problem behavior than it does to prevent it. As a general rule, assume that changing a behavior in your retired racer will take at least as long as it took for him to learn it. If your dog has been pulling on a leash for three years, don't expect him to be walking calmly at your side in three weeks.

In this chapter, I discuss how to fix simple nuisance behaviors like jumping up and leash pulling. I also give you the lowdown on managing sibling rivalry and preventing fights.

Overcoming the Habit of Leash-Pulling

The longer your hound has been rewarded for pulling, the longer it will take to completely change his behavior. If you allow him to pull sometimes, but sometimes you don't allow it, you've turned pulling (as a reward) into a slot machine and fixing this behavior will be very difficult.

If your time schedule doesn't allow you to train consistently on every walk, use a different collar, a retractable leash, a harness, or a head collar so your boy gets a clear signal that this walk or part of the walk is different.

Correcting garden-variety leash-pulling

If you want your hound to learn to walk on a loose leash, it helps if his leash is the same length every time you walk him. Use a soft, 4- to 6-foot leather, nylon, or cotton leash. Tie it around your waist or loop it through your belt — just make sure your hands are off of it. The only reason you need a leash is to keep your hound from wandering off.

If you want your hound to walk on a loose leash outside, start working on this behavior inside. Teach him to walk through the house on a loose leash before you try to retrain him outside. Don't open the door to go out until your Greyhound is sitting or waiting calmly at the door.

If you want him to learn to stay calm outside, you have to begin by getting him to remain calm inside. Don't take a single step out the door until the leash is loose and he remains seated until you release him. Don't move in the direction he wants to go unless the leash is loose. You may need 20 minutes to get to the end of your driveway, but I never said this was going to be quick or easy.

Start slowly. Say a phrase like "let's go." Take two steps with a loose leash. Click to mark this behavior. Take another three steps with a loose leash, and click to mark the behavior. Increase and vary the number of steps you take before clicking so that your hound realizes it's not a certain number of steps that matter, but it's walking with a loose leash that counts.

The first time you work on this behavior, you'll be lucky to get two steps before the leash tightens. As the leash is about to tighten, freeze. Don't move. Sooner or later he'll get the hint and come back to you. When he returns, say "let's go," and start again.

If you don't have the time to train on a particular walk, use a head collar. But remember that this collar is a training tool and *not* a solution. The idea is to wean your hound off the head collar. And help him win by exercising him before you take him for a walk so he's already a little tired.

Doing remedial work for the serious puller

If your Greyhound is a determined leash-puller, you may need to make an extra effort to get him accustomed to walking by your side. Reinforce his understanding by showing him that pulling keeps him from getting what he wants.

First, find a starting line and choose an end point about 20 to 30 feet away. A piece of furniture, a change of flooring texture, a chalk line or a crack on a sidewalk, or a stick are good choices. Just pick something you can easily see. Use a helper if you can. If you're working alone, fasten your hound to something while you set up the starting and ending points. Start in the least distracting environment you can find — inside if you have the room, or the backyard, the street nearest your house, or the hallway outside your apartment, for example.

Show your hound a valued food treat or a new squeaky toy. Choose something that you're confident he will pull to get to. Place the target in plain sight at your end point about 20 to 30 feet away. If you have an assistant, let her hold the target. If necessary, your assistant can squeak the toy or wave the treat to keep your hound interested.

Don't take a step until your retired racer is calm and at your side. Stand still, no matter how long it takes for him to calm down. Say "let's go" to tell him to move ahead. He'll usually start to pull in just a couple of steps the first time you try this. Walk forward until he is about to reach the end of his leash. Immediately begin to walk backward to the start line. Wait behind the starting line until he is not pulling, sniffing, or jumping. Eventually he'll come to your side or sit still.

Start again. Every time the leash is about to tighten, immediately stop and back up to the starting line and wait. Repeat this process until your hound can go the entire distance without pulling.

When you and your hound get to the target, reward him with the treat or toy. The reward should always come from the person walking your hound. If you have someone helping you, she should hand the reward to you and you should give the reward to your hound. If you're working alone and have left a treat or toy sitting on the ground at the end point, stop your hound just out of reach of the reward, so you can get the item and hand it to him. If his reward is a person he is eager to see, let the person get down and greet him with lots of enthusiasm.

Your hound can pull his hardest when his leash is parallel to his back. Change the angle and you change his ability to pull.

Practice this exercise with increased distractions and increased distances to the target.

When your hound has mastered this exercise close to home, take it on the road. Use anything that he is pulling toward as his target. As the leash tightens, stop and take one or two steps back (more if it's a really exciting distraction). Resume forward motion when he returns to your side or the leash isn't tight — whichever you want from him. Just be consistent.

Keeping Your Greyhound from Jumping Up

Jumping up is a very rewarding behavior for dogs. Dogs lick each other's faces as part of their greeting behavior. A dog who jumps up just wants your attention.

When a Greyhound jumps up, he just wants to get to your face. No rule says you can't get down on the floor with your retired racer. If your face is at his level, he doesn't have to jump to get to it.

When you yell something like "no jumping" at your hound while his feet are planted on you, you're actually teaching him to associate the phrase *no jumping* with having his feet on you. In other words, you're telling him exactly the opposite of what you mean to say.

If you're trying to stop your retired racer from jumping up on people, your first job is to manage him so he can't practice jumping. Put his leash on when the doorbell rings. Tie it to something or hold his collar. But don't let him jump up on guests. Put him in another room and wait for him to calm down before you bring him out on a leash if you have to.

To teach him that jumping no longer pays, you need helpers. So invite a friend over. (Friends work better than his live-in family, because your hound is more likely to jump up on guests than he is someone he sees every day.) Leash your boy before your guest arrives. Give him just enough leash to get up and perhaps move one step. Either hold his leash firmly or tie it to an immovable object. When your guest arrives, have the guest take a treat, turn her back on your hound, and remain still until your hound is seated. Remain quiet and still. Hold the dog firmly until he is calm enough to respond to a request for a sit. When he is seated, signal your friend so she can turn and begin to walk toward your hound. Have her hold the treat in her hand so your dog can see it. As long as he remains seated, your friend continues walking. But the instant his butt starts to leave the floor, your friend folds her arms, turns her back, and walks away from him. When his butt goes down again, your friend moves forward. Keep doing this until your friend can get the whole way to your hound. Reward him with the treat only while his butt is on the floor. Have your friend leave by the back door and do it all over again until your hound makes no attempt to jump up.

Repeat this exercise with other friends and other doors until your needlenose will sit quietly when visitors first arrive. You can throw a party and get lots of practice in by having your friends stagger their arrival times.

What do I do when the delivery driver arrives?

Sometimes guests arrive at the door unexpectedly, and you may not be able to train your hound in these moments. If you have no way to train when these situations arise, at least manage your Greyhound so he can't jump up. You can move him to another room, tether him, or put him in his crate so that he doesn't have the opportunity to practice those jumping skills.

When intervention is a must

If you have young children or a frail person in your home who is being or could be injured by a large, obnoxious hound, a mild punishment may be necessary. Get a small spray vial of human breath-freshener. As your hound is about to launch, spray a barrier of scent between him and the intended victim. Don't direct the spray at your dog; use it only to create a scent barrier.

This technique should be used only if absolutely necessary. And only use it if you are training an alternative behavior for which he can be rewarded. Yelling *sit* at a dog who hasn't been trained to sit through distractions doesn't count as an alternative behavior. Until your dog has learned to sit no matter how excited he is, manage your dog. Don't punish him.

If your racer jumps on you when you return from work, find a helper who can manage him when you arrive home. Stay away long enough to get him excited by your return. Then proceed as if *you* were the guest.

If you don't have a helper, do practice sessions by staying away just long enough to let him be excited by your return. Walk in the door. Give no attention of any kind to your boy (including eye contact or touch) unless all four of his feet are on the floor. Simply fold your arms and turn your back until he settles. If he's really obnoxious, wear long sleeves and jeans so you can protect your arms and legs. If you have to lean against a wall to keep from getting knocked over, do that. Just don't move until he has all four feet on the floor. Click to mark his behavior when he plants all four feet on the floor. Respond to any jumping by totally withdrawing all attention. In time, he'll learn that jumping doesn't pay off.

Stopping Your Hound from Counter-Surfing

The first thing to do if you want your hound to stop surfing your countertops in search of food or other goodies to chew is manage the environment. Keep food and other attractive items off the counters. If your dog never finds anything worth stealing on the counter, he'll stop looking for it there.

If you have children or other housemates who can't quite break the habit of leaving food out, use a baby gate to keep your hound out of the kitchen when you can't supervise.

Counter-surfing can be difficult to eliminate if your Greyhound has already been rewarded by stealing food from the counter. Gear your response to your dog's individual personality. Your response has to be strong enough to stop the behavior but not so strong that it causes him to be fearful of other things in the environment. Punishment has to come from the environment or he'll likely learn to wait until you aren't watching and sneak food on the side.

So how do you get the environment to provide the punishment? Use booby traps. You want your hound to eventually be able to roam free in your kitchen without stealing food or even getting up on the counter to check it out. So convince your retired racer that touching the countertops isn't any fun.

If training settle as explained in Chapter 9 hasn't worked, you can set a booby trap. I prefer to use a simple motion sensor device, which can be purchased from a pet supply catalog. It emits a harsh sound for a few seconds then resets itself so it works even if I'm not there and is not too scary for most hounds — even sensitive ones.

If you want a do-it-yourself version using soda cans, here's the recipe. How heavy-handed you have to be when you set your trap depends completely on your hound. What is his reaction to a sharp "ah-ah"? Does he stop whatever he's doing immediately or ignore the noise? If your boy is very sensitive, keep your booby trap mild. If he doesn't seem to notice you, make your trap noisier.

For a sensitive hound, use only a few empty soda cans (perhaps only five). For a real hard-head, you may need 15 or 20 and you may need to put about 20 pennies in each can. Rinse the cans well so the pennies don't stick to the sides. You want them to rattle.

Test his reaction by knocking a few cans off a counter when he's nearby but not watching. Use his reaction as a guide to determine the number of cans you'll need for a trap. Use the fewest number of cans you can get away with and still stop his behavior. Put the cans on sheets of heavy-duty aluminum foil and just set them on the various counters, out of your dog's reach, for several days so he gets used to the sight of them. If you spring the trap too soon, he'll learn to avoid the counters only if the cans are present.

When you're ready to spring the trap, put the dog someplace where he can't watch what you're doing. If you're using the motion sensor, just tape a piece of thread to the sensor that is similar in color to the countertops and tie the other end to a day old bagel (which is just too tough for even a Greyhound to eat quickly) spread with some meat baby food, cream cheese, or peanut butter. Put a drop or two of a scent that he has never smelled before — old-fashioned Listerine works fine — on the counter near the sensor. Turn the sensor on. Bring him back into the kitchen and hang out for a bit. When everything seems normal, leave him alone in the kitchen.

JUST FOR FUN

Surfer gals

Female Greyhounds are usually kept in the upper crates at racing kennels. They routinely jump into those upper crates, and the crates just happen to be roughly the same height as a kitchen counter or a dining room table. You do the math.

If you're using the cans, use an instant adhesive to glue three to five cans onto the foil. Be careful not to get the glue on your countertop. Tie a long piece of thread that is close to the color of your countertops to the tab of the front can or glue it to the foil. Leave about 18 inches of string to use to attach the bait. Tie the other end of the string to the bagel. Stack any remaining cans on top of the base, in the shape of a pyramid. Add the drops of Listerine and bring your hound back into the kitchen and hang out for a bit. When everything seems normal, leave him alone in the kitchen.

If he jumps up and takes the bait, all the cans will come tumbling down or the sensor will go off and your boy will probably be a little scared. Rush in and take the bait before he can recover and eat it. In your dog's mind, the punishment had nothing to do with you. The environment provided the punishment. And after this happens a few times, your Greyhound should learn his lesson if you've been very careful not to leave anything on the counters for him to steal. Continue using a drop or two of Listerine on the countertops for several weeks as a reminder.

Putting an End to Trash Raids

The easiest way to stop your hound from raiding the trash is to put the trash out of your dog's reach — in a cabinet or cupboard, for example. Always put a lid on your trash can. Simple management is usually the best approach to trash raids.

If trash raids only occur when you aren't home or your retired racer shows other signs of destructive behavior when you're gone, these problems may be stress-related. Try working on alone training (see Chapter 6 for more information). Never punish your hound for any behavior that may be caused by fear.

If your hound has gotten rewarded by the trash can and you have no way to move it or keep him from it, use a booby trap. Use the techniques you use to stop counter-surfing (see the preceding section). Stack the cans on the counter but put the bait in the trash can, and put a few drops of Listerine on the edges of the trash can.

Preventing Your Greyhound from Digging Himself into a Hole

The simplest way to stop your hound from digging is to manage his access to the yard. If you take him out on a leash or accompany him on every trip, he can't dig. If you want him to enjoy the yard on his own without constant supervision, you can try a more proactive solution.

Determine why he is digging in the first place. Until you know the reason behind his behavior, you can't fix it. Some dogs dig when they get bored. If you think that's the case with your hound, bring him inside sooner. Many hounds dig to find a cool place to lie down. If that's the case with your boy, bring him in out of the heat or give him a shady place to lie down. Greyhounds are susceptible to heatstroke and heat exhaustion, so they shouldn't be outside for very long if the heat index is over 80 degrees. Some dogs dig to escape or out of fear. If you're leaving your retired racer outside when you go away because he's destructive in the house, you haven't fixed his fear, you've just moved it outside.

If you think your Greyhound is digging because he's bored or because he simply enjoys it, try giving him a *digging pit*. Dig a large hole (about the size your Greyhound would dig) in an area that he likes and one that suits your landscaping. Fill it with loose material that's easy to replace, like pine bark nuggets. Now add really neat toys that are easy to find. At first, partially hide things like a hard chew toy or large biscuits. Dab a little peanut butter on the toys or biscuits or use a food that has a strong odor. Keep hiding new things for him to find. Stuff a Kong, for example. Keep adding neat new things to the digging pit from time to time.

Refill the old holes and put something on top of the area that will discourage him from digging there again — like a large planter or a box. If you can't cover the site of the former hole, try adding something that tastes bad, like hot pepper sauce and alum powder. Pretty soon, your hound will only dig in his digging pit, because that's where he finds the good stuff.

Digging is such a self-rewarding behavior that punishment or corrections are usually effective only when you're watching. If you aren't willing to watch your hound or manage his environment, then you have to choose between allowing him access to the yard or saving your landscaping from his harm.

House-Soiling Troubles

If you have a house-training problem, take your hound to your vet to rule out any possibility of a medical problem. Most house-soiling problems are a result of incomplete house-training. If you haven't house-trained your retired racer following all the instructions in Chapter 6, start over as though your hound just walked through your door for the first time today. Make a clean start. Clean any soiled area, including hardwood floors, tile, and linoleum, with a strong enzyme-based cleaner. If the area is carpeted, soak an area twice as large as you think is affected; urine tends to spread in the padding. Prevent access to the area by covering it with a chair or a piece of foil (if the area is completely dry). If your Greyhound tends to return to the same spot, placing his food dishes on or near the area will probably discourage him from viewing it as a place to eliminate.

Marking territory isn't about house-training. When any dog marks his territory, he's not just having an accident. He's intentionally leaving his scent behind. Territory marking usually involves an upright object, like a wall or the side of a chair. Although most Greyhounds don't tend to mark indoors, even neutered male dogs and female dogs may occasionally try to mark.

If you catch him suspiciously sniffing an upright object, as though he's about to lift his leg, interrupt the behavior with a sharp sound. Immediately take him to the defined outside area. Reward him for urinating or marking there. If he does seem inclined to mark, help him learn to control the behavior by only allowing him to mark on your outside property rather than anywhere he chooses. Pay attention to when and where he's marking. Is he marking in response to a stranger or a strange dog in your home or the sight or sound of a strange dog outside in your yard, for instance? Manage his environment so he can't see or hear the dogs or outside activities that cause him to mark when you aren't home and watch him carefully when you are.

Overcoming Sibling Rivalry among Greyhounds

Most of us succumb to potato chip syndrome — betcha can't have just one retired racer. And many of us already have dogs of another breed before we adopt our first retired racer. So, some basic things about living with more than one dog are very important. Most Greyhounds enjoy the company of other dogs, but that doesn't mean there won't be squabbles. In this section, I tell you what you need to know about the ways dogs communicate with each other and about how you can help resolve problems if they arise.

If your dogs are merely squabbling, let them sort it out. Don't create a problem where one doesn't exist by intervening.

Dogs commonly play-fight with one another (see Figure 10-1). Although this can look like fighting if you've never seen it before, you'll quickly learn the difference.

If a fight does break out, don't punish the aggressor or coddle the loser. They're trying to work out who is in charge. It doesn't matter who you think should be the top dog. They'll decide. The more you interfere, the worse the situation is likely to become.

If you can clearly identify the *alpha* dog (or the leader of the pack) and he is fit enough to maintain his role, reinforce that position by giving him first access to attention, grooming, eating, sleeping, playing, and any other things he may value. This gets tough when you have a favorite old man who is now suffering from chronic health problems. He can't safely protect his alpha status anymore. So don't try to protect it for him. Help him learn his new role by reinforcing the new alpha dog. Most dogs aren't that concerned about where they fit as long as they know exactly where that is.

If you have a problem with your pack, each of your dogs has to understand that you are the leader. All dogs must earn everything they value, including all their meals and social interactions like petting and play. Make sure all your dogs understand that you are the only one with access to the can opener. Reward both dogs (alpha first) for good behavior in each other's presence. Make the presence of the other dog and the absence of squabbling a good thing. And make the absence of the other dog really boring.

Figure 10-1:
Don't confuse play fighting with aggression.

Photograph courtesy of Nancy Beach

Alpha theory

If you have one dog, you have one pack. If you established your relationship, he understands you're the leader. When you add another dog or two or six, you now have two packs, one that includes you and your dogs and one that includes only the dogs. The more dogs you have, the more likely you'll eventually have personality conflicts.

In packs with three or more dogs, things get even more interesting. There is an alpha male, an alpha female (a top male and female), a beta male and a beta female (the second ranking male and female), an omega (the lowest ranking dog in the pack), and everyone in between. Who fits where can get complicated because our presence as part of the bigger pack changes the dynamics among the dogs. The number of dogs you can have before problems arise depends on the breeds of the dogs and the individual personalities. For some breeds or some dogs, even one other dog is one too many.

If you're going to have more than one dog, you need to understand some basic things about real dog packs.

- The dog pack decides who's alpha. Stay out of it.
- There is no such thing as democracy. The alpha dog owns whatever he wants.
- The alpha dog eats first, wins tug games, wins staring contests, and sleeps where he wants. He gets the best of everything if he wants. Watch the pack carefully to see who's really in charge.
- The omega dog shows deference by licking the mouths of other dogs, moving out of the way, looking away when other dogs stare, and freely giving up food, chewies, or toys.
- Pack dynamics aren't constant. Roles change and they overlap. This doesn't just happen over time. It can change many times in the course of a day.
- Most problems occur among dogs of the same sex or among dogs who are uncertain about where they fit. Dogs don't like uncertainty. In a sense, a dog would rather be omega than be uncertain. We, their humans, are often the cause of their uncertainty. We can't resist feeling sorry for the dog who is being bullied or picked on. We scold the dog who is being most aggressive. We want our furry family to "play nice."

Top dog

One of the most confusing things for dog owners is that the dogs may get along fine for months or even years before they start battling. If one of the dogs is just reaching social maturity, the older dog may no longer be willing to put up with bratty behavior that was acceptable from a kid.

When you've identified who fits where in the pack, don't mess with it. If the resident dog is small or elderly or ill, don't baby her or feel sorry for her because your new Greyhound is taking over. If you don't want this to escalate, reinforce the dog who is most likely to be able to physically maintain the alpha role.

The alpha dog eats first, gets petted first, goes out first, gets the best toys, and the first and best choice of sleeping areas. In other words, he gets what he wants when he wants it. Even young puppies establish pack rankings, and they do it at very early ages.

If the challenged dog is submitting but the aggressor continues the attack, and the attacks are getting more ferocious, you will need to keep them separated at all times or find another home for one of the dogs. If you place the challenger, be sure to place him where there are no other dogs.

Spend time with each dog individually away from the other dogs in the pack. You may be surprised at how your dog acts without the support of his own pack. Your omega could be top dog somewhere else and your alpha may be a real pussycat.

Maintaining a peaceful kingdom

If you can tell by postures or behaviors that a scrap is about to begin, let the dogs know with your sharpest "ah-ah" or whatever sound you use to say, "Knock it off, you farm animal." If the argument is already in progress, stay out of it. Don't intervene unless you have to protect a dog from serious injury. Most interactions are simple skirmishes and go nowhere if we don't butt in. In fact, many dogs fight only if one of their humans is in sight. You're part of the larger pack. Your presence changes the dynamics of the pack and may make an uncertain dog feel bold enough to initiate a fight or fight back.

Fights in multi-dog homes often break out along fence lines. This is most likely to happen when

- You come home and your dogs are in the yard.
- A stray or strange dog appears on the other side of the fence.
- You or someone else pays attention to your dogs from the other side of the fence.

Prevent trouble by getting through that gate fast and getting your dogs indoors. All it takes is for one dog to step on the toes of another dog while they're excited and all hell can break loose.

Male dogs are more likely to fight with other males. Females are more likely to fight with other females. If you're adding your second dog, choose a dog of the opposite sex. If you're adding a third dog, evaluate your existing dogs carefully. If your boy is a mellow type who gets along well with other male dogs, add another male dog. Choose a smaller, more submissive dog. If your female is also a mellow dog who gets along with other female dogs, add another male dog anyway. Although males may posture more and act gruff, females are more likely to actually fight. Choose a boy who is not likely to challenge your resident boy. If your heart is set on another female, choose her carefully.

Skirmishes happen in even the most stable packs. Anyone who has even had a sibling or raised children knows that sometimes we get on each other's nerves. When dogs are under stress, they are more likely to squabble. What many folks think of as a dog fight is nothing more than bickering. We just aren't used to bickering with our teeth.

Fights are less likely to occur if your dogs have been taught to follow your lead. If you haven't done any training of manners, do it now. Manage your environment so no one gets injured and so the dogs don't get more practice. Practice does make perfect after all.

- ✔ **Supervise.** I pay close attention to the pack dynamic so I can catch something brewing before it erupts.

- ✔ **Separate all aggressive dogs when you can't supervise.** Use crates and/or baby gates. Avoid conflicts by keeping your dogs separated when they are eating or if they have chew bones or toys they value.

- ✔ **Put different-sounding bells on the instigators so you know where they are and when they are in proximity of one another.**

Handling fights when they happen

Dog fights are horrendous to watch. Most people aren't accustomed to seeing these gentle creatures acting like real dogs.

Be prepared. If you've seen any signs of aggression developing, plan for the possibility that a fight may break out. Store a large blanket in or near each area where the dogs regularly interact. Keep a high-backed chair or a folding chair nearby. Keep ammonia capsules or a citronella spray on hand.

If you have to intervene, stay calm. Yelling doesn't usually help interrupt the fight. But if you have a lot of dogs, a serious yell may be enough to get the attention of the *fringe dogs* (those who are watching but haven't yet entered in) so you can get them out of the area. You have to figure out what is likely to work with your dogs.

Working with a neighborhood bully

If your retired racer is acting aggressively toward strange dogs, his behavior is probably based on fear. Always get professional help to determine the reasons for your dog's reaction to other dogs. And don't forget to examine your own role in your dog's behavior.

I once worked with the owner of a Rottweiler who actually taught her dog to hate a certain Sheltie in her neighborhood. The Rottie was big, even for a Rottie, and out of control. She had been through traditional obedience training and performed well when there were no distractions. But the trainers recommended a prong collar for control on the leash. And whenever the Rottie saw the Sheltie, she tried to lunge, snarling and growling at the other dog. The owner tightened the grip on the leash and pulled her back. The owner yelled at her Rottweiler, took her home, and punished her for this response.

But what she didn't do was consider what message she was communicating to her dog. Think about it. If every time you saw me on the street, someone stuck prongs in your neck, yelled at you, took you home, and spanked you, how well would you like me?

When another dog approaches, do you tighten up on your dog's leash? Do you pull on the leash? Do you yell? All of those things signal your dog that something is wrong. Worse yet, you may be sending signals that encourage him to be aggressive. Dogs are far more likely to bite if their owners are present. And in some kinds of protection training, dogs are actually stimulated to attack by yanking back on their leashes.

Get a head collar and work on deference and training exercises with your hound. Reward him for any good behavior when dogs are around. If another dog can be a block away without a negative reaction from your retired racer, reward him.

You can even try flooding him with incredibly great food only when another dog is present. Remove the treats the instant the other dog disappears. This way, your dog will start to associate other dogs with *positive* events, not negative ones.

Keep your hands out of it. Spray the offending dogs with the citronella or break an ammonia capsule and toss it in the middle of them. Throw a blanket over the dogs and then wedge the back of the chair between them to separate them. After the two dogs are separated, they usually calm quickly. As soon as they begin to settle, remove the aggressor.

If a dog is injured and cries out, the rest of the pack may viciously attack the injured dog. The same thing may happen to a dog who is having a seizure. Always isolate a seizing or injured dog from other dogs. Protect seriously ill dogs from other members of the pack as well. If the pack does attack, the only way to get the fight stopped is to remove the screamer.

Nexcare waterproof bandages are great for patching wounded ears (one of the first casualties in a fight). They're one of the few things that will stick to a furry Greyhound ear. You may need more than one bandage to hold the ear together, but it could save you a trip to the vet and save your dog from anesthesia and stitches.

WARNING!

Pariah dogs

Occasionally a dog comes along who everyone in the pack seems to pick on. Sometimes they'll attack this dog viciously or even kill it. This dog has to be rehomed and placed in a household with no other dogs.

How well sibling rivalry resolves itself depends largely on how you may have inadvertently reinforced the wrong behaviors, how long they've been practicing these behaviors, and how severe the attacks have been. If the fighting worsens (fights are escalating or one or more dogs needs serious patchwork from your veterinarian), get professional help immediately. Supervise or separate the dogs. And always muzzle them when they are outside together if you're dealing with a problem.

Most behavior problems are a result of stress, fear, lack of physical exercise, boredom, or lack of training. This is especially true of any destructive behaviors, such as an adult dog chewing inappropriate things. Destructive chewing is usually the canine equivalent of humans biting their nails.

Many people tend to set their dogs up to fail by not being realistic in their expectations. Learn to speak your dog's language so you really understand what he's trying to tell you. And teach him to speak English so he can understand what you expect.

Many Greyhounds grin when they greet you or when you raise your voice to them. If you've never seen a Greyhound grin and don't know how to read your dog, this may look like a snarl. But nothing could be farther from the truth. Grinning is a submissive behavior meant to show deference. Some Greyhounds nit, which means they take tiny little bits at you with their front teeth when they're excited. This behavior should be discouraged, because it does hurt. If you haven't seen these behaviors before or don't keep in mind what they mean, you could easily make the mistake of thinking that your perfectly sweet Greyhound is being aggressive.

Dogs can be quite dominant with each other — even aggressive — and yet be very submissive to people. Don't assume because one of your hounds is constantly reminding his adopted brother that he's top dog and that his next step will be to growl or bite you or another person.

Don't create problems where there aren't any. A number of popular training books tell you that if your dog leans against you or if he rushes down the stairs ahead of you, he's showing his dominance and you need to put him in his place before he takes over. But guess what? Because of the way

Greyhounds are built, they don't have a lot of choice about rushing down the stairs. And leaning is a common Greyhound trait. Most of the dogs who do it are among the most submissive dogs I know.

The first step with any serious behavior problem is to find good professional help. The sooner you intervene to identify and treat the problem, the better the chance your hand will overcome the problem or at least get it under control. If your hound shows aggression toward you or any other person, get help immediately.

Chapter 11

Helping the Fearful Dog Stand on His Own Four Feet

. . . .

In This Chapter

▶ Avoiding the situations that cause your Greyhound to be afraid

▶ Meeting fears head-on and surviving to tell about it

▶ Helping your dog learn to be alone

. . . .

*M*any dogs are afraid of things, and Greyhounds are no exception. Fear is directly connected to survival. Being fearful to some degree is good. The overly brave dogs are the ones who don't live long enough to reproduce.

Problems arise when your dog's fear creates too much stress or leads to aggression. Dogs respond to fear with either fight or flight. Sometimes they simply freeze like a deer caught in the headlights. And that's also a form of flight. The brain takes off, but the body doesn't get the message to follow. Greyhounds are bred to run, so it shouldn't come as a surprise that most Greyhounds are more likely to flee than they are to fight.

In this chapter, I help you understand and deal with your Greyhound's fears, the ones that are preventing him from enjoying the world around him. Whether your retired racer is afraid of slippery floors, is nipping at strangers, or is terrified of loud noises, the ways to help him overcome those fears are the same. And I'll give you some tips that can help with two common sources of fear — thunderstorms and separation anxiety. But remember serious fears need serious help. Start with a complete physical exam to rule out any physical causes for your hound's behavior. Then ask your vet for a referral to a trainer or behaviorist who can help you determine the exact nature of your hound's problem.

Avoiding Fear

Before you figure out how to retrain a fearful dog, you need to know how you can avoid the fear in the first place. The following sections have all the information you need to stop fear before it starts.

Teaching your retired racer to relax

You can build your Greyhound's confidence by teaching him basic behaviors and introducing him to lots of new experiences, like those in Chapters 6, 7, 8, and 9.

Develop your acting skills. Your dog is watching you. Your reaction — or how he perceives your reaction — usually determines his initial reaction as well. So if you know your hound is afraid of loud noises, don't shower him with well-intentioned comforting at the first sign of thunder and lightning. All this does is teach your dog that thunderstorms are worthy of notice — or worse, that being afraid is something you like, because you rewarded him with all that attention.

Taking it slowly

Take your time when you introduce your Greyhound to new people, places, and things. Don't overwhelm him.

Let him approach new situations instead of forcing him into them. Plan ahead by taking him to new places when they are less likely to be crowded. Reward any and all positive responses to new people, places, or things. This will encourage your needlenose to view new experiences positively, instead of with fear.

Paying attention to your dog

As his leader, your job is to keep bad things from happening to your Greyhound. If you see signs of stress in your hound as you approach something or when he hears something, calmly and quietly remove him from the situation. Move far enough away to counter the stress — that means far enough that you can get a tail wag or other signal that he's no longer anxious. As soon as he's capable of a tail wag, get some eye contact and use some food rewards for a response to a simple behavior cue, such as *sit*. (Throughout this chapter, I use *tail wag* to mean get your dog relaxed enough to take a treat, respond to a simple cue he knows well, and show no signs of stress.)

Don't ask your hound to lie down when he's afraid. Down is too defenseless and submissive for a frightened dog.

If your Greyhound is terrified, back away to a safe distance — a place where he'll eat a treat when offered and seems relaxed. Get eye contact from your dog. Then take him home and proceed more slowly the next time.

Nothing overcomes stress like food. Use it liberally. If your retired racer is refusing food, you can bet he's stressed. Diverting him with food is like psychologically removing him from the stress. Keep your body language neutral. Don't think of food as a reward. Think of it as a tranquilizer. When he's taking food, work on a simple behavior he knows well like targeting your hand.

Let him hang at the edges of the situation and determine his own pace forward. Stay neutral when he's hanging back. Divert his attention for a few moments and let him get accustomed to the sights and sounds. Don't try to bribe or cajole him to move forward. My experience has been that the more you try to get a Greyhound to approach something he's anxious about, the more convinced he'll be you're up to something. Instead, smile and reward any movement forward.

Using a happy word

Find an expression to use when something mild happens that isn't likely to frighten him but will get his attention if he isn't used to it. I say "kaboom." Start using this expression with simple things. Deliberately drop a spoon on the floor. Say "kaboom" and immediately give a great treat. Repeat it over and over again just like you did when you introduced your verbal clicker, until the word itself will get him excited and make him happy. Then when little non-scary things happen, like a chair falls over or you drop a large, empty pot on the floor next to him or he skids on the kitchen floor as he comes running for dinner, say "kaboom" and laugh and give him a treat. Gradually extend it to bigger and scarier things. If he's waiting for you to tell him whether a new bad experience is safe or scary, all you have to do is say "kaboom," and he'll know it's safe.

Not all frightened dogs were once abused

Not all fears are related to abuse or some previous trauma. Most are simply from lack of exposure. Dogs are cautious by nature. If they've never seen something before, they're cautious if not afraid. And some people are more fear-inducing than others. Dogs are more likely to be afraid of men than women, for example. People in hooded clothes or carrying backpacks often spook dogs, as do men with beards. Younger, boisterous children and people with disabilities that affect their motor skills also tend to be frightening at first for dogs, because this isn't the way they are accustomed to seeing people move. Take time to expose your hound to all kinds of people. Most dog bites are fear-related. Teach your dog he has nothing to fear.

Some hounds seem to develop fears easily. Others seem to take the world in stride. Fearfulness has a genetic component. If your hound is the fearful type, he can still be helped, although he may never turn into an adventurer. You'll have to be more careful about exposing him gradually to new situations. Overcoming his fears may take time. But he certainly isn't hopeless.

Some new Greyhound adopters unintentionally teach their retired racers to fear children. They're so careful and so concerned when their retired racer is first introduced to children that they inadvertently telegraph the wrong message to their dogs. For example, if you hold your hound's leash tightly the first time he encounters a child, you're communicating tension to your hound. Your dog may begin to respond by pulling back or acting edgy around children. So you then begin to reassure the dog. The dog thinks you like that behavior, so he does more of it. And before you know it, you have a dog who has been taught that children are scary.

Helping Your Retired Racer Overcome His Fears

Help your needlenose conquer his fears by gradually exposing him to tiny little pieces of the fear in tiny increments. Teach him to associate something happy instead of something bad with the thing he fears.

No matter what your hound is afraid of, you can gradually help him overcome his fear by changing the association to something good and by exposing him carefully in tiny steps. Some fears are easier to treat than others, of course. The most difficult fear to treat is fear of thunderstorms.

Avoid the fear

Controlling — and avoiding — the situations that trigger your dog's fear is one of the most difficult jobs you face. If your hound is afraid of something, you have to prevent him from experiencing that fear while you work on treating it. With a few fears that can be easy to do, but with most it is very difficult.

Identify the triggers surrounding the fear

Before you can start working on your hound's fear, you have to learn all the things that tell him something scary is about to occur. These scary things are the triggers that tell him the big fear is likely to occur. Fear of thunderstorms may be about noise, but chances are it's more complicated than that. Your dog could be afraid of the thunder, the wind, the lightening flashes, the changes in the barometric pressure, the smell of the ionized air, and who knows what else. Maybe he has generalized the fear of thunder to include fear of low-flying jets.

If he's afraid of strangers, the sound of the doorbell may actually be the first trigger. But there are others like the door opening and the sounds of excited voices greeting visitors that could trigger the same response. Maybe he's okay if someone reaches for him slowly but not if they move quickly. Maybe he isn't frightened if they're four feet away, but he's frightened at three feet. One strange person at a time may be no problem, but two make him nervous. Maybe your Greyhound has generalized his initial fear of the mailman to include all people in uniform.

Each fear is more complex than it may originally seem. Your job is to identify, isolate, and treat each trigger separately. You can't treat the problem as one fear — you have to break it down and treat each part of the fear on its own.

Find a way to make him smile

Figure out what really excites your Greyhound. What are his passions? Teach him to associate a word or sound with very positive things and then use it to trigger a happy response instead of a fearful one. Teach this association the same way you taught him to respond to his reward marker. Simply treat him every time he hears the word or sound. Now you always have a way to get his tail wagging with a happy word. When he reacts to the phrase the way he reacts to the sound of the car keys, or his dinner dish, or the sight of his leash, you know you're ready for the next step. If he has more than one fear, teach separate words for each situation.

If you're dealing with mild fear, try simply flooding him with treats whenever the scary thing appears. The instant it disappears, stop the treats. Change the way he views the trigger. This approach works well with a dog who isn't really frightened of children but just isn't sure what they are. Every time a child appears, begin treating him and continue as long as the child is in sight. When he no longer shows signs of stress when a child appears, let the child gently toss the treats from a short distance. In no time, your Greyhound will most likely view children with the same warmth and happiness as he views adults.

Work in tiny steps

Next to keeping him away from his fears, taking tiny steps is the hardest part of training. You don't have to walk before you run, you have to crawl. Don't move ahead until you see his tail wagging at each point along the way. If you move too quickly and he experiences fear, you may actually *lose* ground. The first steps are the slowest and the hardest. After you get past these, things usually progress quickly.

Overcoming a serious fear problem can take weeks, months, or even years to resolve. Be patient.

TIP

Thunderstorms: A dog's worst fear

Fear of thunderstorms is common and difficult to fix.

Here are some suggestions that can help your hound until the thunderstorm season is over and you can get help:

- Turn on some music or a TV to mask the noises until the storm is over.

- Ask your veterinarian for medications to help your hound through it.

- Keep all doors and outside gates closed so that your dog cannot escape (a common reaction to fear of thunderstorms). Keep the windows covered so he can't see outside and try to crash through the window.

- Don't crate or confine your dog. Even if he prefers his crate or a small place, don't lock him in. He may panic in such tight quarters.

- Don't leave your dog outside in a storm.

- Rub his coat with a fabric softener dryer sheet to decrease static — a common result of thunderstorms and one that dogs learn to associate with the storms.

- If your retired racer likes the car, try letting him "ride out" the storm in the car.

- Ignore his fear. Don't comfort or coddle him.

- Keep your own reactions and behavior calm but happy. Act as if absolutely nothing unusual is happening.

When the storm season is over, you can start to work on desensitizing. Ask your veterinarian for a referral to a behavioral consultant.

Find a place to start

After you've identified all the triggers and introduced your happy words, you have to find a place to start. How far removed physically or emotionally from the fear does your hound have to be? If even the sight of the car triggers signs of stress in your retired racer, start on the other side of the door into the garage. If she's terrified of the cast-iron lawn ornament in your neighbor's yard, find out how far away you have to be to see no signs of stress, then get even farther away. You need to be far enough away that you can easily get a tail wagging.

You know it's safe to move ahead when you can get his tail wagging with your voice, a treat, or a favorite toy. Back up when you add another trigger. Expose him to each level under several different circumstances and be sure everything that happens still lets him feel safe. Let's say his tail is wagging when he's sitting in the car. Can you open and close the automatic garage door? Back up before you add that trigger.

Break the exposures into the tiniest steps possible. Don't assume that because he'll greet one person at the door with his tail wagging he's ready for a trip to the mall at Christmas time. He may need a month before he'll happily greet a stranger on the street, but after that, he may need only a few more days to insist on greeting every neighbor on the block. Perhaps in another week, he'll act as though you imagined the whole problem. Learn to read your dog and always give him as much time as he needs.

Working through Separation Anxiety

Separation anxiety is a common problem in dogs, and it seems to be more common in dogs who are adopted as adults. The more often a dog is moved from one home to another, the more likely he is to have separation anxiety.

Most dogs who have separation anxiety show it by being destructive or vocal when they're alone. Sometimes they soil the house. Many dogs internalize their stress. But these dogs are no less stressed than the dog who eats the sofa. They're just busy working on an ulcer instead.

Combine the techniques in this section with the alone training in Chapter 6.

Many owners crate a destructive dog, and the problem, as far as they're concerned, is resolved. Even if you crate your dog and eliminate the destructive behavior, your dog is still in emotional pain. All that's stopped is your financial pain. Take time to fix the problem. Don't just put a Band-Aid on it.

If you work and your hound has a serious problem, you may need to find a place for him to stay during the day and/or rely on special medications from the vet.

Identifying the signs of stress

Look for and identify all signs of stress, including whining, panting, trembling, a drippy nose, a lack of interest in food, stretching, yawning, and scratching. These will start well before you pick up the car keys to leave. The longer the problem has existed, the earlier in your morning routine he'll begin to show stress. Drippy noses, panting, stretching, yawning, and scratching are normal behaviors most of the time. But when they occur in the vet's office or as you're preparing to leave, they're related to stress. Pay attention to context.

Reward calm behavior *before* the signs of stress appear. You may have to start before you even get out of bed.

Responding to the fearful dog

Don't pay any attention to your dog for at least 15 minutes before you leave or for 10 minutes after you return. You want departures and arrivals to be boring for your dog.

Each dog is different. What is reassuring to one dog may cause another dog to panic. Find the right combination for your dog.

Don't tell your dog it's okay in that reassuring voice if he's responding with fear. Even though your intentions are to help calm him down, you're essentially rewarding him for being afraid.

Take your Greyhound for a run or a brisk, long walk each morning. Put that energy to use in a constructive way.

Identify all the cues that tell your retired racer you're leaving. We all have weekday and weekend routines. Shake things up a bit and fool your dog. Put your suit on, but don't go anywhere. Pick up your keys and then go watch TV. Put on your weekend jogging clothes, but go to work and change there. Use a different door. Park the car down the street. If you only wear makeup on weekdays, wear it on Sunday. If you normally only read the paper on weekends, read it on weekdays instead. If there are things you only do on weekdays, do them on weekends instead. Leave your briefcase in the garage. The idea is to keep your dog from knowing whether you're coming or going. Do lots of repetitions of these each day.

The cues you send may be very subtle. Because I wear jeans most of the time, how do my dogs know when I'm leaving if I'm wearing jeans? They've learned I only put a belt on when I dress if I'm going out. And that may be hours before I leave the house. Always identify all the cues and do what you can to shake them up. And don't forget to do lots of repetitions each day.

Leaving a dog who's afraid to be alone

Some dogs find a crate a nice, safe place to be. But many dogs panic in confined spaces. If your dog's crate makes his separation anxiety worse, try a safe room instead. You may have to remove everything that's in the room and line the walls with sheets of acrylic if your hound is really panicked when he's alone.

Close the blinds so he can't see the activity on the street. Or open the blinds if looking outside calms him down. The key here is to know what works for *your* individual dog.

If you normally have a radio or TV on when you are home, turn it on as soon as you get up. Set it at a volume that will mask street noises that may increase his anxiety. If you've been turning the radio or TV on just before you leave, this has probably become a departure cue. Don't turn it on.

Teach your Greyhound coming-home cues. For example, choose a CD you like, play it for your dog, and reward him while the CD is playing. Do it over and over. Then set your CD player and a light on a timer so that the CD comes on shortly before you arrive home. Gradually increase the length and frequency of your absences. And gradually increase the amount of time between when the lights and music come on and when you arrive home, until he's used to having them come on 15 to 30 minutes before your arrival. When you go to work, set the timer to come on about 30 minutes before you arrive home.

Teach him away cues as well. Work on alone training (covered in more detail in Chapter 6) using a frozen stuffed Kong. Hand it to him and then leave. Remove it when you return. He's only allowed to have it when you're out of sight.

Some combination of these techniques should work for most dogs if you can control absences while you work on the techniques and/or combine the techniques with appropriate medication from your vet.

Part IV

Keeping Your Retired Racing Greyhound Healthy

The 5th Wave   By Rich Tennant

"OK, I'LL LET HIM PLAY AS LONG AS YOU STOP SAYING, 'YOU CAN'T TAKE AN OLD DOG'S NEW TRICKS'."

In this part . . .

The chapters in this part cover everything from feeding and grooming your Greyhound to taking care of him when he gets sick. In this part, you'll figure out how to prevent health problems from starting, and you'll get useful information on recognizing and dealing with them if they affect your hound. You'll also find great tips for avoiding emergencies and dealing with them if and when they come up. And finally, I let you know how you can help an ailing hound be as comfortable as possible. If you're looking for information on any facet of your retired racer's health, you've come to the right part.

Chapter 12

Feeding Your Greyhound

Choosing which food to feed your retired racer isn't as simple as walking into the grocery store and buying the biggest, least expensive bag of food on the shelf. When I read a recommendation in a consumer magazine to do exactly that — a recommendation implying that all dog foods are created equal — I was appalled. Greyhounds need a high-quality diet suited to their specific needs.

Although Greyhound lovers agree on how much they love their dogs, they don't always agree on which food is best. So keep in mind that virtually any opinion may be challenged by someone with equally good sources to support his or her opinion. Read the information in this chapter and make your own decision on what works for you and your retired racer.

Understanding How Greyhounds Differ from Other Breeds

The ideal balanced dry food diet for the average healthy retired racer is comprised of 22 to 27 percent protein, 10 to 15 percent fat, and 5 percent fiber. If your hound is a real couch potato, use foods that are at the lower end of these ranges.

As long as your Greyhound's weight is good, his coat is shiny and healthy, and his energy levels are strong, you're doing it right.

Greyhounds that are actively and regularly competing in agility, lure coursing, or other high-energy activities need higher amounts of protein and fat in their diets. The right blend for them would be more like 28 to 30 percent protein, 15 percent fat, and 5 percent fiber. But remember that opinions vary considerably, even among the experts, so try different foods with your Greyhound and see how he responds. Modify his diet according to his specific needs.

If your Greyhound is doing a lot of outdoor activities during cold weather, he may need extra energy to maintain his body temperature. If he spends a lot of time outdoors during hot weather, he will need extra energy to make up for what he uses to pant and stay cool. Just add a bit of extra oil to his diet or use a food with a slightly higher fat content. *Remember:* Keep an eye on the scale and his ribs, so he doesn't gain too much weight.

Taking a Look at the Building Blocks of Good Nutrition

Many years ago, a dog's diet would have been primarily meat. But with the increased use of commercial pet foods, more and more of our dogs' diets are made up of carbohydrates from grains. The purpose of eating, of course, is to provide energy. This energy comes from three sources: protein, fat, and carbohydrates, which I cover in the following sections.

Protein

The amount of energy your Greyhound gets from the protein sources in his diet depends on the quality of the protein and its digestibility. Some proteins are used by dogs more efficiently than others. The highest quality protein sources are eggs, fish, meat, and poultry. Milk can also be a good source of protein, but most adult dogs don't tolerate milk well. Grains can also provide protein, but these are lower quality proteins.

If you start to read up on diet and nutrition, you'll find all kinds of arguments about how much protein your dog should get and from what sources. Some people argue that we are feeding way too little protein to our dogs, that dogs do better on amounts in the 28 to 30 percent range, and that protein should come primarily from meat. Others argue that we are feeding too *much* protein and that amounts shouldn't exceed 20 to 22 percent. Still others argue that dogs can do very well on a vegetarian diet, with no protein from meat.

I take a more moderate stance and recommend feeding your dog a diet that is comprised of 22 to 27 percent protein.

Fat

Fat is a highly concentrated source of energy, supplying more than twice as much energy as proteins and carbohydrates. Fat provides essential fatty acids and transports fat-soluble vitamins. Fat may also make food taste better and may help your dog feel fuller with less food.

Greyhounds who don't get enough of the right kinds of fat generally have coarse, dry coats and dandruff. I recommend feeding your dog a diet that consists of 10 to 15 percent fat.

Many dog food producers use discarded old fat from the restaurant industry. If the brand of food you buy smells rancid, switch brands, or at least return that bag and ask for a replacement.

Carbohydrates

Carbohydrates come in the form of grains, sugars, fruits, and vegetables. Dogs don't need high amounts of carbohydrate in their diet. But commercial dog foods often contain lots of carbohydrates, because they're a less expensive source of energy than protein or fat.

Remembering the Other Elements of a Healthy Diet

In addition to feeding your Greyhound a diet with the correct balance of protein, fat, and carbohydrates, you also need to make sure he's getting enough water, vitamins, and minerals. Check out the following sections for more information on these vital parts of a dog's diet.

Water

Your retired racer should always have a supply of fresh water available. Dogs vary widely in their consumption of water. So the amount of water your hound needs depends on a variety of things, like the temperature, his activity level, and the moisture content of his food. The average 60-pound dog consumes a total of seven cups of water from all sources, including food, every day. But many Greyhounds drink less water than the average dog.

Don't spend a lot of time worrying about the amount of water your dog should drink every day. Instead, just make sure he has a constant supply of fresh water, and he'll drink as much as he needs.

Never withhold water without consulting a veterinarian.

Vitamins and minerals

We know almost nothing about the vitamin and mineral needs of dogs. And we know even less about using vitamins and minerals as supplements to a balanced diet. But that doesn't stop a variety of opinions from being bantered about.

Vitamins are classified as either fat-soluble or water-soluble. Dogs need some vitamins, because they can't manufacture all they need to meet their daily requirements. However, unlike humans, dogs *do* manufacture vitamin C. Because vitamin C is also used as a preservative in commercial dog foods, many knowledgeable people argue that young, healthy dogs rarely need additional amounts of this important vitamin.

Commercial diets include vitamins and minerals. Some people argue that poor storage, use of rancid fats, and the processing of commercial foods breaks down or renders vitamins and minerals unavailable. Others argue that commercial dog foods provide all the vitamins and minerals a healthy dog needs if the food is stored and handled properly.

Making Sense of Your Feeding Choices

Deciding which food to feed your retired racer is a daunting task. So in this section, I guide you through the process of choosing between premium and grocery-store varieties of dog food, help you decipher all the information on your dog food label, and inform you on what the ingredients in your dog's food really mean (including which ones are good and which ones you should avoid).

No matter what choices you make, if you buy a commercial dog food be sure the label specifically says it meets or exceeds the AAFCO standards.

Choosing between premium and grocery-store varieties

Most commercial pet foods are made largely from the wastes from slaughterhouses, grain production, and the restaurant industry. These ingredients are considered unfit for human consumption, but we regularly (and often unknowingly) feed them to our pets.

The better-quality foods are called *premium* brands and are available through pets stores, feed stores, and veterinarians. Price is at least *some* indicator of quality when it comes to dog food. For example, a bag of food that costs $10.95 for 50 pounds isn't likely to have the same quality ingredients as a bag that costs $38.00 for 33 pounds.

Vegetarian hounds?

Because of the concerns over quality of commercial foods, many Greyhound owners have switched to feeding their dogs raw meat and natural food diets. Some are feeding a totally vegetarian diet. Several of these diets are currently in use. But using them requires research and a commitment to making sure your racer's diet is properly balanced. To learn more about these alternative diets, check out the resources in Appendix B.

Look for high-quality foods at lower prices at discount pet supply stores or price clubs. But read the labels carefully, to be sure the food has the nutritional balance your Greyhound needs.

The cheapest food isn't always the cheapest to feed. Food that costs $1.00 a pound may actually be cheaper to feed than a food that costs $0.50 a pound. If you need to feed eight cups a day of the cheap food to give your dog the proper nutrition but it only takes three cups a day of the "expensive" food, which food is actually cheaper?

Reading labels

In order for your dog to get the nutrients she needs from her food, the nutrients in the food have to be digestible. And nothing on pet food labels addresses the issue of digestibility or availability of nutrients. So when you read your dog food label, you can tell whether your food contains the nutrients, but not whether your dog can obtain them from the food. Complicated, isn't it?

The label (see Figure 12-1 for an example) gives you a guaranteed analysis of the crude protein, fat, fiber, and moisture contents of the food. Then it lists in order, by weight, the ingredients. But that isn't as straightforward as it seems. For example, if the ingredients are listed on the label as "chicken, ground corn, corn gluten, ground wheat, corn bran, wheat flour, and wheat bran," you may assume that the primary ingredient is chicken. But when you combine all the corn-based ingredients, you would probably find that the corn far outweighed the chicken. You may even find that the wheat outweighed the chicken. This practice of listing ingredients separately, when they're derived from the same source, is called *splitting*. So the food manufacturer, instead of having to say that the food's main ingredient is corn, can say that the main ingredient is chicken by splitting the corn-based products into smaller groups. If you look closely at dog food labels, you'll often find that two of the top three ingredients in dog foods are grains (if you combine all the grain sources).

If it's good for me, it's good for my dog. . . .

Most veterinarians recommend finding a brand of dog food and sticking to it. And most vets also recommend *never* giving your hound people food. But ask most adopters and they frequently admit that they feed their hounds people food from time to time. My dogs get all kinds of people food. And I frequently use a different brand of food for training or as an addition to their regular diet. The real problem with people food is that we tend to overdo it — we give them all the wrong things and way too much of it. And not *everything* we eat is safe for our dogs. Some of our favorite people foods can be hazardous or even deadly for our dogs.

For example, chocolate is extremely harmful to dogs. Chocolate contains a substance called *theobromine,* which is toxic to dogs. If you have a 50-pound Greyhound, 1 pound of semisweet chocolate, 5 ounces of unsweetened baking chocolate, or 50 ounces of milk chocolate are deadly.

Onions are another harmful human food, because they contain an ingredient that can cause a life-threatening anemia in our canine companions. The garlic plant is a member of the same family but doesn't seem to present the same problem, so garlic powder is safe as a flavoring.

The issue here isn't people food — it's the quality and quantity of the people food you give. What you don't want them to have is junk food that is high in salt, sugar, and chemicals. And you don't want them to have foods that are high

in fats, like turkey skin, ordinary hotdogs, sausage, or the fat trimmed off a juicy steak. Those foods can cause some nasty digestive problems, like pancreatitis, which can be very serious, or even deadly.

Many people like to give their hounds milk products, especially ice cream. But you may have been told not to. Lots of dogs don't tolerate the lactose in milk products. Others have no problem with very small amounts. If you have your heart set on giving your hound a taste of ice cream occasionally, try one of the lactose reduced or lactose-free varieties that can be found in nearly all supermarkets. Reserve these products for very special occasions and use only the low-fat or fat-free versions.

Because yogurt has live bacteria cultures that I believe help digestion, I give my dogs a soup-spoon-sized dollop of plain nonfat yogurt every day.

Greyhounds are some of the best moochers I've ever seen. If you don't think you can say no to those big brown eyes, then save your hound's health and waistline by not giving him anything except his daily allowance of dog food. When you use food for training, subtract it from his daily ration.

If you really want to share with your hound, try fresh, frozen, or canned fruits and vegetables. Try only small amounts to see what he likes and how well he tolerates them.

Most dog owners feed their dogs a commercial dry food. But canned dog food is another option. Some adopters prefer to feed canned foods. Although canned foods are often higher in protein value and may be more digestible, canned foods do increase plaque buildup on teeth. If you are going to use canned foods as your hound's primary food source, you must be willing to spend even more time keeping his teeth clean and his gums healthy. Although dry foods may seem to be higher quality, you have to compare the ingredients to the ingredients in canned foods to be certain.

If you're not sure whether to feed your dog canned or dry, you can compare the ingredients in a canned food with the ingredients in a dry food. But you need to be sure you're comparing apples to apples and not apples to oranges. Here's how:

1. **Examine the label of the dry dog food and determine how much protein and how much moisture the food has.**

   For example, let's say the label shows that the dry food has 24 percent protein and 10 percent moisture. That means the food is made up of 90 percent dry matter.

2. **Divide the protein level of the dry dog food (24 percent) by the amount of dry matter (90 percent) to determine how much protein your dog is really getting.**

   So 0.24 ÷ 0.90 = 0.27, or 27 percent protein.

3. **Now examine the canned food label and determine how much protein and how much moisture the food has.**

   Let's say the label shows that the food has 8 percent protein and 80 percent moisture. That means the food is made up of 20 percent dry matter.

4. **Divide the protein level of the canned dog food (8 percent) by the amount of dry matter (20 percent) to determine how much protein your dog is really getting.**

   So 0.08 ÷ 0.20 = 0.40, or 40 percent protein.

So even though the dry dog food *label* shows that the food contains 24 percent protein and the canned dog food *label* shows that the food contains 8 percent protein, when you take into consideration the moisture content of the foods, you find that the dry dog food really only has 27 percent protein and the canned has 40 percent. Now you can see why comparing apples to apples makes such a big difference.

You can do the same computations with fat content or other nutrient levels. And you can also compare dry foods to one another or canned foods to one another. Simply divide the percentage of the nutrient by the percentage of the dry matter in the food to get the dry matter protein content.

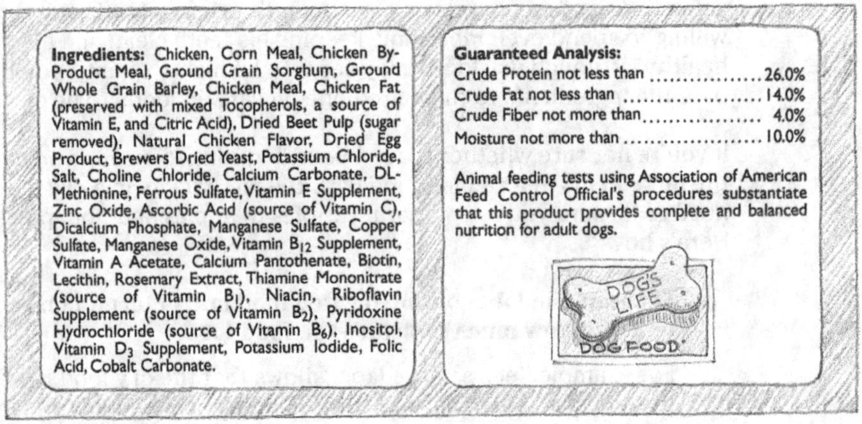

Ingredients: Chicken, Corn Meal, Chicken By-Product Meal, Ground Grain Sorghum, Ground Whole Grain Barley, Chicken Meal, Chicken Fat (preserved with mixed Tocopherols, a source of Vitamin E, and Citric Acid), Dried Beet Pulp (sugar removed), Natural Chicken Flavor, Dried Egg Product, Brewers Dried Yeast, Potassium Chloride, Salt, Choline Chloride, Calcium Carbonate, DL-Methionine, Ferrous Sulfate, Vitamin E Supplement, Zinc Oxide, Ascorbic Acid (source of Vitamin C), Dicalcium Phosphate, Manganese Sulfate, Copper Sulfate, Manganese Oxide, Vitamin B_{12} Supplement, Vitamin A Acetate, Calcium Pantothenate, Biotin, Lecithin, Rosemary Extract, Thiamine Mononitrate (source of Vitamin B_1), Niacin, Riboflavin Supplement (source of Vitamin B_2), Pyridoxine Hydrochloride (source of Vitamin B_6), Inositol, Vitamin D_3 Supplement, Potassium Iodide, Folic Acid, Cobalt Carbonate.

Guaranteed Analysis:
Crude Protein not less than 26.0%
Crude Fat not less than 14.0%
Crude Fiber not more than..................4.0%
Moisture not more than 10.0%

Animal feeding tests using Association of American Feed Control Official's procedures substantiate that this product provides complete and balanced nutrition for adult dogs.

Figure 12-1:
A typical dog food label.

Some adopters like the convenience of semi-moist foods, and most hounds love the taste of these foods. And no wonder: They're high in sugars and salt. Semi-moist foods are often primarily grain-based and include large percentages of soy. And almost all of the inexpensive ones are also loaded with artificial colors and preservatives. They are the worst possible choice for dogs with a tendency toward dental problems. If you use them at all, reserve them for training treats and tend to your hound's dental hygiene religiously.

Understanding what the ingredient list really means to your dog

Making sense of the ingredients listed on a dog food label can raise even the calmest person's blood pressure. In this section, I explain some common ingredients listed on pet food labels and let you know my take on them and how they affect your dog.

Animal by-products

Avoid labels that simply use terms like *animal meal, animal by-products,* or *poultry fat.* Look for labels that identify the exact source of the protein, carbohydrate, or fat. For example, the terms *beef fat* and *chicken fat* tell you something that terms like *poultry fat* and *animal fat* don't. The more specific the better.

Dog food labels list the amount of crude protein in the food, but the amount of crude protein isn't the amount of *digestible* protein. The proteins in pet foods come from a variety of sources that range from human-grade meats, fish, and poultry to all kinds of animal and plant by-products. The meats, fish, or poultry, unless clearly stated otherwise, are usually from dead, diseased, dying, or disabled animals that are not fit for human consumption. Meat, poultry, and fish meals are made from animal tissues. These are the leftover parts of animals, not counting meat, referred to as *animal by-products,* and they include organs, bone, blood, and intestines freed of their contents. By-products cannot contain more than 14 percent of indigestible material, except for amounts that can't be avoided during processing.

I avoid buying foods for my dogs that contain by-products, even if the source of the by-product is identified.

Grains

A common product in pet foods is grains. Dogs can absorb most of the carbo-hydrates from rice, but other grains and carbohydrates are less digestible. In fact, up to 20 percent of some carbohydrates aren't digested at all by dogs and are simply excreted in the form of waste. Carbohydrates that aren't digested have little nutrient value.

Although good quality soy is often the primary ingredient in vegetarian-based dog foods, many dogs don't digest soy well and can end up with gas — something Greyhounds are prone to regardless of which food they eat.

All grain ingredients aren't created equal. Many grains that are added to dog foods are leftovers from the human food industry and have little of their orig-inal nutritional value left. For example, *ground corn* is the entire corn kernel ground or chopped. But *corn gluten meal* is the by-product after the manufac-ture of corn syrup or corn starch and after the bran, germ, and starch have been removed. Look for carbohydrates that are in *ground* form rather than in the form of *meal.*

Fruits and vegetables

Some foods also contain fruits and vegetables. The degree to which they con-tribute to the dog food's overall nutritional value is limited by the amount and quality of the fruits and vegetables.

Knowing How to Feed Your Retired Racer

After you've chosen your dog food, you still need to determine how and when to feed your Greyhound. I feed my dogs several small meals each day. Frequent smaller meals help prevent *bloat.* Bloat is a life threatening condition that can strike without warning. I talk more about bloat later in this chapter and in Chapter 14.

Many people free-feed their hounds (giving them free access to food whenever they want it), but I recommend against it. If you feed your retired racer several small meals, you can immediately tell if he isn't eating well, which may be a symptom of illness or another problem. If you have more than one dog and they all have access to the food all day, you may not notice that one dog isn't eating. If you use food in training and you free-feed your hound, too, you may end up over-feeding him unintentionally. Controlling when and how much food he eats ensures that he won't get too much. Finally, I prefer to have my dogs work for a living. If food is always available and always free, it isn't very valuable as a training tool.

When you feed your retired racer, always measure out the amount of food that goes into his dish and allow him about 30 minutes to eat. At the end of this period of time, remove what he hasn't eaten.

If you stop free-feeding and switch to controlled feeding, your guy may need to see the food disappear for a few days after his 30 minutes are up. But he'll soon catch on that he only has a limited time to eat, and he'll eat all he needs in that time period.

All food should be earned by your Greyhound. Even at mealtime, my dogs have to do something to earn their food, like sit calmly and patiently in front of their dishes until they are released to eat.

Most foods have feeding guidelines on the label. But these are only guidelines; they can be off by an incredible amount. Use your dog's weight, general health, and coat condition as your guide.

Adjust the quantity you feed your retired racer based on how much food you use in training that day, as well as on his daily activity level and how often he is being fed.

Looking at Some Common Feeding Issues

Knowing what to feed your retired racer and how often to feed him is a big help. But some other common issues surrounding feeding come up from time to time, and being knowledgeable about these problems so that you can address them if and when they arise puts you one step ahead.

Poor coat condition

Greyhounds with poor coats may need more good-quality fat in their diets. Try switching to a better-quality food, with a higher-quality fat content. Omega 3 (fish oil) capsules are also a great way to improve a dog's coat. Simply disguise a 1,000 mg capsule in a ball of canned food and give your hound one capsule a day. You can find Omega 3 capsules in the nutritional supplement section of most drug and grocery stores. Expect to wait a month or more to see if a change in diet or the addition of the Omega 3 has made a difference.

Because poor coat condition can also be a sign of other health problems, consult your vet if your hound's coat or skin condition doesn't improve.

Bloat

Many dogs eat their entire daily food requirement in one meal. This isn't a good practice with deep-chested breeds of dogs like Greyhounds. Although Greyhounds are not in the high-risk group, they are susceptible to a life-threatening condition called *bloat*. Because it can kill so quickly, you need to know about it even though retired racers aren't in the highest risk group.

Bloat is a catchall term for *gastric torsion* or *gastric dilation and volvulus syndrome* (GDV). When a dog is suffering from bloat, the stomach can actually twist. When that happens, the blood supply to the stomach and other vital organs is cut off. The cause isn't known but latest studies strongly indicate a genetic link. Only immediate medical intervention can save your hound's life if he bloats. Almost 50 percent of dogs who bloat die.

Bloat is a true medical emergency. Even with medical intervention, an affected dog can die within a few hours from the time the symptoms begin. Symptoms can develop hours after your hound has eaten. The symptoms are excessive salivation, swelling of the stomach, and unsuccessful attempts to vomit. Many dogs with bloat pace and seem visibly uncomfortable and restless. Do not wait to see if the situation gets better. Do not waste time trying home remedies. Call your veterinarian's office and advise them that your hound is showing symptoms of bloat and that you're bringing him for evaluation and treatment. (Calling ahead gives them an opportunity to be ready to begin treatment as soon as you arrive.) Then get him to the veterinarian immediately. Get someone to drive you if possible, because your mind isn't likely to be focused on your driving.

The newly released findings from the most extensive study ever done on the causes and prevention of bloat raise some questions about techniques we have traditionally used to prevent bloat. Based on the most recent study, the most important ways to prevent bloat are as follows:

- ✔ **Feed frequent small meals throughout the day and find ways to slow your hound's eating if he gulps his food.**

- ✔ **Avoid even moderate exercise for one hour before or one hour after a meal. Avoid *strenuous* exercise for at least two hours before and after a meal.**

According to the study, a happy dog is less likely to bloat. Apparently temperament is a major factor. Dogs who are nervous and fearful are more at risk. If your hound is especially fearful or nervous, talk to your vet about medications that can help him. Combine medications with behavioral solutions to address known fears and prevent new ones. Chapter 11 provides some techniques for helping a fearful dog.

In the past, adopters were advised to use raised dishes, but the new study not only found this doesn't help, it concludes that it actually *increases* the risk of bloat. Your adoption group's advice may not reflect this information if the group is not yet aware of it, or your group may choose to ignore this advice until further information is available.

The researchers are still analyzing the data they've collected about specific types of food like canned versus dry, so no new recommendations are available. Until the results are available, these tips may also help reduce the risks:

- ✔ **Put a length of large-link chain into his food dish.** He'll have to eat around and between the links. This works better than using a brick or a Bundt pan where he can simply (and quickly) eat around the obstacle. You can purchase a foot or two of chain at a home supply store.

- ✔ **If your hound gulps his food, try finding a brand of dry food that has large pieces, or use nutritionally balanced large dog biscuits instead of kibble so he'll have to chew before swallowing.**

- ✔ **If you travel with your Greyhound or have to board him in a kennel, keep his food and schedule as close to normal as possible, because stress appears to be an increased risk factor.**

Obesity

Obesity contributes to canine health problems, just like it contributes to health problems in humans. Keep your dog's weight in his normal range by weighing him once a month and adjusting his diet accordingly. ***Remember:*** Greyhounds are the right weight when you are able to see a slight definition of the last two or three ribs.

If you're planning to course or compete in agility, keep your Greyhound within five pounds of his racing weight. Additional weight can cause him to be more prone to injuries.

Spayed or neutered dogs may tend to gain weight. The change in hormone levels affects appetite and activity levels in some dogs. If your racer begins to gain weight after being spayed or neutered, increase the dog's activity level and decrease the amount of food you give by 10 percent. Don't make further reductions without consulting your vet. If reducing his food intake doesn't work, have your Greyhound's thyroid tested. Some anecdotal evidence suggests that thyroid deficiencies may be related to spaying/neutering. Discuss reduced-calorie food formulas with your veterinarian to find one that is right for your Greyhound.

Finicky eaters

If your retired racer isn't eating well, start with a visit to the veterinarian and a thorough exam to determine the source of the problem. Although some dogs tend to be picky eaters, this isn't often a problem with a healthy Greyhound. I have found that some hounds are suspicious of new foods. If it doesn't smell familiar or look familiar, they aren't sure they want to taste it. Just offer it casually on several occasions and chances are your boy will make it a new favorite in no time. And don't be surprised if one of your hounds loves something and another turns his nose up at it.

If your vet rules out health problems and your boy is still being finicky, stop free-feeding him. Free-feeding encourages picky eating. Feed him on a regular schedule, and try a better-quality dog food.

Make diet changes gradually over several days. Start with one-quarter new food and three-quarters old food. Two days later change to one-half new and one-half old. A few days after that move to three-quarters old, one-quarter new, and so on. The change should take about a week. Give your Greyhound at least six to eight weeks to adjust, before you decide if the change in diet is working.

Chapter 13

Grooming Your Dog

. . . .

In This Chapter

▶ Keeping your retired racer looking good

▶ Getting the jump on fleas and ticks

. . . .

*P*eople usually think of grooming as brushing and bathing, but it should also be your primary way of routinely assessing your Greyhound's health. A quick, daily once-over with a brush keeps your hound's coat in good condition and it also gives you the opportunity to catch any nicks or dings that occur during one of his runs around the backyard or the house. Don't just brush your hound; look and touch. Add a little massage — it's a great way to bond with your retired racer and it helps him learn to enjoy handling.

Do a weekly inspection of your retired racer's eyes, ears, teeth, feet, and nails. Use your eyes, your nose, and your fingers as your guide. Lots of little problems may not be noticed by your eyes, but your nose or fingers may pick up on them right away. For example, dogs' ears often develop an odor even before there are any visible signs of irritation or infection. You may not see a minimally chipped tooth, but your fingers will find it before it rips his gums or tongue to shreds.

In addition to giving you a chance to look for early signs of physical problems in your hound, grooming is also about keeping his coat, teeth, and nails in top condition. If you groom him regularly, you can keep him free of ticks and fleas more easily.

Greyhounds are clean animals. Many of them actually groom themselves, like cats do. Personally, I believe some of them may even be a bit vain.

When you first see your retired racer, he may have a bare butt, which may be from contact with his crate. The cause of this bald-thigh syndrome is just another one of the many things no one agrees on. If the coat on his butt doesn't grow back in within several months, it may be a result of other health problems. Talk to your vet. Your new Greyhound may have some dandruff, fleas, or ticks. And his teeth may look dreadful. But don't let this first impression discourage you. In no time, you'll be able to get your boy in tip-top shape by using the tools you gain in this chapter.

Embarrassed by flakes?

Many Greyhounds, especially when they first arrive from the racetrack, have dandruff. You can help get rid of the dandruff by adding a tablespoon of safflower oil to his food each day or by giving him a 1,000 mg Omega 3 fish oil capsule each day. He may also need more liquid. Add liquids that he likes to his water dish (to encourage him to drink more water). Try electrolyte-fluid ice cubes, low-sodium beef broth, or some low-sodium vegetable or tomato juice.

You can also try a colloidal oatmeal shampoo. Moisturizers help offset the dryness and discomfort and help hydrate the skin. Use products formulated for dogs. They are available through your veterinarian, or follow her recommendations for similar products found in pet supply stores.

Don't continue to self-treat any skin condition that is not showing improvement in three to six weeks. If the condition has the appearance of pimples, prickly heat, or is open and runny, it isn't dandruff. Consult your vet.

Caring for Your Retired Racer's Coat and Skin

You want your Greyhound to have a shiny, healthy coat. And in order to do that, you need to brush him, bathe him, and keep him free of fleas and ticks. The following sections explain how to do all these things.

Brushing your new best friend

A gentle daily brushing is ideal. You can get away with less frequent brushings if your hound doesn't have skin problems or doesn't spend a lot of time outdoors.

Instead of looking at brushing as a chore, view it as a special time of bonding between you and your retired racer.

Use a rubber curry comb, a sisal hound glove, or a soft brush to brush your Greyhound. Start at his head and work your way to his tail, using long, gentle strokes.

The goal in brushing a Greyhound is to stimulate the skin and pull the loose fur away. Unless you poke your hound in the eye, it's almost impossible to do this incorrectly.

Make brushing a pleasant experience for your retired racer by talking softly and offering quiet praise when he remains still and calm. Offer him an occasional treat.

Saving money with medicated shampoos

If you have to use a medicated shampoo or conditioner on your Greyhound to address a problem with his coat or skin, you can save money by following these tips:

✔ **If he's particularly dirty or greasy, bathe him with an inexpensive, nonmedicated shampoo first.**

✔ **Use water to dilute the amount of shampoo you're likely to need for the bath.** Diluting

the shampoo makes it easier to distribute the shampoo evenly. Use an old squeeze bottle to apply the diluted shampoo. Don't dilute any shampoo you're storing; only dilute what you'll use that day.

✔ **Leave the shampoo or conditioner on for ten full minutes (or as directed by your vet or the label).** If you rinse it off too soon, you're wasting your money.

Skin problems can be limited greatly by grooming your Greyhound regularly, keeping stress at a minimum, feeding high-quality food, and giving him the appropriate exercise.

Greyhounds are naturally clean. Because they have little oil in their coats, they don't usually need frequent bathing. Your nose and the condition and feel of the dog's coat should be your guide. Recommendations on the frequency of bathing range from once a week to twice a year. Unless you are dealing with a specific skin problem or your hound decided to hug a skunk, once a month should be adequate (and anything more than that may be too much).

Rub-a-dub-dub: Giving your hound a bath

Hundreds of dog shampoos are on the market, and deciding which one to use may seem impossible. Choose a simple, tearless puppy shampoo.

If you need to use a medicated shampoo, put a couple drops of mineral oil in your hound's eyes to protect them or use a tearless shampoo on his head and face, and reserve the medicated shampoo for the rest of his body.

Greyhounds are sensitive to the cold, so there are very few climates where you can bathe him comfortably outside in even the warmest weather. Plan on using your bathtub or taking him to a groomer.

Look in pet supply stores for shower attachments that make bathing your boy in your bathtub easier.

Pepe Le Pew?

Okay, so your hound decided to hug a skunk. How do you get the odor out? First, do not bring your hound inside or your entire house will smell of skunk for weeks.

In a large, clean bucket mix the following ingredients:

8 16-ounce bottles (or 1 gallon) of 3 percent hydrogen peroxide

1 cup baking soda

4 teaspoons dishwashing liquid (not dishwasher detergent)

Apply the solution to your dry Greyhound, carefully avoiding his eyes. Thoroughly work the solution into his fur for five full minutes. Rinse him thoroughly. Repeat the procedure if necessary.

Note: This mixture cannot be stored. Do not place it in a closed container. Discard any remaining solution as soon as you are finished.

Greyhounds have a tendency to collapse when they are in warm water. Don't be alarmed if his legs go out from under him. Work with a helper, so one of you can support him while the other bathes him.

After you're finished bathing your Greyhound, keep him from drafts, especially in the winter. Don't let him outside until he is thoroughly dry, unless it is a very warm day. If the sun is hot, be careful that you don't leave him outside too long (he can get sunburned just like you can).

A second wash/rinse is rarely necessary unless he got into something foul or you're using a medicated shampoo that recommends a second washing. If you are using a medicated shampoo, remember to rinse your hands before you clean his face or get near his eyes.

Keeping fleas from getting a foothold

During the flea season, brush your Greyhound daily and go over his body with a flea comb that has 32 teeth per inch. If you find any fleas, drown them in a bath of alcohol. (Just keep a small, wide-mouthed jar full of alcohol with your grooming supplies.) If you live in some parts of the country or encounter fleas more than rarely, you need something more effective.

If you need to treat your hound dog for fleas, depend on your veterinarian's advice. Avoid pet store collars, medications, and treatments that you apply to your hound or put in contact with his skin except those containing only *pyrethrins*. Pyrethrins are derived from plants and are sighthound safe. And avoid treatments for your hound that contain permethrin — although it sounds the same, it is not the same as pyrethrin. If you are looking for an over-the-counter product, most Greyhound adoption groups recommend the Adams line of flea products, which are used extensively by the racing kennels and are available at almost all pet supply stores. To treat your house or other areas look for products that contain Nylar, Precor, allethrin, resmethrin, pyrethrin, and/or permethrin. Do read all labels carefully and follow the advice of your adoption group and veterinarian. New products appear each year so by the time you read this there may be other safe products available, but don't trust anything you haven't researched and asked about.

Effective flea control requires several necessary steps. Ask your veterinarian to recommend products and procedures to help you:

- ✔ Get rid of the fleas that fell off your hound in your house.
- ✔ Get rid of the fleas on your hound.
- ✔ Get rid of the fleas that are waiting outside to climb on your hound.
- ✔ Keep the fleas from coming back.

There are a number of new treatments on the market to prevent or kill fleas and ticks. The safest and most effective of these are available through your veterinarian. Some work to kill adult fleas, some kill fleas and ticks, some are insect growth regulators, and some work immediately to kill adult fleas.

All flea treatments have risks and benefits. Advantage may not be safe for Greyhounds that are prone to seizures. Some hounds have had reactions to Program and Frontline. Because new products appear almost every year and information about how these products affect Greyhounds is constantly being updated, discuss this with your veterinarian or your adoption group.

What about ticks? Ticks carry some incredibly nasty diseases that can be fatal and can hide in a chronic state for months or years. Currently, Greyhound-safe tick treatment options are Frontline, which is applied once a month, pyrethrins, which is applied to the dog's coat, and Preventic, which is a collar. Frontline and Preventic are available through your veterinarian. Check your hound carefully for ticks any time he has been outside in an area where ticks are common. If you find a tick on your dog, remove it immediately. I explain more about tick-borne diseases in Chapter 14.

Don't attempt to burn the tick with a cigarette or smother it with alcohol or petroleum jelly to get the tick to remove itself from your hound. There are inexpensive and easy-to-use gadgets available at pet stores that are specifically designed for removing ticks. Keep one on hand in case you find a tick on your dog.

Removing ticks

Ticks have to be attached for a period of time before they transmit all those nasty diseases we're concerned about. So getting them off your hound as quickly as possible is important. Here's the short course in removing ticks:

✔ Because ticks can also spread diseases to humans, wear latex gloves or put plastic sandwich bags on your hands to protect yourself. Avoid squeezing or crushing the tick's body.

✔ Use tweezers to get under the tick's head near the dog's body. Pull gently until you feel the tick release. If it looks as though the head remained, talk to your vet.

✔ Dispose of the tick's body in a jar of alcohol. Ticks are very difficult to kill and can live for years, so don't think you can simply wrap it in tissue and throw it in the trash.

✔ Disinfect the area of the bite with an antiseptic cleanser.

✔ Wash your hands with soap and water.

Taking Care of Your Dog's Ears

Check your Greyhound's ears each week. Clean them with a wad of cotton and a cleaner made specifically for the ears of dogs. Some hounds need to have their ears cleaned as frequently as once a week, but most need less-frequent cleaning. Let your nose and your eyes guide you.

Place a piece of cotton or cloth moistened with ear cleaner over your index finger and stick it in your dog's ear. Gently twist your finger around like you're cleaning the inside of a small bottle or a shot glass. Repeat if necessary.

Your hound's ears should have a nice, healthy pink color to them, and they should never have an unpleasant odor. Just as some people have more wax buildup in their ears than others, some hounds have more wax in their ears than others. If your boy is shaking his head or rubbing and scratching his ears, see your vet.

Trimming Your Retired Racer's Nails

If you are planning to trim your dog's nails yourself, do yourself (and your hound) a favor and ask your veterinarian or groomer to teach you how to do it properly (and check out Figure 13-1 for illustrated instructions for trimming your dog's nails). Learn to use a grinder as well as nail clippers.

When you trim your dog's nails, you want to take off only the part of the nail in front of the quick. You can see the quick as the pointed area in the center of the nail in the second illustration in Figure 13-1. On hounds with white or light nails, the quick is pink when you see the nail in the light. If your hound has darker nails, try finding the quick by shining a flashlight from behind the nails, or ask your vet or a groomer for help. Because Greyhounds have thick nails, it helps to make an additional cut from the top of the nail as shown in the third illustration in Figure 13-1.

If you accidentally cut the quick of the nail, it will bleed quite a bit and scare not only your hound, but you as well. Even when you know what you're doing, you're bound to catch the quick once in a while.

If you do your own clipping, get *styptic powder* from the vet, groomer, or pet store. Styptic powder is an effective way to stop bleeding if you accidentally cut the quick of your hound's nail.

If you don't have styptic powder, use flour, cornstarch, a crayon, or a wet tea bag (from regular tea, not the herbal variety) instead.

How do you stop a bleeding quick? Dip the bleeding nail into the styptic powder, flour, or cornstarch and apply pressure; or push the nail into a crayon; or hold a wet tea bag against the nail for a full five minutes. Do not disturb the styptic powder, flour, or cornstarch or try to remove it when the bleeding stops. If you cannot successfully stop the bleeding in five minutes, call your vet.

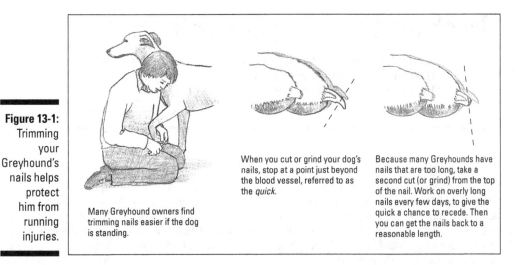

Figure 13-1:
Trimming your Greyhound's nails helps protect him from running injuries.

Many Greyhound owners find trimming nails easier if the dog is standing.

When you cut or grind your dog's nails, stop at a point just beyond the blood vessel, referred to as the *quick*.

Because many Greyhounds have nails that are too long, take a second cut (or grind) from the top of the nail. Work on overly long nails every few days, to give the quick a chance to recede. Then you can get the nails back to a reasonable length.

Make nail trimming easy on both you and your Greyhound by giving him lots of time to get used to it. Have him stand up so you can get at him more easily. Try putting a dab of peanut butter on the refrigerator door at his nose level so he can lick at it while you trim. At first, do just one nail at a time, then give him a treat and stop. As he gets accustomed to your handling, increase the number of nails you do in each session until you can do them all in one session. If your guy is squirrelly about having his nails done, get a helper. One of you can hold him and give him treats while the other one trims.

Follow these tips as well:

- **Use a heavy-duty, scissors-type nail clipper.** The guillotine type of nail clipper is usually not tough enough to handle really heavy nails, and it gets dull quickly.

- **Be sure your clippers are sharp.** Dull clippers hurt. If he flinches and you know you haven't cut the quick of the nail, your clippers are probably dull. Replace them.

- **Take off only a tiny bit at a time.**

- **Use a cordless grinder instead of clippers, or use it to file the rest of the nail down.** But don't try to use a cordless grinder without desensitizing him to the sound and feel first. Cordless grinders are less noisy than the ones with cords, plus they're rechargeable. But remember, a grinder can build up heat quickly so only work on each nail for a second or two. Cordless grinders can be purchased at any home supply store.

Brushing Your Greyhound's Teeth

Some dogs don't need a lot of work to keep their teeth healthy. Unfortunately, Greyhounds aren't those dogs. Keeping your retired racer's teeth and gums healthy is a true challenge. Be sure to brush your dog's teeth *every day*.

Yogurt: Your dog's best friend

Besides tasting good, yogurt may help ward off the Big D (diarrhea). Use this simple formula to know how much yogurt to feed your dog: Give ¼ cup of plain yogurt with active cultures per 25 pounds of dog per week. That's about 2 tablespoons per day for a 75 pound dog.

Many dog owners swear by yogurt — including me. When my dogs, Greyhound and otherwise, are getting their yogurt regularly, they seem less susceptible to the tummy upsets and gas that come with diet changes and stress.

Let your retired racer get comfortable with the process of brushing his teeth. Gently and slowly teach him to enjoy having his mouth handled. Start with merely touching his muzzle. Then lift a lip and peak in. Gradually make your handling more intrusive. At the end of each day's handling session, give him a dollop of yogurt from a metal spoon. This will help him get used to the feel of a strange object in his mouth and make it easier to introduce a toothbrush. Work to make this pleasant, not just tolerable.

Use toothpastes and gels specifically designed for dogs. These products contain ingredients like zinc ascorbate, chlorhexidrine, or an enzyme. Most veterinarians carry one or more of these products. Start with a finger brush like the one shown in Figure 13-2 or a finger wrapped in gauze. Look for finger brushes at your pet supply store or vet's office. By working slowly and patiently, I've taught my hounds to accept brushing with an electric toothbrush.

As you brush your dog's teeth, always be gentle. Try to get all the nooks and crannies. At least once or twice a week, use a dental cleanser/mouthwash that contains zinc ascorbate or chlorhexidrine.

If your Greyhound has bad breath, have him checked by your vet. Bad breath should never be ignored. Dental disease is the primary cause, and untreated dental disease can cause serious health problems.

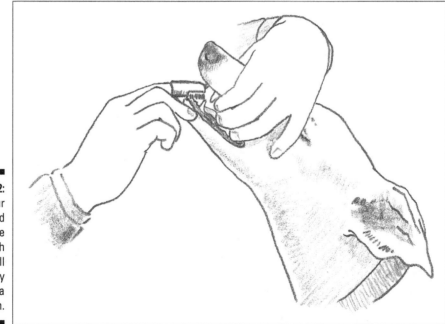

Figure 13-2:
Your Greyhound may not like a toothbrush but will readily accept a finger brush.

Even when you take care of your dog's teeth on a daily basis, you'll still have to get them cleaned and polished professionally. You can't get under the gum line yourself or remove stains. Only a professional polishing can remove the stains and get under the gum line.

By spending a few minutes each day, your actions can reduce the number of times your hound will have to be anesthetized for dental cleaning.

Try using one of the commercial tartar control treats on the market. The best of these are available through veterinarians' offices. And don't forget the various non-edible dental toys, if you can get your hound to chew on them. Dab a touch of peanut butter on the hard ones or dip the rope ones in a bit of bouillon and freeze them to increase the appeal. Using raw bones as a dental aid is highly controversial. Almost all vets warn that you should never let a dog have a real bone. Some vets who practice alternative medicine have other thoughts. If you want to know more, see Appendix B for books and Web sites that have links to alternative veterinary medicine and nutrition sites.

Chapter 14

Preventing Health Problems

● ●

In This Chapter

▶ Doing everything you can to help your Greyhound avoid health problems

▶ Knowing which illnesses your retired racer may be especially susceptible to

▶ Keeping an eye out for some common canine illnesses

● ●

*I*n this chapter, you'll find basic information on keeping your retired racer healthy and on health issues that are important for your hound. This isn't a medical textbook, and it's definitely not a substitute for medical advice. The best thing you can do to keep your retired racer healthy is to develop a good relationship with a veterinarian who believes in continuing education and who is knowledgeable about Greyhounds (or is willing to learn).

Medical information is constantly changing. Print or online Greyhound magazines and e-mail lists, general dog interest magazines, and the Internet can help you keep up with new information. Although the Internet is a great source of information, not all of it is accurate and some of it is downright dangerous. So don't let any resource become a substitute for professional advice.

Veterinarians often disagree among themselves about the best approach to a particular situation. Because medicine is constantly changing, there are often no "right" answers. And today's hot, new, "right" answers may be discredited tomorrow.

Avoiding Health Problems Before They Come Up

The best way to treat a health problem is to prevent it. Spend time learning what your retired racer looks like, smells like, and feels like and how he behaves when he is healthy, and you'll know quickly when something isn't quite right.

Dogs are experts at hiding signs of illness and injury. Maybe this is a leftover trait from their wild ancestors. In the wild, a dog who is sick or injured is in danger — even from his own pack. If a dog is ill or injured, weaker members of the pack may take advantage of the situation to improve their own place in the pack.

Routine checkups

Schedule a wellness visit for your retired racer as soon as he comes to live with you. Let your retired racer and your veterinarian meet each other when your boy is well so your vet will know how your hound looks and acts when he's healthy. And a simple visit without a lot of yucky stuff helps your hound be more comfortable at the veterinarian's office in the future. I make it a point to stop by my vet's office occasionally to weigh my dogs, give them biscuits, and then leave so that sometimes only good things happen when we go to the vet's office.

A healthy dog should have a routine physical exam at least once a year until the age of seven. Before he reaches that age, talk to your vet about when would be the best time to do a geriatric profile. This evaluation will give your vet a good baseline in case a problem develops in later years.

Vaccinations

What should you vaccinate for? How often should you vaccinate? Should you vaccinate at all? This is becoming one of the most fiercely debated issues of the decade for pet owners.

Why is vaccination such a big issue? Vaccinations challenge your hound's immune system. Some researchers feel that this is contributing to the increase in health problems like cancer, allergies, and other immune system related diseases and problems.

But there is a reason we vaccinate. That reason is to protect our pals from serious illnesses that can disable and kill. And some diseases like rabies can be passed along to humans.

While the experts work it out, I've decided to space out my dogs' vaccinations. Rather than having all the vaccines given at one time, I'm scheduling each type of vaccination separately at least two or more weeks apart. This way, their immune systems aren't getting so much of a jolt at one time.

Talk to your vet about the risks and benefits of vaccinating and the diseases that are prevalent in your specific geographic location. Work out a plan with your veterinarian that's acceptable for both of you.

Regardless of the choices you and your veterinarian make, a wellness visit at least once a year will help identify illnesses while they are still in the early, more treatable stages. Annual blood screening to establish your hound's baseline and to monitor him for disease and undiagnosed health problems should begin at age two or as soon as you adopt your retired racer.

Taking a Look at Special Health Concerns

Greyhounds are healthy dogs. But it's easy to lose sight of that when you read long lists of Greyhound-specific problems or spend time reading e-mail lists where all folks seem to talk about is what is wrong with their hounds. Many of the problems we see in Greyhounds are common to many different breeds. Others are more uncommon but are still not limited to just Greyhounds. A few require special mention, because your vet may not see them very often if she doesn't have a lot of retired racers as patients. I cover these problems in the following sections.

Because Greyhounds have so little body fat and because of the way their livers process drugs, they are especially sensitive to certain drugs and chemicals. This high level of sensitivity could result in death. Greyhounds also have blood chemistries that differ from other breeds. Try to find a veterinarian who is aware of these issues and takes them into consideration when she is doing diagnostic procedures.

Anesthesia and drug sensitivity

Greyhounds are especially sensitive to certain anesthetic agents. Some drugs should *never* be used on your Greyhound. If your veterinarian isn't willing to use the right drugs for your Greyhound, find a veterinarian who will. Greyhounds take much longer to recover from anesthesia than other dogs. So be sure your vet uses anesthetic agents that wear off quickly.

Ask your vet to use anesthetic agents that are unlikely to cause *malignant hyperthermia,* a condition that occurs when your dog's body rapidly and dangerously overheats. This condition can happen during or following anesthesia and affects humans and swine, in addition to dogs. Greyhounds seem to be at a higher risk than other dog breeds and can also experience malignant hyperthermia following exercise or after ingesting hops. The condition is often fatal, and Dantrolene is the only medication currently available to treat it.

Some of the medications used before surgery can also cause problems for Greyhounds. For example, Greyhounds should never be given barbiturates. Most veterinarians are now aware of these issues and use the appropriate combinations of medications. Check Appendix B for sources of up-to-date information.

Bloat

Bloat is a life-threatening condition. The symptoms of bloat include retching without an ability to vomit, an abdomen that feels or looks full and swollen, pacing or restlessness, or other signs of distress. These symptoms can occur soon after a meal or hours later. Although Greyhounds are not as prone to bloat as many breeds, they are at risk. If your retired racer shows any symptoms of bloat, do not wait to see if he gets better; get him to a veterinarian immediately. Bloat can kill very quickly. Check out Chapter 12 for more information on bloat and what you can do to prevent it.

Breed-specific conditions

Even with the dings and bangs that go with living the life of a professional athlete, Greyhounds really are healthy dogs. They are prone to few of the many genetic or inherited diseases that affect many breeds. But, just as many human families are predisposed to certain health conditions like diabetes or heart disease, Greyhounds are predisposed to certain conditions as well. Here is a list of conditions that sometimes affect Greyhounds:

- ✔ **Hemophilia:** Greyhounds, like nearly every other breed of dog, are susceptible to hemophilia — a hereditary disorder that affects the ability of the blood to clot properly. As in humans, although hemophilia is passed through the female, only males have the problem (except in vary rare cases when females are also affected).

- ✔ **Von Willebrand's:** This disorder is a clotting disorder similar to hemophilia. Von Willebrand's is also hereditary, but it affects both males and females. Stress is a contributing factor to the disorder. Most dogs with the ailment can live normal lives. But precautions need to be taken if the dog requires surgery or suffers a serious injury.

✔ **Progressive retinal atrophy:** This is an inherited condition of the eye, which leads to blindness and is common in many breeds. There is no effective treatment at this time.

✔ **Hypothyroidism:** Hypothyroidism may be a hereditary or genetic problem and is common in virtually every breed. Some veterinarians argue that environmental causes, including over-vaccination, may be partially responsible for the increase in thyroid disease in dogs. Regardless of its causes, hypothyroidism is a very treatable condition.

The most common symptoms of hypothyroidism are dry scaly skin, a dull coat, bilateral hair loss, weight gain, cold intolerance, exercise intolerance, and mental dullness, but many dogs show no physical symptoms. Undiagnosed thyroid disease can cause all kinds of behavior changes in dogs, including aggression. If your hound develops a behavioral problem, always ask your vet to do a thyroid panel to check your hound's thyroid function.

✔ **Benign and malignant tumors:** Tumors aren't as common in Greyhounds as they are in most other breeds. However, growing evidence suggests that Greyhounds and other large breeds may be susceptible to bone cancer — particularly in the long bones of the legs. Greyhounds may also be more susceptible to cutaneous hemangioma/hemangiosarcoma.

✔ **Arthritis:** Arthritis affects almost any dog who lives long enough. Greyhounds experience plenty of wear and tear on their joints because of their early training and vocation and their sheer joy of running. But lots of dogs who have never been anything but couch potatoes develop arthritis as well.

✔ **Pannus:** An inherited progressive disorder that can lead to blindness, Pannus isn't curable, but aggressive treatment can control it.

✔ **Tick-borne illnesses:** Greyhounds may be more susceptible than other breeds to some of the tick-borne illnesses, specifically ehrlichiosis and babesiosis.

Other ailments may affect your retired racer but are uncommon enough in many veterinary practices that your vet may not be familiar with them. If your vet doesn't treat a lot of Greyhounds, she may appreciate your sharing this information with her:

✔ **Pemphigus/Lupoid Onchodystrophy.** This is an autoimmune disease affecting only the nails. There are no systemic changes. Multiple nails separate at the quick and fall off. Treatment includes prednisone/chlorpheniramine and/or niacinamide/tetracycline.

✔ **Dysuria or "Tying Up."** This is a problem that some male Greyhounds experience when stressed (like after racing, lure coursing, long periods of travel, anesthesia, or hospitalization). They develop urethral spasms. A Greyhound with this problem stands for long periods of time straining to urinate, but only drops come out. Treatment is medication to relax the urethra such as Dibenzyline or Ismelin.

✔ **Cramping.** Some retired racers are prone to muscle cramps. Cold weather or exercise usually bring these on. One or more legs stiffen and the gait becomes rigid. Immediate treatment is to get the dog inside and walk him around where it's warm. Long term treatment, which will usually eliminate the problem, is a daily potassium supplement.

Female Greyhounds may develop a red, polyp-like "growth" on the vulva. This is actually a clitoral hypertrophy caused by the testosterone used to keep them from coming in heat when they are at the track. It is not a tumor and is not a problem. In fact, it usually (but not always) goes away on its own.

Undiagnosed diarrhea may also be a problem for your hound, especially when he first arrives. Retired racers, because they are housed with so many dogs from all parts of the country, frequently have parasites that some vets in some parts of the country rarely if ever see. It doesn't matter whether your hound has been wormed, or has had ten negative fecal exams (some parasites like whipworm don't show up in fecal exams). De-worm again with Panacur and Droncit before subjecting him to intrusive and expensive diagnostic procedures. Insist if you have to, and don't settle for a lesser worming medication if your vet doesn't have Panacur (and chances are he may not). It can't hurt, and it may just be the solution to all your hound's woes. If the Panacur and Droncit are effective, be sure to de-worm again in three weeks and again in three months.

Knowing What to Watch for in Your Retired Racer

Many of the health problems that can affect your hound are treatable or even preventable. You just have to know what to watch for. And in the following sections, I give you the inside scoop.

Heartworm

Heartworm is spread by mosquitoes and is found all over the United States. Before your Greyhound can be put on a heartworm preventive, he has to be tested to be sure he doesn't already have heartworm. Medications can be used daily or monthly to prevent the disease. Most adopters use these medications year-round. But your hound needs to be tested regularly, even if he takes year-round preventives. Some preventives are now combined with medications that treat other parasites, and one even controls fleas.

Not all medications are safe for Greyhounds. Some are safe in one form but not another. Some are safe for most Greyhounds but not all. The medications most Greyhound groups agree are safe are Interceptor, Sentinel, Filiarabits (daily dose), and Heartgard.

Roundworms, hookworms, tapeworms, and whipworms

Roundworms, hookworms, tapeworms, and whipworms are internal parasites. They are common wherever groups of dogs live. And that almost guarantees that your retired racer will have one or more of these varieties of parasites when you first get him from the track. Even if your retired racer was wormed before you got him, a follow-up treatment is usually necessary.

The good news for you and your Greyhound is that Interceptor and Sentinel (heartworm preventives) work on all these parasites except tapeworms. Sentinel is a combination of Interceptor (a heartworm preventive) and Program (a flea preventive) so it controls fleas, too. The best way to prevent tapeworms is to control fleas. Regardless of which medications your dog takes, your veterinarian will probably want to check a fecal sample once a year to make sure there aren't any parasites.

Tick-borne diseases

The most common tick-borne diseases are babesiosis, ehrlichiosis, Lyme disease, and Rocky Mountain spotted fever. They can go dormant for long periods of time — even years. And when they *do* rear their ugly heads, their symptoms are subtle and mimic a lot of other conditions, making tick-borne diseases very difficult to identify. They can be fatal if they aren't diagnosed and treated soon enough. Symptoms include lameness, fatigue, loss of appetite, fever vomiting, spontaneous bleeding, depression, or weight loss. These symptoms can occur and then lessen or disappear, so don't ignore them if they go away in a few days. If your retired racer develops symptoms that can't be diagnosed, ask your vet to draw blood for a tick panel.

Tick-borne diseases are usually diagnosed by drawing blood and submitting it to a laboratory for a tick panel. The blood is measured for antibodies to the organisms. The presence of the antibodies doesn't mean that your retired racer has the disease. It means he has been exposed to it. The more antibodies the dog is producing, the more likely it is that there is an active infection. If the levels, called *titers,* are above a certain number, your veterinarian will recommend treatment.

Some groups feel the danger of tick-borne diseases is so great that all retired racers should be tested. A few argue that all retired racers should be treated with an appropriate antibiotic just in case. Other groups take the position that only retired racers with symptoms need to be tested or treated. The opinions are so diverse that you can't get anyone to agree on anything, except that the diseases are really nasty.

Tick panels

When your vet says she's drawing blood for a tick panel on your retired racer, she probably means a panel that tests for Rocky Mountain spotted fever, Lyme disease, babesia, and Ehrlichia Canis — the most common disease-causing organisms. But these aren't the only disease-causing organisms. If the tick panel shows that your hound doesn't have any of these organisms, but your hound has symptoms, you can also discuss having him tested specifically for all strains of Ehrlichia. Unless your vet is very specific that she wants all strains tested, most labs don't do it. Ask the lab to screen for *E. canis, E. risticii, E. platys,* and *E. equi.* Not all that long ago, only a few labs were doing tick panels. Now, many are. Be sure that your veterinarian sends the blood sample to a lab that will test for antibodies for at least the four most common tick-borne problems.

Chapter 15

Avoiding Emergencies

In This Chapter

▶ Understanding what is — and isn't — an emergency

▶ Removing hazards from your home and yard

▶ Keeping your retired racer safe at home and on the road

*B*eing able to help your retired racer in the case of emergency is part of your responsibility as a pet owner. But a book or video on pet first aid is useless if you aren't willing to take the time to study and practice. If you really have an emergency, you won't have time to look up instructions in a book. And you sure won't be able to take the time to put a video in the VCR and follow the instructions for doing CPR. The very nature of emergencies is that they require immediate attention. In this chapter, I don't offer a crash course in first aid. That would be impossible in just a few pages. I do, however, provide you with lots of information on how to keep your hound safe and happy in lots of situations. And I tell you what to look for so you'll know when it's time to call the vet.

If you have an emergency, don't waste your retired racer's time and possibly his life trying to look up emergency first-aid measures. Get him to help immediately. If possible, call ahead so your vet or emergency clinic can be prepared to start treatment the moment you arrive.

Knowing What Constitutes an Emergency

Some people consider even the slightest problem an emergency, and others decide to wait and see when they should be calling a vet. Knowing when to call your veterinarian is important.

Here are some situations in which you need to call a veterinarian immediately:

- ✔ Any loss of appetite that continues for more than 24 hours.
- ✔ Vomiting or diarrhea that persists for more than 24 hours or any vomiting or diarrhea in a dog more than eight years of age.
- ✔ Symptoms of bloat, such as unsuccessful attempts to vomit, rapid shallow breathing, distressed appearance, and painful or enlarged abdomen.
- ✔ A first seizure, recurrent seizures, or any seizure that lasts more than three minutes.
- ✔ A body temperature above 104 degrees or below 100 degrees.
- ✔ A serious fall or blow to the head, chest, or abdomen even if your hound doesn't appear to be injured.
- ✔ Any encounter with a moving vehicle.
- ✔ Any open wound or injury in which bleeding continues for more than five minutes, despite your efforts to control it.
- ✔ Difficulty breathing.
- ✔ Collapse or unconsciousness.
- ✔ Snake bite.
- ✔ Heatstroke.
- ✔ Poisoning.
- ✔ Burns.
- ✔ Straining or difficulty urinating or defecating.

You can do a lot to prevent emergencies by learning how your hound behaves when he is well and by dog-proofing your home.

I carry index cards in my car — one for each dog — in case I'm injured and can't care for the dogs myself. Each card lists the dog's name, age, and description (and ear tattoo numbers for my retired racers), my veterinarian's telephone number, a backup emergency contact number in case I'm traveling, the dog's vaccination information, and a list of any medications he is taking. I use a different color index card for each dog so that if I need more than one card to hold all the information, it's easy to see which card belongs with each dog.

Responding to a Dog in Distress

If your dog becomes ill or injured, you need to know how to get him to treatment as calmly and efficiently as possible. Check out the following sections for more information on safely handling and transporting your hound if an emergency occurs.

Remove any loose animals or extra people from the area. The injured dog is stressed enough without having to deal with bystanders or other dogs. Deal with any nearby dogs calmly and quietly. Assume any dog is aggressive in this situation, and act accordingly.

You can use a leash to form an emergency snare to capture a loose dog (assuming you can get close enough and the dog is showing no signs of aggression). Simply put the clip end through the leash handle. Hold it open with one hand. Slip it over the dog's neck without touching the dog, and tighten. (Check out Figure 15-1 for illustrated instructions for making an emergency snare.)

Never muzzle a dog who is vomiting, coughing, or having difficulty breathing.

Even the most gentle hound — even your sweetie, may bite if he is frightened or in pain. Muzzle your hound before you attempt to restrain him or transport him. If you don't have a muzzle on hand, you can fashion an emergency muzzle by following the steps in Figure 15-2.

You can use any long, soft item. A scarf or old panty hose are ideal. The item needs to be soft, at least 30 inches long, and 2 to 4 inches wide.

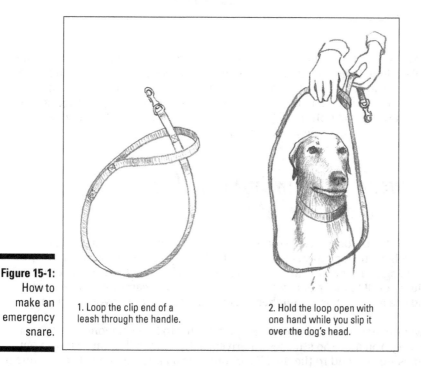

Figure 15-1:
How to make an emergency snare.

1. Loop the clip end of a leash through the handle.

2. Hold the loop open with one hand while you slip it over the dog's head.

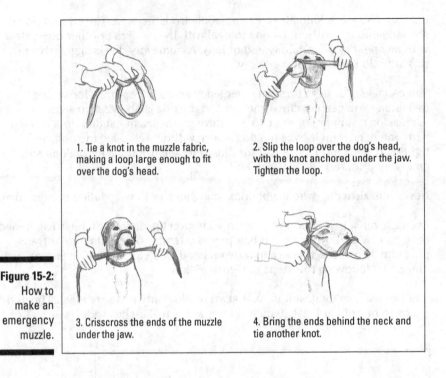

Figure 15-2:
How to
make an
emergency
muzzle.

1. Tie a knot in the muzzle fabric, making a loop large enough to fit over the dog's head.

2. Slip the loop over the dog's head, with the knot anchored under the jaw. Tighten the loop.

3. Crisscross the ends of the muzzle under the jaw.

4. Bring the ends behind the neck and tie another knot.

Tie a knot in the middle of the item to act as an anchor under the dog's jaw. Make a loop large enough to drop over the dog's nose without having to get close to the dog's mouth. From above and behind the dog's head, slip the loop over the nose and tighten (but don't restrict breathing). Bring the ends down around the bottom of the lower jaw and crisscross. Bring the ends to the back of the neck and tie securely in a bow.

Transporting an injured dog to a veterinary clinic

If your dog is conscious, assist him into the car by putting his front paws into the vehicle then simply scooping his butt up into the vehicle. Even a 90-pound weakling can get a dog into a vehicle this way. If he isn't conscious or is too injured or ill to move and he's too heavy for you to carry alone, get a helper and use a blanket as a stretcher to get him into and out of your vehicle.

If your needlenose needs emergency care, try to find someone else to do the driving. You'll be too stressed to drive safely, and you'll want to have your hands free to tend to the dog. If a phone is available, call ahead so treatment can be started as soon as you arrive.

Keeping Your Retired Racer Safe and Happy

Emergencies happen, but there are a lot of things you can do to keep your hound from harm and to prevent emergencies at home or when you travel. It's easier on you and on your hound if you keep life safe and stress-free. In the following sections I help you learn how.

Hidden hazards

Homes and yards are a treasure chest of dangers for hounds. If you get down to his eye level (on all fours, if you can) and look around, you'll be amazed at what you'll notice. There are all kinds of things your hound can reach that may be dangerous. Dogs have been known to swallow many objects that we wouldn't think of as edible. Veterinarians have removed strings, yarn, and panty hose from the bellies of dogs. So as you look around your house, ask yourself what kinds of little knickknacks your Greyhound could steal from low places, like the coffee table, and choke on? What kinds of cleaning products are hiding under your kitchen sink that may be harmful if your hound tries to snack on them? And where is that box of chocolates you were given for your birthday? All these items pose potential risks for your Greyhound, so be sure to keep them out of your hound's reach.

Don't think that hiding forbidden items in a closed cupboard will be any more effective in keeping out a Greyhound than it is in keeping out a toddler; some Greyhounds excel at figuring out how to open doors. If you've adopted a skinny, furry Houdini, you'll figure out how to be very creative.

By now you've probably introduced him to the things in your home that may be harmful, but what about the things he may encounter when you take him to someone else's home? Seriously think about what things could present a danger to a Greyhound who has never encountered them before and take precautions so that he doesn't get hurt. For example, he needs to learn that swimming pools are not solid objects. Take the time to introduce him to these kinds of things. Show them to him and, where possible, let him touch it with a nose or paw. If that isn't possible, at least tap on it or do something to help him understand what the object is.

If you are planning to let your hound run with other Greyhounds, you need to have a *turn-out muzzle*. Turn-out muzzles are a plastic, basket style muzzle like the ones used by the racing kennels when the dogs are turned out for exercise. If one isn't provided when you adopt your retired racer or you can't purchase one from your group, check out the resources in Appendix B.

Greyhounds should be muzzled while they're running together. Greyhounds seem incredibly mellow when they're with you one-on-one, but when they're running, they're entirely different creatures. They can become very competitive. If they bump into each other, they may snap or nip, and muzzles help protect their delicate skin from injury.

One of the best things you can do for your needlenose is to be sure he has lots of identification so he can always find his way home — even if it takes a little help. Your adoption group will probably provide an ID tag with their contact information. Consider this a back-up form of identification, not the primary information. As soon as you know what you'll name your retired racer, get him his own ID tag.

ID tags can get lost or become unreadable, and ear tattoos can fade in time — if they were even legible to begin with. Talk to your vet about microchipping. A tiny chip is inserted just under the skin using a needle and syringe much like your vet uses to give a vaccination. Virtually all animal shelters, animal control organizations, and vet's offices that do microchipping have readers. Although not all readers can read all microchips, the presence of a chip says someone cares about the animal and is trying to find him.

Another way to keep your hound safe and to keep identification on him at all times is to use a breakaway collar like the one shown in Figure 15-3. Many injuries and even strangling deaths are caused when dogs get their collars caught in their crates or on things in the house and yard or while playing with other dogs. A breakaway collar pops open if a certain amount of pressure is applied, but can be kept from opening if you have to use a leash on your hound. Contact Chinook and Company at 800-643-5109 or check them out online at www.breakawaycollar.com.

Chocolate lovers beware

Chocolate contains a substance called *theo-bromine*, which is poisonous to dogs. Different kinds of chocolate contain different amounts of theobromine. As little as 1 pound of dark baking chocolate can be a deadly dose for a 50-pound dog, so always keep chocolate out of the reach of your retired racer. Thinking about giving your hound a little bite from time to time? Would *you* snack on a little arsenic?

Figure 15-3:
A breakaway collar is a great option for Greyhounds.

Your big backyard

Dog-proof your yard. Look for hidden and unsuspected hazards in your yard. Avoid lawn chemicals and pesticides if at all possible. Keep your needlenose safely inside while you mow so he can't fall under a mower if he's startled and trying to get away. If you tie your hound out while you work in the yard or garden, always use a harness instead of a collar. And be certain the tie out is far from anything that may be dangerous. Supervise him carefully and keep him in sight.

Check your yard for holes your hound may trip in or branches or broken fences that could puncture or impale a running or excited dog. A cut-off shrub or a broken post can impale your racer when he's running. A low-swinging tree branch can gouge a Greyhound's eye.

Many of the ornamental plants and shrubs you worked so hard to cultivate are poisonous if eaten by dogs. And all those chemicals you're using to make your lawn the envy of the neighborhood are probably not safe either.

Leaving any dog tied outside alone is risky, especially if he's wearing a collar instead of a harness. If your racer is tied outside, can he wrap the line around one of his legs and break it as he chases after a squirrel? Or, worse, he could rush to the end of the line, break his neck, and hang himself. What kinds of wild animals could come onto your property? For example, are there venomous snakes about or is rabies a serious concern?

When retired racers are running at high speeds, they can and do run into clearly visible objects. Try to keep all obstacles out of your hound's path. And they'll crash into fences if they're running together in unknown territory. When they're running with other dogs, they tend to run at each other and can run right into a fence post if you let them start alongside each other in the middle of the area. If you're letting more than one dog run, let them start at the fence line on opposite sides.

Swimming pools can be a real adventure the first time your hound sees one. We thought we'd done everything right. When we first visited a friend with a pool, we showed our boy that the pool was liquid by splashing a bit of water on him and touching his paw to the water. No problem. He showed no interest in investigating further. Before our next visit, we had him to the shore where he discovered the joys of wading and lying in the surf. Next time he saw the pool, he dipped his paw in to check it out. You guessed it. Before we could stop him, he stepped in because it seemed just like the surf to him. And if your hound has never seen a covered pool he may think it's a solid surface and try to walk out on it. This is extremely dangerous since a soft pool cover can close in around him and trap him under water.

If you have a pool, take the time to teach your hound how to safely get out of the water at the shallow end or how to use the steps if your pool has them.

When the weather outside is frightful

My boy is a real sun puppy. He'd spend hours basking in the sun if I'd let him. Too much of a good thing can be dangerous, though. Use sunscreen on bare butts and bellies, tips of ears and noses. Sunscreen made for infants works well. Avoid his eyes.

But sunburn isn't the only warm weather hazard. Avoid heatstroke by providing shade, a constant supply of fresh water, and controlling the amount of time your dog's outside when the heat index is above 80 degrees Fahrenheit. Limit exercise on hot days and exercise only in the cool of the morning or evening. Watch out for his paws when you're on hot pavement. If you have to walk him on hot pavement, use dog booties to protect his feet. And never leave your hound in a car in warm weather — even with the windows open.

Winter has it's own dangers. Retired racers don't have much insulation to protect them from winter's chill. Put a coat on your hound if the windchill is really bad or if he's going out for more than a quick potty break. Look for ice-melting products for your sidewalk or driveway that are safe for your hound. And put booties on him to protect his feet from the cold, the chemicals used to treat roads and sidewalks, and to keep his feet from being cut by the ice. Most dogs enjoy a romp in the snow. Just don't let him overdo it. If you're cold, you can bet he is, so protect him from harm. And don't forget to put his coat on him after a cold weather run.

WARNING!

The toxicity of plants

Many indoor and outdoor plants are toxic to animals. So unless you check with a veterinarian to determine whether a specific plant can harm your hound, you're better off assuming that *all* plants have the potential to be toxic. When in doubt, ask your veterinarian.

If you suspect your retired racer has ingested something poisonous, don't wait to see if he'll be okay. With many poisons, there is only a small window of treatment opportunity. If you wait to see if your hound's okay, you may have sentenced him to death. Immediately call your vet, not a human poison control center. (Treatment for dogs and people differs.)

Remember your senior hound is even more susceptible to weather extremes than a young healthy hound.

Fencing should be at least four feet high, preferably five feet, and not have spiked or broken slats. Electronic or hidden fencing, which works by putting a collar on your dog that produces a shock to his neck when he crosses a certain boundary, isn't appropriate for Greyhounds. It won't keep marauding dogs out. And it usually doesn't keep Greyhounds in. Electronic fences don't contain many high-prey dogs because they're so focused on the prey they either don't notice or don't care about the pain. Many escape but are afraid to return because of the fear of being shocked as they re-enter the yard.

So what do you do about household and backyard hazards? Wish I could give you an easy answer that was right for everyone. City dwellers face different hazards than rural residents. Folks who live in the mountains have different concerns than folks in the desert. Because each environment has its own backyard hazards, there is no simple recipe I can give you for protecting your retired racer. The best advice I can offer is talk to your vet about which common household products, plants, and animals are a concern in your area, and then remove them or think of ways to keep your hound safely away from them.

Close Encounters of the Canine Kind

There are leash laws in nearly every community, but most of them are ignored. If they were only ignored by people with well-trained, friendly dogs it wouldn't be so bad. But only well-trained folks tend to have well-trained dogs. The people who let their dogs run loose are the ones who have obnoxious if not aggressive dogs. Of course that description often fits the owner, too.

I have very strong opinions about how to deal with dogs who are off-leash and presenting a possible threat to my dogs. My job as leader is to protect my dogs. If I have to scare or injure a loose dog to accomplish that, I will. Better it should be that dog who is injured than one of my dogs. This information is about dog-dog encounters. I'm assuming the marauding dog is *not* a threat to you.

I assume any loose dog is aggressive and do anything I can to avoid meeting him. I calmly and quietly try to get out of his range of vision. I never turn my back on a dog who sees me and is advancing toward me. I also try to identify an escape route.

If I can't avoid the loose dog, I intervene before he can get to my dogs. I physically place myself between the oncoming dog and my dogs. I calmly move my dogs behind me and keep them there.

I try to carry a tennis ball and food, and I always carry smelling salts or a citronella spray. Ammonia capsules (smelling salts) are easy to carry, easy to break, and easy to throw. Wind direction isn't a big issue as it is with pepper spray. They can also be effective for dog fights. Check a local medical supply house or ask your doctor for a few.

I try to divert the loose dog's attention. I keep my voice calm and quiet because excited, loud, or high pitched voices incite a dog who is already wired. If he doesn't seem too intent on me, I try things to get his tail wagging. "Wanna go for a ride," will do it for most dogs. Or I calmly toss a ball. If I don't have a ball handy, I'll toss anything he may chase including the bag of "goodies" I cleaned up after my dogs. That may give me time to retreat or think of something else to do. If tossing a ball doesn't work, I toss a big handful food. I toss it as far away from the direction in which I hope to retreat as I can. I back away as far as I can. Maybe I'll get out of the loose dog's perceived territory.

If you're absolutely sure that your hound is the target, and you can't divert the loose dog or retreat, keep yourself between your hound and the attacker. Behavior has to be interrupted before it is in progress. Stand tall and still. Say "no" in your deepest, calmest, growliest tone. Maybe he'll at least pause. Break the ammonia capsule and gently toss it at the dog's feet. Keep another handy in case your aim is lousy.

An alternative to ammonia is a citronella spray. These are relatively new and are more effective but less difficult to manage than a pepper spray. It can be purchased with a holster that attaches to your belt so it's always handy.

If he continues the attack, use any weapon you can find to safely stop him. Do whatever you have to do to protect yourself and your hound. Don't worry about being a nice guy or a good neighbor. If the owner is nearby, don't expect her to intervene. (They usually just stand there staring.) Report any incidents to animal control. The owner of the loose dog is usually responsible for any medical costs for injury to your hound as long as he was leashed — even if your hound fights back.

If You Go Away

Leave detailed contact information with the sitter, the kennel, your veterinarian, the day care facility, or whoever is going to care for your hound. Include an alternate contact in case something happens to you. Write detailed feeding, medication, and care instructions. Write down a list of all appropriate words your hound knows well and how you use them so your caregiver can communicate.

At some time almost everyone has to board or hospitalize their hounds. If you have to board your boy, here's the scoop on making that experience easier for him.

Private boarding facilities range from doggie spas to not fit for a dog. Ask your veterinarian, groomer, pet supply retailer, friends, or neighbors for referrals. If your referral is from a pet professional, ask if they have actually visited or used the facility. Many refer as a courtesy to a good client or customer and have no idea what the kennel is like.

Call to schedule a visit. When you call, ask if you may drop by unannounced during scheduled pick-up or drop-off hours.

When you make your inspection visit, pay attention to the following:

✔ How does the facility look and smell? If you don't like what you see or smell, don't leave your hound there.

✔ Are the runs heated and air-conditioned? If heat or air-conditioning are necessary in your climate, ask at what temperatures they are turned on. Never leave your retired racer in a place where he could suffer from extremes in temperature.

✔ How much time each day will your dog be confined to the run? Some kennels allow for individual walks or play times. Take advantage of these special features if you can, even if they cost a little more money. Your dog will thank you for it.

✔ Be sure the kennel has arrangement for 24-hour emergency veterinary coverage. Find out when a person is actually on the premises and how often your hound will be checked on.

✔ Do they allow multiple dogs to be loose together in a common area? If so, be sure all the dogs are always muzzled and supervised by a responsible adult when they're together.

Make sure you can bring your own bedding. Even a short stay in a kennel can result in elbow *hygromas* (a swelling over a bone or pressure point caused by lying on hard surfaces) and pressure sores. If you leave bedding at the hospital or kennel, chances are it will be removed when it gets wet, dirty, or shredded.

Blankets tend to get balled up in a corner, and your poor hound ends up sleeping on a cold, hard floor. You need a good, cushiony, waterproof bed that can be hosed down and will dry quickly. What's wrong with a bed that's machine washable? Machine washable doesn't help much if:

- ✔ The bed doesn't fit in the washing machine.
- ✔ The bed fits in the washing machine but takes several loads to do the outer cover, then the guts, and then the inner cover.
- ✔ The facility holds twenty dogs but only has one washing machine.

Look at the Comfy Bed from H & H Industries. These are cushion and cot beds (which can be purchased separately) that can be custom made in exactly the right size for your retired racer. They are nearly indestructible and have a surface that is easy to hose down or disinfect and dries quickly. They are superior to similar products found in stores and catalogs. H & H Industries is online at www.hh-industries.com. Or you can call them at 877-266-3923.

Taking your hound across the country

If your hound loves to travel and you aren't going to spend all your time off sightseeing, take him along for the ride. People often leave their pals at home because they believe hotels don't allow dogs. Many do. Traveling with your hound requires some work on your part. But if he really enjoys travel, it may be a less stressful alternative to kenneling for both of you. A little planning is all it takes to enjoy vacations with your hound.

Start with basic manners training so he'll be welcome at hotels, camp grounds, or rest stops. Teach him to stay quietly in the car until you release him so he doesn't bolt into traffic during a pit stop.

Make sure the information on his identification tag is up to date. If you're on the road with him and he escapes or you are injured, no one will know whom to notify. Add a second tag that includes an alternate contact name and number.

Carry a copy of your NGA pet certificate and a recent photo of each of your hounds so you can prove ownership if necessary. Carry a copy of his medical records including vaccinations in case he becomes ill or you need to provide proof of vaccination when you cross into another state.

Pack a bag that includes favorite toys, his favorite food and treats, his medications, a sleeping pad or bed, paper towels, plenty of water, bowls, and clean up supplies. Carry a first aid kit in your car (and learn how to use it). Identify emergency veterinarian clinics in each of your destination areas.

Let him travel in his crate, use a doggie seat belt, or use a harness to secure him to the back seat, if you can. If you have an accident, he could be injured if he flies through the car like a projectile. Attach his leash before you open any car door. Better yet, keep a second leash permanently attached inside your vehicle; then you can change him from that leash to your walking leash without ever risking escape. If he's excited or anxious, he may try to bolt.

Don't let your hound ride with his nose or head sticking out of an open window. Insects and dirt can irritate his eyes, ears, nose, and throat.

Identify possible hazards like heartworm or ticks in your travel areas. Discuss preventives with your vet well in advance of your trip.

Whether you're traveling across town or across the country, never leave your hound in a parked car during warm weather even if the windows are open. Temperatures can rise to dangerous levels quickly. In cooler weather, open all windows as far as you can. Be sure your hound can't escape. Never leave him in a car alone if you can avoid it. Dogs are stolen from parked cars. Use good judgment.

Finding a dog-friendly hotel

If you'll need to stay in a hotel with your hound, make reservations in advance, especially important during busy travel seasons. Expect to pay a nonrefundable security deposit. Not every hotel allows pets, and many restrict pets to a specific block of rooms. In many cases these are also the smoking rooms. If you have an allergy, ask about this in advance.

Protect the motel's bed linens from fur by covering the beds with old sheets you brought from home. Always clean up after your hound. Don't leave him alone in the room if he's susceptible to separation anxiety. If you have to leave your dog alone, always put the "do not disturb" sign on your door. You may even want to add a sign to the door that says "loose dog in room." Be sensitive to the stress he may experience being alone. Limit your absences and keep them short.

Spray the room with air freshener as you leave to check out.

If Disaster Strikes

Virtually any part of the world is susceptible to some form of natural disaster. Someday you may have to evacuate with your hounds. You can learn more about preparing you and your hound for evacuation by going to the Emergency Animal Rescue Service (EARS) Web site at uan.org/programs/ears/articles.cfm. But here are a few tips to help keep you and your hound together in an emergency.

Animals are not permitted in Red Cross evacuation centers. These shelters are not even permitted by most state health laws to allow service dogs. And it isn't just a health law issue. Many people are frightened of dogs and even more are seriously allergic. The presence of animals in a shelter would add to some people's stress levels.

So make your own plans. Compile a list of dog-friendly motels and hotels that are 25 to 50 miles from your home. Check the AAA travel guide for your area or get one of the pet travel guides that are now available. Keep a copy of the names, addresses, and restrictions with your disaster/evacuation supplies.

Along with the preparation you make for yourself, prepare a disaster kit for your hound. If possible, prepare a separate kit for each hound. Keep the supplies in a plastic container with a secure lid. The EARS Web site tells you what to include.

Discuss disaster planning with your veterinarian. Find out what plans she has in place in case your hound needs care during an emergency. Have at least two back-up vets or a vet with multiple locations.

Should you leave your hound if you have to evacuate? If it is not safe enough to leave a child, it is not safe enough to leave your dog.

Set up a buddy system with a friend or neighbor in case your hound is isolated when the disaster or evacuation occurs and you can't get home to him.

Just because you're on vacation doesn't mean hurricane season is. Find out what plans your kennel or the person caring for your pet have if they have to evacuate should while you're away. Get the emergency contact number so you can check on your hound at the alternate location.

If you have to leave your hound with someone, be sure he's confined. A stressed animal is very likely to try to escape and make his way home. The tendency of Greyhounds to bolt when frightened makes this even more important than it is with other dogs.

While you're away from home and for a while after you are able to return, your hound may be stressed. Let him decide how much contact he wants. Reassure if it helps, but don't coddle. Coddling reinforces fear. Some dogs need distance; some need closeness. If symptoms of stress, particularly loss of appetite or mild diarrhea, continue for more than a week, see a veterinarian. Other symptoms of stress include changes in sleep behavior, aggression, desire to hide, jumpiness, clinginess, and nervousness.

Chapter 16

Knowing What to Do When Your Retired Racer Gets Sick

▶ Giving your Greyhound medication

▶ Knowing how to treat common ailments

▶ Helping your Greyhound recover from illness or surgery

▶ Being there for your retired racer as he ages

▶ Saying goodbye to your best friend when the time comes

*I*f you pay close attention to how your hound looks and acts when he is well, you'll be able to tell quickly when he is ill. Ask your vet to show you how to monitor your hound's vital signs so you'll identify potential problems early. In this chapter, I guide you through the process of caring for your hound until you can get veterinary attention. Don't consider this a substitute for information from your vet. Just consider it a primer on caring for your ailing dog.

Giving Your Hound the Medicine He Needs

If you have a sick pup at home, the first thing you need to know is how to give him pills or liquid medications.

Never give medications by mouth to any dog when he is unconscious, vomiting, aggressive, seizing, or lying flat on his side.

Give all medications until they are gone, unless directed otherwise by your veterinarian. Every eight hours and three times a day are *not* the same thing. Some medications must be given on a very precise schedule. Give the medications exactly as directed. If you have questions or can't follow the dosing schedule, talk to your vet.

Giving liquid medicines

The easiest way to get your hound to take a liquid medicine is to mix the medicine with a small amount of plain lamb or chicken baby food. Use only enough food to add flavor and offer it to your hound. Ask your veterinarian before you mix medication with anything, just to be sure it's okay.

If your hound is unwilling to take the medication this way, you have to administer it into his mouth with a syringe. Use only enough baby food to flavor the medication while still leaving it liquid enough to get into a syringe. Ask your vet for a large syringe when he prescribes the medication, or use a turkey baster.

To administer liquid medications, follow these steps (and check out Figure 16-1 for illustrated instructions):

1. **Get down on the floor with your hound and prop the side of his head against your chest or abdomen.**

   Elevate his head only slightly, or you'll make it difficult for him to swallow.

2. **Pull his lower lip out to form a pouch.**

3. **Place the tip of the syringe inside his mouth, just behind the canine teeth, angling the syringe toward the back of his mouth past the lower teeth but not into his throat.**

4. **Depress the plunger into the syringe slowly as he swallows.**

Do not try to administer liquid medications quickly. You may scare your dog and could cause him to choke. At the very least, if he has a bad experience, it'll be even more difficult when you have to give him the next dose.

Giving pills

Unless your hound is not allowed any solid food, try deception. Simply hide the pill in a small amount of food — peanut butter, cheese spread, cream cheese, or really yummy canned dog food are good choices. I've never met a dog who doesn't love one of these and because dogs rarely bother to chew, the pill will be down before he knows it's in there.

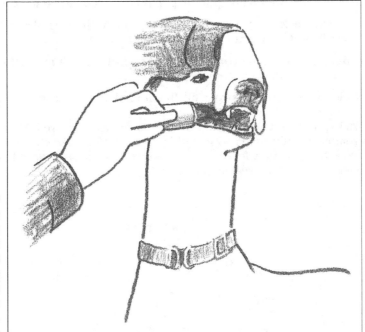

Figure 16-1:
Giving a
Greyhound
liquid
medications
with the
help of a
syringe.

Another option is to use a pill crusher, available at any pharmacy or at some larger pet supply stores. Crush the pill and mix it with canned food. If your hound has a chronic condition that requires daily medications for months or years, this is your best choice. I've found that, over time, some dogs figure out a way to get the peanut butter without taking the pill. But if it's crushed, they have no choice.

Check with your vet first to be sure crushing the pill is acceptable. Some pills, like time-released ones, shouldn't be crushed.

If you have to give the medication in pill or capsule form, follow these steps (and check out Figure 16-2 for illustrated instructions):

1. **Sit your hound in a corner so he can't easily get up or run away.**

2. **Hold the pill in the fingers of one of your hands.**

3. **With the other hand, take hold of his upper jaw by wrapping your thumb over one side and your fingers over the other.**

4. **Tilt his head slightly toward the ceiling.**

5. **Use your thumb and forefinger to wedge open his mouth.**

   Keep his cheeks between his teeth and your fingers so he'll be less likely to bite down while your fingers are in his mouth.

6. **With your other hand, put the pill as far back on the tongue as you can.**

   Use as much of your free hand as you can. A whole hand in his mouth is less likely to get bitten than a finger or two.

7. **Remove your hand from your poor hound's mouth and hold his mouth gently closed.**

   Blow on his nose or stroke his throat until he licks his nose or swallows.

Learn to give liquid medicines to your hound when he is well. Make it part of his routine handling and use something he really likes like chicken broth mixed with some baby food. The process won't seem so strange to him when you have to do it with real medicine.

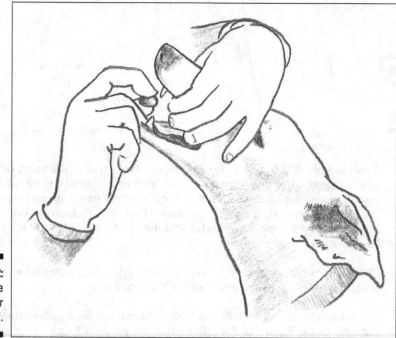

Figure 16-2:
How to give pills to your hound.

Knowing How to Treat Common Ailments

Some illnesses and injuries respond well to home care. The most common ones are described in the following sections. Always discuss any home treatment plan with your veterinarian first and always defer to her recommendations.

Here are some common human medicines to keep on hand for treating simple problems in your hound:

- ✔ Benadryl for allergies and insect bites
- ✔ Dramamine for motion sickness
- ✔ Imodium A-D for diarrhea
- ✔ Enteric-coated aspirin for pain, inflammation, swelling, or fever
- ✔ Tagamet for upset stomach

Your veterinarian can tell you what dosage is appropriate for your hound.

If your hound has had more than three to four episodes of vomiting or diarrhea in the last 24 hours, has blood in his stools or vomit, or has projectile vomiting or explosive diarrhea, don't treat him at home without talking to your veterinarian first.

Diarrhea

Sooner or later, you're bound to be faced with caring for an ailing Greyhound. In the case of diarrhea, it's likely to be sooner rather than later. Greyhounds are particularly prone to diarrhea. Stress and sudden changes in diet seem to be the common causes. So are undiagnosed parasites.

Just because diarrhea is common, don't assume it's harmless. Even if the episodes of diarrhea are mild, if they occur frequently you should let your veterinarian determine the underlying cause.

If your hound's diarrhea is mild and this isn't a persistent problem, you can follow the suggestions in this section before you consult your veterinarian. But if your Greyhound shows signs of illness in addition to diarrhea, such as dehydration, listlessness, or depression, or if the episodes occur greater than six times a day or there is blood present, your hound requires veterinary care and may require hospitalization to replenish fluids.

Diarrhea has many causes. The usual culprits are stress, sudden changes in diet, and dietary indiscretion and intolerance (including spoiled foods, foreign matter, too much fat, and overeating). More serious causes can be infectious agents, intestinal parasites, drugs and toxins, hemorrhagic gastroenteritis, and liver and pancreatic diseases. Your veterinarian can help to determine the underlying causes. If there is no obvious cause and no emergency, before you subject your hound to needless or expensive diagnostic tests, insist that your vet try de-worming with Droncit or Panacur first, even if your hound's fecal exam was negative. Even if he's been de-wormed, if Panacur and Droncit weren't used, try these before you do other testing. This extra step won't harm your hound, but it may keep him from intrusive tests or unnecessary exploratory surgery. If the Panacur and Droncit are effective, be sure to de-worm again in three weeks and still again in three months.

Initial treatment of mild diarrhea, regardless of cause, is the same. Use Imodium A-D after the first loose bowel movement or as directed by your veterinarian. Don't let your hound have any food for at least 24 hours. Then gradually introduce a bland diet that consists primarily of carbohydrates and protein. Keep him from gulping water by adding ice cubes to the water in his dish. If he shows no improvement after the first 24 hours, contact your veterinarian.

If the diarrhea is particularly bad and you're worried about dehydration before you can get to the vet, use the electrolyte replacements available for children. Either freeze Pedialyte into cubes or buy the freezable version. Simply add this to the water in his dish or use it as a substitute for his water. Avoid fats and lactose (found in milk products). Diarrhea usually resolves itself after three to five days. You can then *gradually* reintroduce his regular diet over several days.

A quick way to check for dehydration is to *lightly* hold the skin over your hound's lumbar region (that's his lower back over his spine) between your thumb and forefinger, and pull up. The skin should return to its normal position in one to two seconds. If it takes longer for his skin to return to a normal position, chances are your hound is dehydrated. Dehydration requires prompt veterinary attention.

Age and malnutrition cause skin to lose its elasticity, so this test may not be reliable on geriatric or exceptionally skinny hounds. In that case, check the gums. If the animal is not drooling and the gums feel dry and sticky, that can also be an indicator of dehydration.

Vomiting

Vomiting results from many of the same causes as diarrhea. Veterinary attention is required if there is projectile vomiting or if the vomit contains blood.

My hound ate my homework!

Ingested string, pantyhose (don't laugh, it's been done), or similar items are dangerous for your hound. Don't make any attempt to remove the ends of these items from his mouth or anus.

Doing so may tear his intestines. Instead, call your veterinarian immediately. Endoscopes may be used to retrieve them if you act immediately. Otherwise, surgery will be necessary.

Feeding your hound a bland diet

¼ pound sautéed lean ground beef, fat drained

2 cups cooked white rice

1 hard-cooked egg, finely chopped

1 cup plain nonfat or low-fat yogurt or cottage cheese

Mix together all ingredients. The recipe yields about 2 pounds.

For a 40-pound dog, feed about 1½ pounds of the bland diet per day; for a 60-pound dog, feed about 2 pounds; for an 80-pound dog, feed about 2½ pounds; and for a 100-pound dog, feed about 3 pounds.

Feed in six to eight evenly divided doses every three to four hours. Greyhounds tend to eat their food quickly, so give your dog a tablespoon or two at a time.

Treatment for mild, occasional vomiting is similar to treatment for mild diarrhea, except your hound may not have food or water for the first eight to twelve hours and you reintroduce food a bit more gradually. After eight to twelve hours, offer him ice chips every two or three hours. Ice chips or cubes are even more important when your hound has been vomiting, because gulping quantities of water will almost certainly cause him to throw up again.

If the ice stays down, begin giving your hound Pedialyte. Use frozen Pedialyte cubes equal to about ½ cup every two or three hours. If he's still okay, begin to introduce a bland diet, like the one listed in the nearby sidebar. After the next 48 to 72 hours, you can begin to gradually reintroduce his regular food. If the vomiting recurs or doesn't stop when food and water is withheld, see your veterinarian immediately.

Fever

A persistent or recurring fever shouldn't be treated at home without first talking to your veterinarian. A sudden, high fever (104 degrees or higher) requires prompt medical attention. A dog's normal temperature is 100.2 degrees to 102.8 degrees.

Caring for Your Recovering Hound

We'd all like to believe that our needlenoses will be happy and healthy for their entire lives, but we know better. At some point, every one of us will have a hound who is recovering from an illness, an injury, or surgery. So in the following sections I guide you through some simple things you can do to make it easier on your hound.

Encourage him to eat and drink

If your retired racer has no dietary restrictions, you can do a number of things to make food taste better as he recovers. If these suggestions don't work or your hound is on a special diet, there are special products and medications that you can get from your veterinarian to help:

✔ **Moisten his food and improve the flavor of it.** Use a broth, all-meat baby food, yogurt, cottage cheese, hard-cooked egg, cooked chicken or liver, honey, and/or V8 100% Vegetable Juice to improve the taste of your dog's food and to moisten it.

✔ **Feed him small amounts of food by hand.** A hound who won't eat from his dish will often take bits of food from your hand or may take single bites of food dropped on the floor in front of him.

✔ **Warm the food to body temperature.** Warming your hound's food helps release the smells, which may make the food more appealing. Refrigerated foods should definitely be heated, because the coolness tends to take away some of the natural odor dogs love, but even dry food can benefit from a second or two in the microwave.

✔ **Substitute apple juice, V8, Gatorade, or chicken or beef broth for water.** Try ice cubes or ice chips made of these ingredients if your dog won't drink them from her bowl.

Because a Greyhound who stops eating can become critically ill very quickly, you may have to force-feed your boy. Check with your vet to see if this is necessary and for suggestions on how to do it. *Never force-feed your Greyhound without consulting your vet, and never force-feed a dog who is vomiting.*

Lend a hand

Pay close attention to your hound's vital signs, behavior, eating, and elimination patterns during convalescence. Watch for adverse reactions that may be caused by medications. If he has diarrhea or is vomiting, confine him to a small, enclosed area that is easy to clean.

Because of their thin skin and bony bodies, Greyhounds are especially prone to bed sores. So if your retired racer is unable to move about, get medical grade, egg-crate foam for the bedding or try the Comfy Bed I tell you about in Chapter 15. Turn your hound every few hours. Keep the bedding dry. You may need to have more than one bed so you can do this. Any contact your hound's skin has with urine, feces, or moisture will almost guarantee bed sores.

If your boy is unable to walk without assistance, use a strong scarf or a towel to help him. But only try this if you're strong enough to help without injuring yourself. Simply wrap the towel around his belly and hold the ends up behind his back to give him some extra support while he walks.

For minor, fast-healing wounds, ask your vet for Banguard or a similar product to keep your hound from biting at sutures or wounds. Apply as directed. Don't use Bitter Apple — commonly used by dog owners to prevent their dogs from chewing furniture or other undesirable objects. It has alcohol in it and burns like crazy when applied to an open wound. Get a product specifically made for use on skin and wounds. And remember, most products in spray bottles contain alcohol and will cause a burning sensation.

To prevent your boy from biting at sutures or sores that may take more than a few days to heal, get a cervical-type collar from the vet or pet supply catalog. These collars work for most sites on your hound's body. You can also protect wounds or incisions by simply dressing your hound in an old, large undershirt, under shorts, or a pair of pajama bottoms that cover the affected area.

If your hound is scratching at something rather than biting, use thick toddler's socks to fashion booties and secure them in place with a self-adhesive wrap you can find in any pharmacy's first aid section. Ask your vet for a taste deterrent, to prevent your hound from trying to bite the booties. If your vet says it's okay, increase the padding/dressing over the wound to provide more protection.

Watching the amount of exercise your hound gets

Follow your vet's exercise recommendations *precisely.* Don't improvise just because your hound seems to be feeling better and wants to be more active. If he shows signs of fatigue, like excess panting or lying down, discontinue any activity and consult with your veterinarian. Depending on the type of injury or illness he has had, letting him overexert can do a lot of harm.

Tender-loving care

The last, but most important element in your dog's recovery is regular old-fashioned TLC. Just as people respond to love and reassurance when they are ill, injured, or stressed, so do retired racers. If possible, spend some time at home with him while he's recovering. What's a vacation day or two if it helps speed up your hound's recovery or allows you to better monitor his progress when he's still in shaky condition?

Helping the Aging Greyhound

Although you can't stop your hound from growing older, you can do more to understand what is happening to him as he ages. You can also make some adjustments that will maintain your retired racer's quality of life for as long as possible.

Recognizing the signs of aging

Aging is the gradual deterioration of various bodily and mental functions. Some signs of aging are decreased strength and flexibility, pain or stiffness, decreased tolerance of heat and cold, decreased immunity, increased suscep- tibility to some illnesses, decline in metabolic rate, and gradual deterioration of organ and system functions, including mental function. Just as some humans have a slowdown or even a breakdown in mental processes as they age, so do some dogs.

If you see changes in your retired racer's physical or mental state, talk to your vet. Don't wait until your boy's next checkup. Some changes may be part of the normal aging process. But that doesn't mean there's nothing that can be done to relieve pain in those achy old joints or boost a thyroid that isn't working as efficiently as it used to.

Most age-related changes occur slowly. If you notice any *sudden* changes, seek prompt veterinary attention.

You can help your friend through these years in many ways. Let him keep his favorite sleeping areas or accommodate him if he finds new ones. He may have difficulty getting up and down stairs and may no longer want to share your bed because it just hurts too much to get into it. Get him thicker bed- ding as he grows older. As he becomes intolerant of heat and cold, help him compensate. Get him a heavier coat for outdoor use. He may need a light sweater even inside if you live in a particularly cold climate. Consider getting a heated bed. As your needlenose ages, consider supplementing his diet with a high-quality vitamin and mineral supplement formulated especially for senior dogs.

Dealing with some common problems that come with aging

As your hound ages, he may encounter some common problems that you can help him through. Turn to the following sections for information on specific ailments that are common to aging dogs.

Arthritis

Talk to your veterinarian about some of the new medications available to treat arthritis. The results are often amazing. For most dogs, these medications have few side effects, but no medication is without risk. Talk with your veterinarian about the different alternatives you have for making your hound's life happier and more comfortable.

In addition to trying medication to treat arthritis, you can cover slippery floors with mats or nonskid carpets to make walking easier on your hound.

Keep his sleeping area warm, well padded, and free of drafts. Give him a light sweater for cold nights, and cover him in cold weather. Use a heating pad and massage to soothe achy bones. Keep his weight down and keep him moving with daily walks.

Incontinence

As dogs get older, some begin to lose bladder control and need more frequent trips outside. Some medications can help with incontinence, so consult your veterinarian to see what options you have.

If incontinence or other elimination problems occur, don't banish your hound from your living areas. Instead, use pads specifically designed for this purpose or baby crib pads on the floors and furniture. Use special doggie diapers if you have to, but keep him as involved as possible with the family. Build ramps to help him get to the backyard or fashion a large litter box on the deck or porch and train him to use it. Put in a dog door so he can get out when he needs to. Hire a pet sitter so he can get out more often if you can't be home to take him out.

If you have a hound with an incontinence problem and you still want to provide him with a heated bed, check out the new heated pads that don't require electricity. You'll avoid electrocuting your hound if he urinates while he's sleeping.

If he's incontinent, your retired racer may need more grooming to keep him feeling and smelling fresh. Check out the various waterless shampoos or try a dampened microfiber cloth and spend a little more time on grooming. Just like humans, our hounds feel better when they're clean and spruced up.

Hearing

If your Greyhound develops hearing problems, teach him hand signals so you can communicate. Buy some small beanbags to throw in his direction to get his attention if his back is turned. Or get a small laser pointer to carry with you so you can bounce a light off the wall or floor to get his attention (just be sure not to flash the light in his eyes, because that can cause damage to his vision). Take the time to teach your boy to respond to the light or beanbag and to keep his attention focused on you. A stomp on the floor will also work to get attention, because dogs can sense the vibrations.

Vision

If your Greyhound's vision is seriously impaired, keep all the furniture and his things in the same place so he won't get disoriented or injure himself. Dogs, even Greyhounds, don't rely on their sense of sight as heavily as we do. They can function quite reasonably with even badly diminished eyesight.

If you have to rearrange furniture or remodel or move, take your Greyhound on a tour of the new living arrangement, so he knows what to expect.

If your retired racer needs help, use a light scent that you reserve for this purpose to mark upright obstacles like doorways and table legs, so he isn't as likely to run into them. Use a different light scent on the floor several inches from stairs. Then teach him what those scents mean by leading him to the obstacle or hazard and touching his paw or nose to it. If his hearing is okay, wear a charm bracelet or a small bell attached to your wrist or belt so he can keep track of you.

Teach him cues like *oops* or *watch it* to warn him of stairs or obstacles. If he also has a hearing problem, use laser light cues or foot stomps to warn him of obstacles instead.

Behavior

As dogs age, their behavior may change in ways you wouldn't expect. For example, your retired racer may no longer remember what *sit* means. Or he may not recognize familiar faces. Some aging dogs begin to withdraw from family activities. These problems are referred to collectively as *cognitive dysfunction.* New medications are available that help with the mental confusion aging dogs may face, so talk with your veterinarian about your options.

Dogs thrive on structure and continuity. If you have a major lifestyle change, like a new spouse, a child going away to college, the death of a household member (including one of your furry friends), a schedule change because of a new job, or a move, you may see some behavioral changes in your hound. Never assume something has a behavioral cause rather than a physical cause without seeing your vet for a thorough checkup.

As your hound ages, he will sleep more soundly and may even seem confused when he wakens. Remember to call his name and let him gently awake from sleep.

As senses and body functions change, eating will become more and more the center of your needlenose's day, so let him enjoy it. Give him less food more often. Add bits of meat baby food to his kibble to make it more interesting.

One of the best ways to take care of your aging pal is to continue training and to keep the mental facilities challenged. Remember, training isn't about teaching your hound to sit, it's about interacting and communicating. Give him a reason to get up in the morning. Be patient, and the continuing mental challenge will pay off for your dog.

Knowing when it's time to say goodbye

When illness and infirmity can no longer be kept at bay, love your retired racer enough to say goodbye. Dogs live in the present. They don't regret what used to be, and they don't understand that tomorrow may be better. Don't let your Greyhound suffer because you are unable to face an excruciating decision. Let him make the journey when you know there is no chance for better tomorrows and the present is filled with fear or suffering.

Choosing euthanasia and knowing what to expect

If you're uncertain about your decision to go through with euthanasia, ask to speak with your veterinarian. He may be able to help you determine whether you're making the right choice. He can also reassure you if you're certain it's the right time but are having trouble going through with it. Your veterinarian may want to see your hound before he schedules the euthanasia. You can also discuss any special arrangements you want to make for your hound's body, such as burial in a pet cemetery or being present at his cremation.

When you and your family have made the difficult decision to free your hound of pain and suffering, schedule an appointment. Be sure the receptionist knows what your appointment is for so it can be scheduled in a way that allows you whatever time you need to be alone with your hound. The last appointment of the day may be the best, so you have the time you need. Just be sure to do what feels right for you.

Before you leave for the clinic with your retired racer, call to see whether they're running on schedule, so you don't have a long wait.

Some veterinarians will come to your home if you prefer. If you want your retired racer to die at home and your vet can't comply, many areas now have mobile vet clinics. Explore those options if they feel right.

Many dogs are very stressed by trips to the vet. If you're dealing with an illness that is likely to end in euthanasia, you can ask your vet in advance to give you a sedative to give to your hound before you take him to the clinic. She'll tell you how to administer the medication so it will take effect at the proper time.

On your trip to the veterinarian's office, get someone else to do the driving. When you arrive, let the receptionist know you are there. You may have paperwork to complete. You can arrange to take your hound for burial or have the receptionist make arrangements for a private or communal cremation or burial in a pet cemetery. You may prefer to wait in the car with your hound until the veterinarian is ready for you. Ask that someone come for you when the vet is ready. This may help ease your hound's stress. You shouldn't have to wait alone in the exam room for more than a couple of minutes before the vet arrives.

Understanding cremation

You can make cremation arrangements for your hound's remains even if he dies at home and isn't euthanized. Call your veterinarian's office and make arrangements They'll explain the procedures.

Charges for cremation are based on your hound's weight, whether his remains are cremated communally (with other animals) or privately, and the kind of container in which you wish to have his remains returned. If you choose private cremation, your hound's remains will be returned to you in a few weeks, sealed in an attractive container.

When it comes time to say the final goodbye, be at your hound's side. Hold him and calm him, if you can. You owe him that. After all, he trusts you and needs you in his final moments. Being with your hound until the very end is incredibly difficult, and many people can't handle it emotionally. But if you view your retired racer as a member of your family, try to be with him just as you would any other family member.

The euthanasia process takes only seconds. The vet administers a special solution directly into one of your hound's veins. Your boy will take a deep breath and then fade into unconsciousness within seconds of when the drug is administered. He may take several more deep breaths and there may be some unconscious movement.

Your veterinarian should let you spend whatever time you need with your hound after he has died.

Many pet owners keep a collar or ask for a bit of fur as a remembrance. Others may ask that a photo, poem, or other special item like a favorite blanket be cremated with their pet. Do whatever feels right to you. This is your special friend.

Know that you performed the kindest possible act. Then take the time to grieve and to mourn the lose of your friend.

Grieving

Most people cry — but there is nothing wrong with not crying. Grieve in whatever way is right for *you*. And grieve for as long as you need to. No one can tell you how much grief is appropriate or how long the mourning period should be.

Feeling grief when you lose your beloved friend isn't ridiculous — it's normal. Just because that friend had fur, doesn't make him any less important or valuable in your life.

Sometimes mourning the loss of your pet is more difficult, because friends and families don't understand your attachment to your retired racer. If you don't have a supportive family or social circle, or if you need more help than they can give, find a support group or call a pet loss hotline. Don't be embarrassed.

If you have access to the Internet, try taking part in the grief support chat for Greyhound owners that takes place every month at *A Breed Apart,* a Web site for Greyhound owners. Just go to www.abap.org. Or ask your veterinarian for the name of a local organization you can join for support.

Part V
The Part of Tens

The 5th Wave   By Rich Tennant

Canine SAT exam

HIGH FREQUENCY WORD LIST

STAY!
SIT!
BAD!
DOWN!
FETCH!
OBSEQUIOUS!
SHUTUP!

In this part . . .

This is the place to turn if you want a lot of information but only have a few minutes to spare. Here you can find reasons to adopt a retired racer, ways to prepare your home for your new friend's arrival, tips on training, and suggestions for ways to have fun with your hound.

Chapter 17

Ten Reasons to Adopt a Retired Racer

. . . .

In This Chapter

▶ Dispelling some common myths about retired racing Greyhounds

▶ Looking at some unique benefits Greyhounds have to offer

. . . .

I can give you almost 25,000 reasons to adopt a retired racer. That's the estimated number of retired racers who were available for adoption each of the last three years (based on calculations from the National Greyhound Association and the American Greyhound Council). Only 18,000 retired racers are being adopted annually, which means that more than 7,000 Greyhounds are still needlessly being put to death every year.

But, just because I can't think of any reasons *not* to adopt a retired racer, doesn't mean they're the right dogs for *you* and your lifestyle. Do your research carefully before you make a retired racer — or any dog — a part of your life.

You Know What You're Getting When You Adopt an Adult Dog

Regardless of breed, adult dogs make good adoption choices. You can easily put your common sense aside when you look at a cute little puppy and make choices only from your heart. But many people who get a dog because they couldn't resist that cute puppy face live to regret it, because they don't realize what they're in for. Looking at an 80-pound dog is good reality therapy.

When you adopt an adult dog, you get to see the adult personality and temperament. The personality and temperament a dog has as an adult is often very different than what you would have seen in the same dog as a puppy. You also get to see the physical characteristics of a full-grown dog. You know exactly what size the dog is going to be — and that can make it easier to make a good choice.

Plus, aside from getting a great companion, you just plain feel good about adopting a grown dog whose fate is otherwise uncertain at best.

Adult Dogs Involve Less Work Than Puppies Do

As cute as puppies are, they are a *lot* of work. Aside from having to be house-trained, puppies teethe, chew, and need much more exercise and attention than adult dogs. And the work doesn't last for just a few weeks. Many breeds have the characteristics of puppies until they are well over two years old.

All dogs require a commitment of time, exercise, attention, and affection. Retired racers are no exception. If you can't or won't provide that, be honest with yourself and don't adopt a dog of any age or breed. You'll be doing yourself, and the dog, a huge favor.

Retired Racers Are Great Housemates

Retired racers are low-maintenance. They require minimal grooming; their exercise needs are low to moderate for a dog of their size; and they're compliant, with a personality that helps them adapt quickly to a new lifestyle. Most Greyhounds are naturally laid-back, well mannered, and sensitive. Plus, they're intelligent and respond well to the right training methods. Sounds like a great housemate to me!

Retired Racers Adapt to a Variety of Lifestyles

A retired racer isn't perfect for every family, but he can fit perfectly into almost any lifestyle, as long as you take the time to pick the right retired racer and teach him what he needs to know to be a valued family member. Retired racers are adaptable and do well in loving homes with families who understand their needs. They deserve no less.

Greyhounds do best in a relaxed environment, so homes with lots of rambunctious children or harsh, loud adults aren't ideal. They are sensitive dogs, so heavy-handed owners and training methods are totally inappropriate for Greyhounds.

Greyhounds adjust to many climates, but their light coats, fragile skin, lack of body fat, and sensitivity to extremes of heat and cold make them totally unsuited to living outdoors.

Greyhounds Are Gentle and Quiet

One of the misconceptions about retired racers is that they are aggressive dogs. But most people have only seen photos of Greyhounds racing, with muzzles covering their faces. The muzzles are used to help protect the racers from injury and to determine the winners of close races. Outside of the racetrack, however, Greyhounds are usually quiet, gentle, docile, and compliant. (If you're looking for a watchdog, choose another breed.) They blend well into families with well-mannered children. Most Greyhounds love the company of other dogs, and many live happily with cats as well. Some Greyhounds adapt well to homes with very small animals.

Some retired racers will never be safe with cats, small animals, or even toy breeds of dogs. Work with the adoption group or racetrack kennel to find a retired racer that is right for your family environment.

Greyhounds Don't Need Much Exercise

Another myth about Greyhounds is that, because they're bred to race, they need lots of room to run and constant exercise. But Greyhounds aren't marathon runners; they're sprinters. At the track, they only race once or twice a week. In homes, however, they romp for short bursts and then turn back into couch potatoes. Although daily access to a fenced yard is best, a daily walk or two and a chance to run in a fenced yard or field from time to time are sufficient.

Greyhounds Are Very Clean

The coat of Greyhounds is so light and short that grooming is a breeze. Many Greyhounds groom and clean themselves much like cats do. They also don't have oily coats, so they aren't as prone to doggy odor as some breeds are.

Retired Racers Are Healthy

Retired racers are free of many of the inherited ailments that plague other breeds. For example, hip dysplasia is virtually unheard of among Greyhounds. Their average life expectancy is longer than that of most large breeds — 12 years or more.

But because the bones in Greyhounds' legs are long and thin, they are more prone to breaks. So are those long, skinny tails. Greyhounds' skin is fragile and can tear easily, so almost all Greyhounds will need stitches at some time in their lives. And like all sighthounds, Greyhounds are sensitive to certain kinds of drugs and chemicals.

You Can Find the Racer Right for You

With nearly 25,000 retired racing Greyhounds available each year, you can design your perfect dog. Know what color you want? You can find a Greyhound to match. Know what size you want, from 40 to 100 pounds? You can find a racer to fit your needs. Want a couch potato or a fishing buddy? No problem. Need a dog who can live happily in the city? You'll find him. Want a companion for your aging mother? There's one that'll fill the bill. Whatever you're looking for, somewhere there is a retired racer waiting to race into your life and into your heart.

Greyhounds Are Fun

Many adoption groups have an annual reunion picnic and sell the obligatory event T-shirt. Our group's T-shirt from last year's reunion picnic said it all: "Life with a Greyhound is one big picnic." And that's why most of us have more than one.

Chapter 18

Ten Things to Do Before You Bring Home a Retired Racer

In This Chapter

▶ Doing your homework to determine whether a retired racer is right for you

▶ Preparing your children or other pets for the arrival of their new housemate

▶ Getting ready to welcome your Greyhound into your home with open arms

*A*dding a retired racer to your life is easier if you plan carefully and prepare in advance. Your first job is to decide if a retired racer is the right dog for you and your family.

Do Your Homework

Talk to adoption group representatives, not just Greyhound owners. People who own and love retired racers love their dogs, and in their enthusiasm they sometimes forget that what *they* think is the perfect dog may not be perfect for *you*. Because most adoption representatives have heard the hundreds of lame excuses people give for returning an adopted dog, they know which questions to ask you so that you make the best choice. And that choice may *not* be a retired racer.

Evaluate Your Lifestyle

Take a close look at yourself, your personality, and your lifestyle, and decide whether you're capable of being a loving and responsible adopter. Some things to consider are the financial costs, your family structure, other pets you may have, and your other time and life commitments.

Decide What You Need and Want

If you believe you can give a retired racer a great new life, decide what kind of dog will best fit your lifestyle. Decide what's most important to you. Distinguish between what you want and what you need in a new best friend. What kind of personality will make the best fit? What size or energy level is best? Is gender important? Can you open your heart to one of the many senior retired racers who need loving homes?

Train Your Other Pets Before Your Greyhound Arrives

If you have other pets, now is the time to help them prepare for the new arrival. If your pets have any behavior problems, get them under control before your retired racer arrives.

Teach Your Children How to Behave around Your New Dog

If you have children, or if children are frequent visitors in your home, you have a responsibility to keep them safe. Most children have never been taught to interact properly with a dog. They haven't learned how to greet a dog or how to play with a dog properly. The time you spend on this before your retired racer arrives is critical to the well-being of your children and your new dog. Plan to separate the children from the dog when you can't supervise all their interactions.

Find the Right Retired Racer for You

Nearly 250 adoption groups exist in the United States and Canada, and most racetracks have adoption programs. So finding a retired racer has never been easier. You can go directly to the racetrack and choose your own dog or work with an adoption group that allows you come to their kennel and pick a dog. However, if you aren't an experienced dog owner, your best choice may be an adoption group or track kennel that helps you find the right dog based on your needs and lifestyle.

Take time to understand exactly what services the adoption program provides and what is or is not included in the fee.

Dog-Proof Your Home

If you don't have other pets or young children, your home and yard may be full of hidden dangers. Try to think like a dog who has no experience in a house. Look at the world from his level. You'll be amazed at all the things that are waiting to be explored. Like small children, dogs explore their worlds with their mouths. Manage the environment to keep your new dog safe.

Think about where you want your Greyhound to sleep. Decide where he'll eat and where you want him to eliminate. If your yard is home to dangerous plants, get rid of them or fence off part of the yard so your retired racer can't access it.

Plan to Keep Your Small Pets Safe When Your Greyhound Arrives

Think about how you will keep any small pets, such as cats, safe when the new addition arrives. How can you keep your cat separated from your Greyhound when you aren't there to supervise?

Think about where your cat's litter box is going to be and how you'll keep your Greyhound away from it. If you haven't had a dog *and* a cat before, your dog's interest in the litter box may come as an unpleasant surprise.

Purchase the Essentials in Advance

Be prepared for your Greyhound's arrival. Transitions are smoother when they are well planned. Most adoption groups provide a leash and a special collar for every retired racer they place in a new home. If your dog won't have those items, get advice on where to purchase them. Prepare an identification tag in advance so you can put it on your retired racer before you bring him home.

In addition to the obvious things like dishes and a large, soft bed, you'll need some other items, like baby gates, a crate, or an exercise pen, to help you create a safe environment. Use these management tools to keep your Greyhound out of trouble and away from harm while you teach him what is expected of him.

Include some toys and safe chew items in your preliminary purchases. For supervised play, choose furry squeaky toys. Most Greyhounds love them. Safe chew toys include Kongs, which can be stuffed with goodies, and fruit Nylabones.

Prepare Your Mind for the Arrival

Learn the basics of training and behavior before your retired racer walks in the door. Think about what words you'll use in your training as verbal cues. Decide which behaviors are important to you and decide in advance which behaviors are and are not acceptable. Will your Greyhound be allowed on the furniture? Will certain areas of the house or yard be off-limits? What are the rules going to be? Discuss these issues with your whole family and agree on what is and isn't allowed.

Decide who will take responsibility for chores like training, feeding, walking, and yard cleanup.

Your new friend will be confused about this new world. Make his transition easier by learning how dogs communicate and teaching him what is expected in a clear and gentle way. Take time to understand the world he's coming from and how that may affect his behavior. Figure out how you can help him make the adjustment from life at the racetrack to life in your living room.

Chapter 19

Ten Rules for Training a Retired Racer

In This Chapter
▶ Gaining the skills to train your retired racer effectively
▶ Remembering what works and what doesn't when it comes to training
▶ Building a good relationship with your retired racer through positive learning experiences

Training your retired racer will help him live more comfortably and happily in your home. In this chapter, I give you ten simple rules to follow when training your hound.

Know How to Speak Greyhound

Take the time to learn how retired racers think and how they respond. The more you understand about the breed and how his previous life affects his present behavior, the better you'll be at interpreting what he's trying to tell you.

Your Greyhound's racing life exposed him to lots of people and lots of other Greyhounds, but he has no experience with the new world you've adopted him into. As a rule, Greyhounds are suspicious of things they've never seen before. And very little in your Greyhound's new life is like what he has seen before. Take that into account when you take him somewhere new or train him in anything but a familiar place. Always make new experiences positive.

Although other dogs get hyper and noisy and flit from place to place when they're stressed, Greyhounds tend to turn into statues. When they're in this mode, they aren't learning, so back off and let them decide when it's safe to continue.

Greyhounds have incredibly quick reaction times and tend to startle easily. When they're startled or frightened, they tend to bolt. And their body type makes backing out of a collar very easy. When they're in that flight mode, they can be in the next county before they stop running. So using a properly fitted special Greyhound collar and sturdy leash are essential anytime you're outdoors. Fenced yards and secure areas are necessary for any off-leash activities or training.

Remember That You're Teaching Your Greyhound Even When You Don't Realize It

Learning happens every moment your retired racer is alive. He learns whether you teach or not. He learns from everything that happens to him. Because every interaction with you is a learning experience, whether you intend it to be or not, try to take advantage of it.

How your Greyhound responds is related to his training and his history. If your Greyhound continues to do something you don't want him to do, figure out how this negative behavior is being rewarded. If you want him to repeat something good, figure out how to reward that instead.

Build a Winning Relationship

Even if you don't care if your Greyhound ever sits, don't shortchange him by thinking that training is strictly about manners and obedience. Training is really about building a good relationship and having good communication. So train your Greyhound early and often to build that relationship and open those lines of communication.

Greyhounds are sensitive to your moods and actions. Your retired racer will get stressed if he thinks you're upset. And harshness is almost guaranteed to offend him. If he doesn't like what's happening or if he's had enough, he'll shut down and go into statue mode.

Although some breeds are very forgiving of events that frighten them, retired racers can take a long time to forgive and forget. Bad memories can last a long time. Try to avoid situations that are likely to scare him.

Set Him Up to Win

While your Greyhound is learning new manners, manage his world so he can't get into trouble. Use gates, leashes, and crates to keep him out of trouble. Keep appealing but forbidden items out or reach or out of sight. Reward the behaviors you want from him, and use management to keep him from the behaviors you don't want. If it's safe to do so, ignore the behaviors you don't want. Management, not punishment, is the key.

Catch Him Doing Something Right

People are too accustomed to finding mistakes and correcting them. Most of us barely notice our hound if he's being quiet or chewing on a bone instead of a slipper. But we sure let him know about it if we catch him raiding the trash or chewing a sneaker. Train your Greyhound to do lots of behaviors that you can reward him for. Pay attention to him so you can catch him doing something right, and reward that good behavior.

Know That There Are No Magic Wands in Training

Don't be fooled by trainers who do infomercials or make celebrity appearances on late-night TV. No ten-minute cures exist for dogs with behavior problems. Training isn't a six-second sound bite. It's a process.

Reliability is a direct function of your relationship with your retired racer and your commitment to training, combined with your dog's inherent temperament and character. If your hound isn't doing it right, you didn't train him right. If he continues to do something bad, it's because whatever reward he's getting from the bad behavior is more effective than whatever you're doing to reward him for being good.

Make It Fun

Draw on your dog's natural abilities and interests. Try to find ways to incorporate his love of running, his need to chase, and his response to prey-like noises into your training. Be creative. Act silly. Make watching you more fun than anything else going on around him.

Use the things your Greyhound wants as rewards. If he wants to chase a butterfly, ask for a sit, then release him to chase it as long as it's safe for him to do so. Pay attention to the things that are most interesting and important to him. Think of ways you can use these things or provide access to them as rewards. Turn life into a reward for the behaviors you want instead of something he has to escape from you in order to get.

Keep It Simple

Break everything into small pieces. If your Greyhound is not doing it right, chances are you're moving too fast or trying to teach too much at once. Even the simplest behaviors have multiple parts or actions. The more complex the behavior, the more important it is to break it into small pieces and teach each piece separately. When you make one part of a behavior more difficult, you have to make the other parts easier.

Keep It Short

Greyhounds do not like lots of repetition. After three or four times of doing the same exercise, you'll start to see your Greyhound's attention stray and his eyes glaze over. If he's doing something correctly, just do it once or twice, and then move on. If he isn't doing it correctly, back up to something simpler so he can win. Then quit or move on to something different.

Keep your training session short. A few minutes a day is all you need to teach simple good manners. Incorporate training into your daily routine. Work on behaviors for a few seconds before you feed him or before you open the door to take him for a walk. Mix things up so he isn't doing the same thing several times in a row. Train at different times and in lots of different places so he never knows what to expect.

Even gentle learning is stressful. Learn to recognize the subtle signs that your retired racer is stressed, and stop before he gets to that point.

Keep It Sweet

Corrections have no place in training new behaviors. Being a bully doesn't do anything to build trust in your relationship. And training is all about having a good relationship.

Rewards — and plenty of them — are key to successfully training a retired racer. But rewards shouldn't be bribes. If you bribe your hound to respond, he'll never have reason to respect your leadership.

Make your rewards memorable, and keep him guessing about what you'll do next. Be creative. Be unpredictable. And always leave him wanting more.

Chapter 20

Ten Fun Things to Do with Your Hound

In This Chapter

▷ Exploring new ways to have fun with your Greyhound

▷ Finding ways to help your Greyhound help others

▷ Expanding your fun by adopting more than one

*P*art of the reason owning a retired racer is so wonderful is the fact that they're a lot of fun to have around. And making your Greyhound's life fun is one of the ways you can help him adjust to his new life beyond the racetrack. Check out some of the suggestions in this chapter for ways to have fun with your hound.

For more fun activities and tips for enjoying life with your hound, check out the Lifestyle section and links at my Web site at www.retiredracinggreyhounds.com.

Train Your Retired Racer

If you do it right, training should be fun for both you and your dog. It gives you a way to communicate, because he learns more words and signals. And the more he understands you, the better your relationship will be.

Go Lure Coursing

Lure coursing is an incredibly beautiful thing to watch, and it's as close as anything you can do with your hound that corresponds with what he's been bred to do for thousands of years. In lure coursing, a pair of sighthounds of the same breed compete to see who is fastest and most agile. They chase a lure, usually a white plastic bag, along a prescribed course to a finish line. It's a rigorous sport for dogs who are in excellent condition and have no history of injuries. Watching the amazing transformation of these gentle dogs from mellow companion to keen predator in response to the sight and the sound of the lure is a tremendous learning experience. It's also a great reminder that within that velvet exterior is a core of iron.

Work on Agility

Working on agility isn't just about teaching our dogs to walk on planks or run through tunnels or jump over hurdles. It's also about teaching him body awareness, balance, coordination, self-confidence, and socialization. Agility work is also a great way to burn off energy and help your dog stay in shape — especially if you don't have a fenced-in yard for him to run in. Best of all, agility is truly about teamwork and is a great way to bond with your dog.

Attend Meet-and-Greets

Chances are, you met your first retired racer at a *meet-and-greet,* one of the many public get-togethers at malls, parades, and pet supply stores. A meet-and-greet is an informal way to educate the public about Greyhounds and the need that retired racers have for good homes. It's also a great opportunity to give your retired racer some time with other Greyhounds — an activity they always love.

Teach Your Dog Tricks

No, tricks aren't silly or undignified. Dogs have brains and they need to use them. Many of us get way too serious and demanding about training. Working on tricks is a great way to help him learn and to have fun together while *you* learn how to train. Teaching your Greyhound tricks is great preparation for training the important stuff. Who cares if you mess up teaching him to do a bow or offer a paw?

Give Your Greyhound a Job

You can't send your Greyhound off to chase down rabbits for dinner, so you need to help him find a job. He needs a reason to get up in the morning just like you do. Many behavior problems I see are a result of what I can only call boredom. If your dog can't do what he was genetically programmed to do, find alternatives that put that brain to work. Believe me, if you don't find a job for him, chances are you won't like the ones he makes up on his own if he gets bored.

Teach your dog games that let him use his keen sense of smell. Just because he's a sighthound doesn't mean he can't smell. He may not have the sense of smell that a beagle has, but he still can have fun using his nose.

Get involved in dog-related sports or activities. Look for resources on games and activities you can do that help keep your dog's mind busy.

Take Your Hound on the Road

Traveling with pets is getting easier. If your Greyhound enjoys travel, take him with you whenever it is safe to do so. The more interesting places your dog visits, and the more pleasant and diverse people your dog meets, the more well-adjusted, happy, and confident he'll be.

When you take your dog out, be a responsible caretaker. Obey all the pet rules wherever you stop or stay. Take the time to train basic good manners so he's welcome wherever you go. And most important, *always* clean up after your dog. You wouldn't think of discarding a used baby diaper on someone's property would you?

Sample Other Canine Sports

Flyball is a great sport for a higher-energy, confident dog. In this sport, relay teams of dogs race each other to retrieve a ball and return with it.

Freestyle is Arthur Murray for dogs and their people. It's great exercise for both of you and requires a tremendous amount of teamwork.

Obedience competition is another sport. For too many years, most dog trainers and even most Greyhound adopters thought that Greyhounds were too dumb or untrainable to participate in competition obedience. Only a few brave souls out there were even willing to give it a try. As gentler methods of training more suited to the Greyhound character evolved, more people saw what these dogs are capable of.

Get Some Therapy

Another job for which retired racers are well-suited is that of therapy dog. Almost any well-mannered dog can get involved in therapy work in some form. Greyhounds are so well-suited to this activity that many adoption groups have their own therapy programs.

Greyhounds are an ideal size, because people in wheelchairs (see Figure 20-1) or with mobility problems don't have to bend to pet them. And they are gentle enough that even people who are afraid of dogs often look forward to visits from a retired racer. Many long-term-care facilities welcome visits from retired racers. In fact, some have even adopted their own retired racers to live in the facility.

Watching a face light up when your dog approaches is as therapeutic for you and your dog as it is for the folks you're visiting.

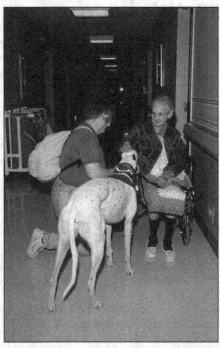

Figure 20-1: Greyhound visits are a great therapy for elderly people or people with mobility problems.

Photograph courtesy of Close Encounters of the Furry Kind

Get Your Dog a Buddy

Ask almost any adopter of a retired racer and he'll tell you that two Greyhounds are better than one. Racers spend their lives in the company of other Greyhounds and seem to genuinely enjoy the company of other dogs — particularly other Greyhounds. Those of us who have more than one Greyhound can't ever imagine life with only one. Although having more than one dog is more work, more costly, and brings with it more responsibility, it's also a lot of fun for you and your dogs.

Appendix A

The NGA Pet Certificate

*I*f you'd like to become your hound's *registered* owner, you can obtain a pet certificate from the National Greyhound Association (NGA). The benefits of registering your dog with the NGA include having a solid way to prove your ownership of your dog if he is ever lost or separated from you. Plus, your registration certificate includes a two-generation pedigree (see Figure A-1) and the Bertillon Card (see Figure A-2), providing a detailed description of your dog. For an additional $15, you can get a five-generation pedigree for your dog.

If you're interested in obtaining a pet certificate from the NGA, you can write to the organization at the following address: National Greyhound Association, P.O. Box 543, Abilene, Kansas 67410. They'll provide you with more details on the registration process. Or you can also check out the NGA Web site at nga.jc.net/ngatop.htm and request the pet transfer form via e-mail.

You'll need your Greyhound's racing name (if you have it), and the tattoos from your Greyhound's right and left ear. If his tattoos are difficult to read, let them know which numbers you can't read, and they'll try to identify the existing owner. The NGA will send you a blue pet-transfer form (which includes the name and address of the registered owner) that you'll then need to have the owner sign. After you get the owner's signature, you return the signed form to the NGA.

Send the blue pet-transfer form to the owner by registered mail. Most owners are cooperative, and many are delighted to hear that one of their dogs has been placed in a good home. Take the time to write a few words about what a great pal you've adopted and send a photo if you'd like. Tell the registered owner how much you appreciate his willingness to make the dog available for adoption. Don't forget to include a self-addressed stamped envelope in which the registered owner can return the pet-transfer form to you. Make this process as easy as possible for the owner, so that you've done everything you can to ensure that he'll cooperate.

TIP

If you haven't heard from the registered owner within four to six weeks, send him a short note as a reminder. Follow this in another week with a phone call if you have a phone number — but only call once. You can't do much if the registered owner isn't willing to respond. Being a pest won't help. Just hug your hound and be grateful you have him. Don't worry about the paperwork, and don't be worried because you didn't get a response.

Some adopters worry that if they contact the registered owner, the owner may want the dog returned. I know of no instances in which this has happened. In truth, some adoption groups do sometimes take dogs under questionable circumstances and may not want you to make contact with the registered owner. If you have any question about the nature of the adoption, check with the adoption group before you proceed.

Figure A-1:
The front of an NGA pet certificate.

Certificate of Registration
of Retired Racing Greyhound
NATIONAL GREYHOUND ASSOCIATION

Abilene, Kansas

I hereby Certify the Greyhound

TOTAL EXPORT   CHACO
                  also known as (pet name)
color BD.   sex M   whelped 07/13/1994

has been registered to

BENJAMIN C. & LEE C. LIVINGOOD

as a retired racing Greyhound.

Pedigree

Sire:		Dam:	
DUTCH DUGAN	DUTCH BAHAMA	I'M HAPPY NOW	HB'S COMMANDER
	GH'S FULL O PEP		ARCADE BUCK

Gary Guccione   04/21/99

Gary Guccione, Secretary-Treasurer, National Greyhound Association   Date
Above Greyhound is certified with the NGA as a retired Greyhound and cannot be used for breeding or pari-mutuel racing purposes.

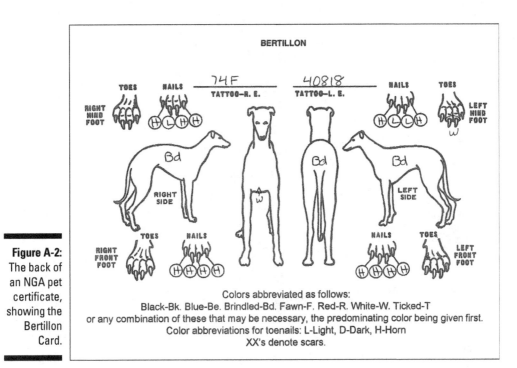

Figure A-2:
The back of
an NGA pet
certificate,
showing the
Bertillon
Card.

Appendix B

Resources

Greyhound Information and Supplies

In this section, I provide resources so that you can find an adoption group or kennel near you, places to go to find supplies for your dog, and where to learn more about retired racers.

If you want to learn more about retired racing Greyhounds, adoption, or life with a retired racer, start by checking out these resources:

- ✔ *A Breed Apart.* To read this online magazine and gain additional information, check it out at www.abap.org.

- ✔ *Celebrating Greyhounds: The Magazine.* A magazine published by The Greyhound Project, Inc., *Celebrating Greyhounds* is a great resource for information on Greyhounds. Check it out online at www.adopt-a-greyhound.org/treats/body_books-per-cgmag.html. Or to subscribe to the magazine, write to The Greyhound Project, Inc., P.O. Box 173, Holbrook, Massachusetts 02343.

- ✔ **The Greyhound-L.** This great e-mail and Web site whose purpose is to provide support to adopters and adoption groups. Web site: www.greyhoundlist.org.

- ✔ *Sighthound Review.* This magazine deals with issues related to all aspects of sighthound ownership and activities. For subscription information, visit them online at www.sighthoundreview.com, or call 785-485-2992.

If you're ready to adopt, contact any of the following three organizations to get a referral to an adoption group or breed rescue group near you:

- ✔ **The Greyhound Club of America.** This site has lots of good breed information. The club can help you find a good breeder if you have your heart set on a puppy or can point you to a rescue coordinator if you are interested in adopting an AKC Greyhound. Web site: www.greyhoundclubofamerica.org.

- **Greyhound Pets of America.** Greyhound Pets of America is a nation-wide, volunteer organization dedicated to Greyhound adoption. If you contact them, they will put you in touch with their local chapter. That chapter may not be the closest one to you. Telephone: 800-366-1472; Web site: www.greyhoundpets.org.

- **The Greyhound Project.** The Greyhound Project is a volunteer, non-profit organization dedicated to providing information about retired racing Greyhounds. They have the most complete and up-to-date listing of adoption groups available. They are not affiliated with any adoption program or organization. Telephone: 617-333-4982 or 617-527-8843; Web site: www.adopt-a-Greyhound.org.

Turn to the following Web sites if you want to know more about the racing industry.

- **American Greyhound Track Operators Association,** www.agtoa.com. Visit this site for links to racetrack kennel adoptions.

- **The National Greyhound Association,** nga.jc.net. Visit this great site for information on Greyhounds, as well as instructions for obtaining the NGA pet certificate, turnout muzzles and other supplies, and links to other Web sites.

Check out these sites for special Greyhound supplies:

- **Adopt-a-Greyhound of Central Canada, Inc.,** www.adopt-a-greyhound.com. Great source of supplies and gifts and they'll help you find a nearby adoption group.

- **The Berry Best Pet Bakery,** bbpetbakery.tripod.com (610-921-0537). A great selection of natural baked "cookies" and biscuits for your hound — including special treats for special diets. A portion of the proceeds go to Greyhound adoption.

- **Chinook and Company,** www.breakawaycollar.com (800-643-5109). Here's a way to keep ID on your hound and keep him safe from collar injuries or even death.

- **H & H Industries**, www.hh-industries.com (or call 877-266-3923). If you need a durable, waterproof, portable bed, check out the Comfy Bed.

- **Karen's Kollars,** www.halcyon.com/greyhounds. When you're looking for a really special collar for your hound, stop here.

- **Montana Dogware,** www.montanadogware.com (406-388-6593). Check out their great midweight coats with attached snoods.

- **Orvis,** www.orvis.com (or call toll-free at 800-541-3541). Visit this site to buy high-quality dog nest beds for your hound.

- **Personalized Greyhounds, Inc.,** www.pgreys.org. Surf over to this site for information on Greyhounds, supplies, and links to other Greyhound Web sites.

- ✔ **Premiere Pet Products,** www.gentleleader.com (800-933-5595). Contact them for the nearest source of the Gentle Leader headcollar and the Sure-fit Harness.

- ✔ **Running with the Big Dogs,** www.retiredracinggreyhounds.com. Check out my Web site for Greyhound resources and product reviews and tips on caring for and training your retired racer.

- ✔ **Silk Road Collars,** www.silkroadcollars.com (253-841-3005). If one kind of fancy collar isn't enough, check out this site.

- ✔ **Toastie Coats and Paws,** www.toastiecoats.com (914-361-3843). Look here for a wide selection of coats, booties, and other items just for hounds.

The following resources are also great if you're looking for dog supplies not often found in pet stores:

- ✔ **Direct Pet/Valley Vet,** www.valleyvet.com (800-360-4838).

- ✔ **Doctors Foster and Smith,** www.DrsFosterSmith.com (800-826-7206).

- ✔ **J&J Dog Supplies,** www.jandjdog.com (800-642-2050).

- ✔ **Jeffers Pet Catalog,** www.jefferspet.com (800-533-3377).

- ✔ **KV Vet Supply,** www.kvvet.com (800-423-8211).

- ✔ **New England Serum Company,** www.NESerum.com (888-637-3786).

- ✔ **UPCO,** www.UPCO.com (800-254-8726).

Training and Behavior

If you want to know more about dog training and behavior, you can turn to books, videos, Web sites, and e-mail lists. In the following sections, I list some of my favorites.

Books

Behavior Problems in Dogs, by William E. Campbell (BehavioRx Systems, 1999).

The Cautious Canine, by Patricia B. McConnell, Ph.D. (Dog's Best Friend, Ltd., 1998).

Clicker Training for Dogs, by Karen Pryor (Sunshine Books, 1999).

Clicker Training for Obedience, by Morgan Spector (Sunshine Books, 1999).

Dog Behavior: An Owner's Guide to a Happy Healthy Pet, by Dr. Ian Dunbar (IDG Books Worldwide, Inc., 1998).

Dogwise: The Natural Way to Train Your Dog, by John Fisher (Souvenir Press, Ltd., 1996).

Don't Shoot the Dog: The New Art of Teaching and Training, by Karen Pryor (Bantam Doubleday Dell, 1999).

Fun and Games with Dogs, by Roy Hunter (Howlin Moon Press, 1993).

How to Be the Leader of the Pack . . . and Have Your Dog Love You For It, by Patricia B. McConnell, Ph.D. (Dog's Best Friend, Ltd., 1996).

How to Teach a New Dog Old Tricks, by Dr. Ian Dunbar (James and Kenneth Publishers, 1998).

More Fun and Games with Dogs, by Roy Hunter (Howlin Moon Press, 1997).

Think Dog: An Owner's Guide to Canine Psychology, by John Fisher (Trafalgar Square, 1995).

The Toolbox for Remodeling Your Problem Dog, by Terry Ryan (IDG Books Worldwide, Inc., 1998).

Video

Click! & Treat Training Kit, 1.1, produced by Click and Treat Products (1995).

On Target, produced by Click and Treat Products (1996).

The Power of Positive Training (five-part video), produced by Positive Power Productions (1996).

Proof Positive (five-part video), produced by Positive Power Productions (1997).

Clicker Magic, produced by Sunshine Books (1997).

Take a Bow, Wow, produced by Metro Media Productions (1995).

Bow Wow Take 2, produced by Virginia Broitman (1997).

Web sites

4M Enterprises
(dog books)
www.4mdogbooks.com
800-847-9867

The Association of Pet Dog Trainers
(books and videos on training; references to pet trainers in your area)
www.apdt.com

Direct Book Service, Inc.
(books on training and behavior, training supplies, and a source for the
Gentle Leader)
800-776-2665
www.dogwise.com

Legacy By Mail
(books, videos, and supplies on training and behavior and fun activities)
legacy-by-mail.com

SitStay GoOut Store
(books and videos on training, training supplies, and a source for the Gentle
Leader and Sure-Fit harness)
www.sitstay.com

For information on clicker training, check out the following Web sites:

- **Click-1 E-mail list:** www.click-1.com
- **Gary Wilkes Click and Treat Training:** www.clickandtreat.com
- **Sunshine Books:** www.dontshootthedog.com

Health

The books and Web sites listed in this section are a great place to start when
looking for information on your dog's health. But remember to always consult
your veterinarian when it comes to health issues.

Books

Caring for Your Older Dog, by Chris C. Pinney (Barron's Educational
Series, 1995).

The Dog Owner's Home Veterinary Handbook, 3rd Edition, by James M. Giffen,
M.D. and Lisa D. Carlson, D.V.M. (IDG Books Worldwide, Inc.,1999).

Dr. Pitcairn's Complete Guide to Natural Health for Cats and Dogs, by Richard H
Pitcairn, D.V.M., Ph.D., and Susan Hubble Pitcairn (Rodale Press, 1995).

Old Dogs, Old Friends: Enjoying Your Older Dog, by Bonnie Wilcox, D.V.M., and
Chris Walkowicz (IDG Books Worldwide, Inc., 1991).

Peak Performance: Coaching the Canine Athlete, by M. Christine Zink, D.V.M., Ph.D. (Canine Sports Productions, 1998).

UC Davis School of Veterinary Medicine Book of Dogs: A Complete Medical Reference Guide for Dogs and Puppies, edited by Mordecai Siegal (HarperCollins, 1995).

Web sites

AltVetMed
(alternative medicine and links)
www.altvetmed.com

American Canine Sports Medicine Association
www.acsma.com

American Veterinary Medical Association
www.avma.org

NetVet Veterinary Resources and The Electronic Zoo
www.netvet.wustl.edu

Pet Loss/Grief
(pet loss links)
www.hsc.usc.edu/~rneville/losslink.html

Your Animal's Health
www.belfield.com/home.html

Activities

You can have lots of fun with your hound thanks to all the things you can see and do together. Or you can lend a helping hand or indulge in Greyhound crafts. Just check out the following resources.

AAA
(information on traveling with your pet)
Web site: www.aaa.com

American Dog Owners Association
(information on public issues and on safely traveling with dogs)
Telephone: 518-477-8469
Web site: www.adoa.org

American Humane Association
(information on animal welfare)
Telephone: 303-792-9900
Web site: www.americanhumane.org

American Kennel Club
(information on obedience, agility, and lure coursing)
Telephone: 919-233-9767
Web site: www.akc.org

American Sighthound Field Association
(information on lure coursing)
Web site: www.asfa.org

Delta Society
(information on therapy work and certification)
Telephone: 800-869-6898
Web site: petsforum.com/deltasociety/default.html

Dog-Play
(information on fun activities to do with your dog)
Web site: www.dog-play.com

Emergency Animal Rescue Service (EARS)
Telephone: 916-429-2457
Web site: www.uan.org/programs/ears/index.htm

Greyhound Manor
(Greyhound-related craft patterns)
Web site: www.greyhoundmanor.com

Pet Vacations
Web site: www.petvacations.com

petswelcome.com
Web site: www.petswelcome.com

Therapy Dogs International, Inc.
(therapy dog information)
Web site: www.tdi-dog.org

TravelDog
Web site: www.traveldog.com

United Kennel Club, Inc.
(information on obedience and agility)
Telephone: 616-343-9020
Web site: www.ukcdogs.com

Index

Notes

Notes

Notes

Notes

Notes

BUSINESS, CAREERS & PERSONAL FINANCE

0-7645-9847-3   0-7645-2431-3

Also available:
- Business Plans Kit For Dummies
  0-7645-9794-9
- Economics For Dummies
  0-7645-5726-2
- Grant Writing For Dummies
  0-7645-8416-2
- Home Buying For Dummies
  0-7645-5331-3
- Managing For Dummies
  0-7645-1771-6
- Marketing For Dummies
  0-7645-5600-2

- Personal Finance For Dummies
  0-7645-2590-5*
- Resumes For Dummies
  0-7645-5471-9
- Selling For Dummies
  0-7645-5363-1
- Six Sigma For Dummies
  0-7645-6798-5
- Small Business Kit For Dummies
  0-7645-5984-2
- Starting an eBay Business For Dummies
  0-7645-6924-4
- Your Dream Career For Dummies
  0-7645-9795-7

HOME & BUSINESS COMPUTER BASICS

0-470-05432-8   0-471-75421-8

Also available:
- Cleaning Windows Vista For Dummies
  0-471-78293-9
- Excel 2007 For Dummies
  0-470-03737-7
- Mac OS X Tiger For Dummies
  0-7645-7675-5
- MacBook For Dummies
  0-470-04859-X
- Macs For Dummies
  0-470-04849-2
- Office 2007 For Dummies
  0-470-00923-3

- Outlook 2007 For Dummies
  0-470-03830-6
- PCs For Dummies
  0-7645-8958-X
- Salesforce.com For Dummies
  0-470-04893-X
- Upgrading & Fixing Laptops For Dummies
  0-7645-8959-8
- Word 2007 For Dummies
  0-470-03658-3
- Quicken 2007 For Dummies
  0-470-04600-7

FOOD, HOME, GARDEN, HOBBIES, MUSIC & PETS

0-7645-8404-9   0-7645-9904-6

Also available:
- Candy Making For Dummies
  0-7645-9734-5
- Card Games For Dummies
  0-7645-9910-0
- Crocheting For Dummies
  0-7645-4151-X
- Dog Training For Dummies
  0-7645-8418-9
- Healthy Carb Cookbook For Dummies
  0-7645-8476-6
- Home Maintenance For Dummies
  0-7645-5215-5

- Horses For Dummies
  0-7645-9797-3
- Jewelry Making & Beading For Dummies
  0-7645-2571-9
- Orchids For Dummies
  0-7645-6759-4
- Puppies For Dummies
  0-7645-5255-4
- Rock Guitar For Dummies
  0-7645-5356-9
- Sewing For Dummies
  0-7645-6847-7
- Singing For Dummies
  0-7645-2475-5

INTERNET & DIGITAL MEDIA

0-470-04529-9   0-470-04894-8

Also available:
- Blogging For Dummies
  0-471-77084-1
- Digital Photography For Dummies
  0-7645-9802-3
- Digital Photography All-in-One Desk Reference For Dummies
  0-470-03743-1
- Digital SLR Cameras and Photography For Dummies
  0-7645-9803-1
- eBay Business All-in-One Desk Reference For Dummies
  0-7645-8438-3
- HDTV For Dummies
  0-470-09673-X

- Home Entertainment PCs For Dummies
  0-470-05523-5
- MySpace For Dummies
  0-470-09529-6
- Search Engine Optimization For Dummies
  0-471-97998-8
- Skype For Dummies
  0-470-04891-3
- The Internet For Dummies
  0-7645-8996-2
- Wiring Your Digital Home For Dummies
  0-471-91830-X

* Separate Canadian edition also available
† Separate U.K. edition also available

Available wherever books are sold. For more information or to order direct: U.S. customers visit www.dummies.com or call 1-877-762-2974.
U.K. customers visit www.wileyeurope.com or call 0800 243407. Canadian customers visit www.wiley.ca or call 1-800-567-4797.

SPORTS, FITNESS, PARENTING, RELIGION & SPIRITUALITY

0-471-76871-5

0-7645-7841-3

Also available:

- Catholicism For Dummies
  0-7645-5391-7
- Exercise Balls For Dummies
  0-7645-5623-1
- Fitness For Dummies
  0-7645-7851-0
- Football For Dummies
  0-7645-3936-1
- Judaism For Dummies
  0-7645-5299-6
- Potty Training For Dummies
  0-7645-5417-4
- Buddhism For Dummies
  0-7645-5359-3

- Pregnancy For Dummies
  0-7645-4483-7 †
- Ten Minute Tone-Ups For Dummies
  0-7645-7207-5
- NASCAR For Dummies
  0-7645-7681-X
- Religion For Dummies
  0-7645-5264-3
- Soccer For Dummies
  0-7645-5229-5
- Women in the Bible For Dummies
  0-7645-8475-8

TRAVEL

0-7645-7749-2

0-7645-6945-7

Also available:

- Alaska For Dummies
  0-7645-7746-8
- Cruise Vacations For Dummies
  0-7645-6941-4
- England For Dummies
  0-7645-4276-1
- Europe For Dummies
  0-7645-7529-5
- Germany For Dummies
  0-7645-7823-5
- Hawaii For Dummies
  0-7645-7402-7

- Italy For Dummies
  0-7645-7386-1
- Las Vegas For Dummies
  0-7645-7382-9
- London For Dummies
  0-7645-4277-X
- Paris For Dummies
  0-7645-7630-5
- RV Vacations For Dummies
  0-7645-4442-X
- Walt Disney World & Orlando
  For Dummies
  0-7645-9660-8

GRAPHICS, DESIGN & WEB DEVELOPMENT

0-7645-8815-X

0-7645-9571-7

Also available:

- 3D Game Animation For Dummies
  0-7645-8789-7
- AutoCAD 2006 For Dummies
  0-7645-8925-3
- Building a Web Site For Dummies
  0-7645-7144-3
- Creating Web Pages For Dummies
  0-470-08030-2
- Creating Web Pages All-in-One Desk
  Reference For Dummies
  0-7645-4345-8
- Dreamweaver 8 For Dummies
  0-7645-9649-7

- InDesign CS2 For Dummies
  0-7645-9572-5
- Macromedia Flash 8 For Dummies
  0-7645-9691-8
- Photoshop CS2 and Digital
  Photography For Dummies
  0-7645-9580-6
- Photoshop Elements 4 For Dummies
  0-471-77483-9
- Syndicating Web Sites with RSS Feeds
  For Dummies
  0-7645-8848-6
- Yahoo! SiteBuilder For Dummies
  0-7645-9800-7

NETWORKING, SECURITY, PROGRAMMING & DATABASES

0-7645-7728-X

0-471-74940-0

Also available:

- Access 2007 For Dummies
  0-470-04612-0
- ASP.NET 2 For Dummies
  0-7645-7907-X
- C# 2005 For Dummies
  0-7645-9704-3
- Hacking For Dummies
  0-470-05235-X
- Hacking Wireless Networks
  For Dummies
  0-7645-9730-2
- Java For Dummies
  0-470-08716-1

- Microsoft SQL Server 2005 For Dummies
  0-7645-7755-7
- Networking All-in-One Desk Reference
  For Dummies
  0-7645-9939-9
- Preventing Identity Theft For Dummies
  0-7645-7336-5
- Telecom For Dummies
  0-471-77085-X
- Visual Studio 2005 All-in-One Desk
  Reference For Dummies
  0-7645-9775-2
- XML For Dummies
  0-7645-8845-1

HEALTH & SELF-HELP

0-7645-8450-2

0-7645-4149-8

Also available:
- Bipolar Disorder For Dummies
  0-7645-8451-0
- Chemotherapy and Radiation
  For Dummies
  0-7645-7832-4
- Controlling Cholesterol For Dummies
  0-7645-5440-9
- Diabetes For Dummies
  0-7645-6820-5* †
- Divorce For Dummies
  0-7645-8417-0 †

- Fibromyalgia For Dummies
  0-7645-5441-7
- Low-Calorie Dieting For Dummies
  0-7645-9905-4
- Meditation For Dummies
  0-471-77774-9
- Osteoporosis For Dummies
  0-7645-7621-6
- Overcoming Anxiety For Dummies
  0-7645-5447-6
- Reiki For Dummies
  0-7645-9907-0
- Stress Management For Dummies
  0-7645-5144-2

EDUCATION, HISTORY, REFERENCE & TEST PREPARATION

0-7645-8381-6

0-7645-9554-7

Also available:
- The ACT For Dummies
  0-7645-9652-7
- Algebra For Dummies
  0-7645-5325-9
- Algebra Workbook For Dummies
  0-7645-8467-7
- Astronomy For Dummies
  0-7645-8465-0
- Calculus For Dummies
  0-7645-2498-4
- Chemistry For Dummies
  0-7645-5430-1
- Forensics For Dummies
  0-7645-5580-4

- Freemasons For Dummies
  0-7645-9796-5
- French For Dummies
  0-7645-5193-0
- Geometry For Dummies
  0-7645-5324-0
- Organic Chemistry I For Dummies
  0-7645-6902-3
- The SAT I For Dummies
  0-7645-7193-1
- Spanish For Dummies
  0-7645-5194-9
- Statistics For Dummies
  0-7645-5423-9

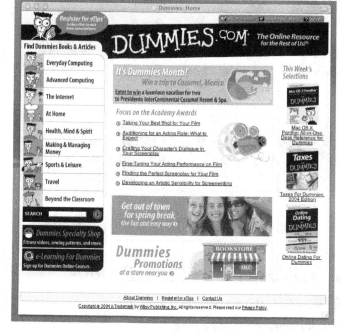

Get smart @ dummies.com®

- **Find a full list of Dummies titles**
- **Look into loads of FREE on-site articles**
- **Sign up for FREE eTips e-mailed to you weekly**
- **See what other products carry the Dummies name**
- **Shop directly from the Dummies bookstore**
- **Enter to win new prizes every month!**

* Separate Canadian edition also available
† Separate U.K. edition also available

Available wherever books are sold. For more information or to order direct: U.S. customers visit www.dummies.com or call 1-877-762-2974.
U.K. customers visit www.wileyeurope.com or call 0800 243407. Canadian customers visit www.wiley.ca or call 1-800-567-4797.